P9-BYM-141

MAXIMUM
SPORTS
PERFORMANCE

BOOKS BY JAMES F. FIXX

Games for the Superintelligent (1972)
More Games for the Superintelligent (1976)
The Complete Book of Running (1977)
Solve It! (1978)
The Complete Runner's Day-by-Day Log and Calendar (annually since 1979)
Jim Fixx's Second Book of Running (1980)
Jackpot! (1982)
Maximum Sports Performance (1985)

MAXIMUM SPORTS PERFORMANCE

James F. Fixx

with the Nike Sport Research Laboratory

Random House
New York

Copyright © 1985 by the Estate of James F. Fixx

All rights reserved under International and Pan-American Copyright Conventions.
Published in the United States by Random House, Inc., New York, and
simultaneously in Canada by Random House of Canada Limited, Toronto.

*Grateful acknowledgment is made to the following for permission to
reprint previously published material:*

Academic Press: Table by Gordon Stoddard from *Sports Medicine,*
by Allan J. Ryan, M.D., and Fred Allman, M.D. (eds.),
Academic Press, New York, 1974.

Family Media, Inc.: Chart of "Our Guide to the Best Sports for
Your Health," by Bud Wilkinson. Reprinted from *Today's Health,*
May 1972, by special permission. Copyright © 1972 by
Family Media, Inc. All rights reserved.

Miller Brewing Company: Two charts from "The Miller Lite Report
on American Attitudes Towards Sports," © 1983 by
Miller Brewing Company, 3939 West Highland Boulevard,
Milwaukee, Wisconsin 53201.

William Morrow & Company, Inc., and Knox Burger Associates Ltd:
Chart on p. 55 "World Class level" down to "Weekend level" in *The
Competitive Edge,* by Col. James L. Anderson and Martin Cohen.
Copyright © 1981 by Col. James L. Anderson and Martin Cohen. By
permission of William Morrow & Company, and Knox Burger Associates Ltd.

Ross Laboratories: Chart on Relative Body Fat Values by
Robert Hodges, from *Medical Times,* Vol. 109, © 1980 Ross
Laboratories. Reprinted with permission of Ross Laboratories,
Columbus, OH 43216.

St. Martin's Press, Inc.: Two illustrations and one chart from
The Sports Fan's Ultimate Book of Sports Comparisons, by
The Diagram Group. Copyright © 1982 by Diagram Visual
Information Ltd. St. Martin's Press, Inc., New York.

Time-Life Books Inc.: Table from *Life Science Library*/THE BODY,
by Alan E. Nourse and the Editors of LIFE.
© 1964 Time-Life Books Inc.

Track & Field News, Inc.: Two charts compiled from data published
in *Track & Field News,* July 1983, Los Altos, California.

John Wiley and Sons, Inc.: Two figures of the heart from
Being Fit: A Personal Guide, by Bud Getchell with Wayne Anderson,
John Wiley and Sons, New York, 1982. Copyright © 1982 by
John Wiley and Sons, Inc. Reprinted by permission.

Library of Congress Cataloging in Publication Data

Fixx, James F.
Maximum sports performance.

Bibliography: p.
Includes index.
1. Sports—Physiological aspects. 2. Sports—
Psychological aspects. 3. Physical fitness. I. Title.
RC1235.F56 1985 612'.044 84-17963

ISBN: 0–394–53682–7

Manufactured in the United States of America

2 3 4 5 6 7 8 9

FIRST EDITION

*Charts by Carol Grobe
Illustrations by Pat Stewart*

Designed by Carole Lowenstein

To Peggy—
Who made the early and last years
of the author's life happy.

The family of James F. Fixx

In front of excellence,
the immortal gods have put sweat,
and long and steep is the way to it.

—HESIOD, c. 700 B.C.

On the Purposes
of This Book

Maximum Sports Performance is a compilation of current knowledge about the attainment of excellence across the range of contemporary sports. Its chief purpose is to gather into one place the principal facts about athletic accomplishment, including the crucially important psychological aspect, and thereby enable athletes of all kinds, from beginners to the most accomplished, to perform more expertly and derive more enjoyment from their achievements.

Much of the material assembled here has been unearthed only during the past few years by researchers who in vastly increasing numbers find themselves fascinated by the various frontiers of sport—physiology, biomechanics, psychology and so forth. In order to buttress their discoveries with specific applications, many if not most of their scientific conclusions have been augmented by commentary from leading athletes and other authorities.

The need for a book of this kind first suggested itself nearly a decade ago when, in the course of conducting research for *The Complete Book of Running*, the author had occasion to interview a distinguished physiologist, David L. Costill. As director of the Human Performance Laboratory at Ball State University, Costill had spent much of his life seeking to discover how the human body functions when it is placed under stresses of various sorts—high temperatures, fluid deprivation, physical exhaustion and the like. Having learned a great deal about the subject, and because he himself had long been a running enthusiast, he had written an illuminating and enormously useful manuscript that he called *A Scientific Approach to Distance Running*. He said, however, that despite persistent effort he had been unable to find a publisher willing to issue it as a book.*

Costill's entirely undeserved frustration was no bizarre or isolated instance but was unhappily symptomatic of the uneasy relationship, in our own country and in others, between athletes and the sources of knowledge they need in order to perform at their best. The primary purpose of the present book, therefore, is to provide a report, unencumbered by forbidding technical language, on what has recently been learned about the most effective nurturing of the various athletic capacities.

In writing *Maximum Sports Performance* the author has enjoyed the invaluable assistance of the research staff of Nike, Inc., whose director of research, Dr. E. C. Frederick, is widely recognized as an inventive pioneer in the investigation of sports physiology. Nike's laboratory in Exeter, New Hampshire, which Dr. Frederick oversees, has for some two decades been looking closely at the scientific basis of sport and not only has made numerous significant discoveries about how the human body functions as it makes various kinds of athletic efforts but has, in the process, toppled more than a few myths.

Unlike the usual volume of athletic instruction, this book is not arranged according to the several sports but is based on the specific skills upon which those sports depend. Speed, after all, is nonetheless speed whether it is used in running the sixty-yard dash or in covering a squash court, and a marathon runner's endurance is cut from the same cloth as a cross-country skier's. Similarly, the agility of a gymnast has close application to the needs of tennis and basketball players, while the strength upon which a wrestler relies is directly relevant to the challenge faced by a fullback charging through a defensive line. For this reason it is not unlikely that

---

* Atonement for this sin of omission has since been made by the editors of *Track and Field News*.

useful information will be found in contexts that may at first glance appear unpromising.

It will perhaps not surprise readers that throughout these pages considerable emphasis has been placed on the numerous scientific findings that have emerged from studies of distance running. Part of this is attributable to pure bias. The author not only cherishes the sport of running but, having written two books and much else about its intricacies and ramifications, has become more familiar with it than with any other athletic enterprise.

By chance, however, this bias turns out to parallel the preoccupations of large numbers of medical, physiological and psychological investigators. The reason is that running, because most of its effects are so promptly arrived at and so unmistakably meaurable, is a prime choice of scientific researchers. To the extent that bias is present in these pages, therefore, it is widely shared and not solely idiosyncratic.

If *Maximum Sports Performance* succeeds in its goals, it will be largely because of the many athletes and other authorities who have temporarily laid aside their training, their research and in some cases substantial segments of their personal lives by generously agreeing to provide interviews and other forms of indispensable assistance.

In particular my thanks go to Colonel James L. Anderson, director, Department of Physical Education, the United States Military Academy; Franz Beckenbauer, Hubert Birkenmeier and Vladislav Bogicevic, the New York Cosmos; Keith F. Bell, Ph.D.; Rosemary Casals; Robert W. Christina, director, Motor Behavior Laboratory, The Pennsylvania State University; Cynthia Croteau, Nike, Inc.; Bill Curry, DP Industries; Karen Dewis, the University of California at Los Angeles; Stanley Edelman, M.D.: Gary Fencik, the Chicago Bears; Joe Fields, the New York Jets; Peter Fleming; Tom Fleming; Lawrence Folinsbee, Ph.D., Institute of Environmental Stress, the University of California at Santa Barbara; E. C. Frederick, Ph.D., research director, Nike, Inc.; Jeff Galloway, president, Phidippides International; Vitas Gerulaitis; Gayle Godwin, head coach, women's tennis team, the University of California at Los Angeles; Austin Gontang, Ph.D.; William J. Gonyea, Ph.D., the University of Texas; Ken Griffey, the New York Yankees; Abraham Grossfeld, gymnastics coach, Southern Connecticut University; Tim Gullikson; Tom Gullikson; Allen Guttman, professor of American studies, Amherst College; Mike Haffner; Wayne Harer, the

New York Yankees; Franco Harris, the Seattle Seahawks; Jim Hart, the St. Louis Cardinals; Buffie Heath, Nike, Inc.; John Hiebert, M.D.; Jay Howell, the New York Yankees; Mike Isaacson, Nike, Inc.; Dr. J. Arthur Jackson; Jeff Johnson, Nike, Inc.; Ernst Jokl, M.D.; Peter Jokl, M.D.; Sheldon P. Konecke, D.P.M.; Robert S. Loeb; James E. Loehr, Ph.D.; John Lucas, Ph.D., The Pennsylvania State University; Lynn McCutcheon, Northern Virginia Community College; Rob Roy McGregor, D.P.M.; Mark MacIntyre; Archie Manning, the Houston Oilers; Edward Mather; Sandy Mayer; Patricia Mihevic, Institute of Environmental Stress, the University of California at Santa Barbara; Harvey Misel; Gene Monahan, trainer, the New York Yankees; Bill Mongovan, track and cross-country coach, St. Mary High School, Greenwich, Connecticut; Art Monk, the Washington Redskins; Jonathan Nelson, associate professor, Northern Michigan University; Bruce C. Ogilvie, Ph.D., San Jose State University; Lillis O. Palmer; Van Rensselaer Potter, M.D.; Michael Quinn; Allan J. Ryan, M.D., editor, *The Physician and Sportsmedicine*; Alberto Salazar; Carl Scheer, president and general manager, the Denver Nuggets; Julius Segal, Ph.D., United States Department of Health and Human Services; Lee Roy Selmon, the Tampa Bay Buccaneers; Geoff Smith; Jon Spaventa, the University of California at Santa Barbara; Rusty Staub, the New York Mets; Charles Steinmetz, M.D.: Tim Sutton; Sandra Swan; Kathrine Switzer; Kelly Tripucka, the Detroit Pistons; Grete Waitz; Herschel Walker, the New Jersey Generals; Jack Welch, Nike, Inc.; Mark E. Wolpa, D.P.M.

Todd Benoit was tireless in his research efforts.

—J.F.F.

Contents

MAXIMUM
SPORTS
PERFORMANCE

CHAPTER 1

The Science Explosion

There's too much information that's not based
on science at all. These days, it doesn't
have to be that way.

—TIM SUTTON, *track coach*

NEVER BEFORE has so much been known about the sources of athletic excellence and the most effective ways to achieve superior performance. There has been an unprecedented growth in scientific knowledge about exactly how the human body functions and how we can coax the most out of its various systems. Until only recently athletes and their coaches used mostly guesswork, tempered by whatever experience they were able to draw upon, in formulating training regimens. In the past several years, however, the introduction of detailed, exactingly quantified information about physiology, biomechanics, nutrition, equipment, and the psychological aspects of sport have made it possible to devise unprecedentedly precise programs for improvement.

These advances began nearly a century ago, when physiologists Wallace O. Fenn and Rodolfo Margaria foresaw that science might profitably be applied to sport. Fenn investigated such subjects as the elasticity and internal friction of human muscle and the force it is able to exert as it functions at various speeds. Margaria looked closely at the sources of muscular strength and the various influences on it—oxygen debt, lactic acid, gravity and so forth—and vastly increased our knowledge of exactly what occurs in athletic movements. "I find the physiology of muscular exercise one of the most stimulating branches of biology," he once wrote.

In 1922 a British biophysicist and physiologist, A. V. Hill, was awarded a Nobel Prize for his studies of human muscle. It was Hill who, long before the notion appears to have occurred to anyone else, saw that scientific principles might profitably be applied to sport. "If . . . physiology can aid in the development of athletics as a science and an art," Hill told the British Association for the Advancement of Science in 1925, "I think it will deserve well of mankind."

The most publicly visible early manifestation of the marriage between science and sport, however, took place in Cambridge, Massachusetts, in 1927. Here, under the prodding of Lawrence J. Henderson, a portly, bearded professor of medicine, the celebrated Harvard Fatigue Laboratory came into being in the basement of

Lawrence J. Henderson

a brick building known as Morgan Hall. During the institution's twenty-year life span its pioneering researchers looked into human responses to cold, wind, altitude, nutritional alterations and deprivations, and the rigors of exercise. Beginning in the late 1920's, as reports of the Harvard Fatigue Laboratory's research began to reach the world beyond Cambridge, guesswork in athletic training began, at first haltingly and then with increasing speed, to give way to scientific principles. As the first research facility of its kind, the Harvard Fatigue Laboratory was the forerunner of the hundreds that are in operation around the world today.

These laboratories permit us to scrutinize the chemical tides of our very cells and thus, for the first time, to measure aspects of physiology that were once thought forever beyond the reach of scientific analysis—fatigue, for example, and the evanescent sense of being fully ready to compete. Sports psychologists, employing the arcane armamentarium of their trade, are discovering how best to nourish the flames of competitiveness, enthusiasm and desire. (One observer recently referred to "the widespread realization that the mind could be one's most prized or most problematic piece of athletic equipment.") Finally, new testing procedures permit us to evaluate, with an accuracy never before possible, the most elusively subtle characteristics of all manner of athletic equipment, needed and unneeded, useful and ridiculous.

Inherent in this plethora of information, however, is a frustrating paradox. It is that, for whatever reason, there remains a gulf between the source of such information—professional physiologists, university research laboratories, and the like—and those who might most clearly benefit from it. In Eastern Europe the typical researcher, laden with Ph.D. degrees and up-to-the-minute athletic lore, serves as coach as well, swiftly transmitting his findings directly to the athletes in his charge. That, however, is not the way of the West. Although Western researchers perform work that is in many instances every bit as imaginative and accomplished as that of the East Germans and the Soviets, for the most part its immediate destination is not the playing field at all but the pages of professional journals that few coaches bother to consult.

For one thing, these publications make formidably difficult reading, filled as they are with graphs, charts, and so many obscure scientific terms that by comparison *Finnegans Wake* seems as simple as *Goldilocks and the Three Bears*. Not long ago a midwestern coach, asked whether he made a point of keeping up with the scientific literature, replied, "I certainly do. I read *Sports Illustrated* every week."

Researchers themselves are dismayed, and in some cases quietly aggrieved, by the discrepancy between the information they so painstakingly ferret out and what athletes do—or, more to the point, fail to do—with it. "The problem, basically, is one of communication," says one prominent investigator. "The coach can't understand the scientist's language, and the scientist doesn't want to compromise the accuracy and precision of his work enough to get it out to people in a language they might be able to understand."

This is a costly shame, for during the past several years, as mentioned, scientific researchers have turned up an unprecedented trove of information on how athletes of all kinds can wrest maximum performance from their minds and bodies. In running, for example, we are now able to distinguish not just two fundamental varieties of locomotion—aerobic (with oxygen) and anaerobic (without oxygen)—but two distinct types of muscle—so-called fast twitch and slow—and are therefore able to devise training programs cunningly tuned to the precise abilities and goals of individual athletes. Similarly, in the high jump, the pole vault and a diversity of other events, biomechanical research has led to significant refinements of technique. (As this is being written, a twenty-year-old Soviet pole vaulter, Sergei Bubka, has set an indoor record of 19 feet 1½ inches using a revolutionary grip.)

With only rare exceptions, however, little of this new knowledge finds its way out of the scientific community until years or even decades have elapsed. "There's too much information that's not based on science at all," declares Tim Sutton, a Missouri track coach. "These days it doesn't have to be that way. Too much coaching is just based on word of mouth—Moses Malone does this, Alberto Salazar does that. And of course a lot of coaches don't really do any coaching that's worthy of the name. They just look for good athletes."

That Sutton's criticism is true is unarguable. It is also unfortunate, for the research that has been undertaken during the past few years, despite the obscurity of much of it thus far, has begun to shed light on an impressive range of long-standing perplexities:

- Are athletes born or made?
- How is strength best developed? Speed? Endurance? Agility?
- What foods should athletes eat (and what foods avoid) in order to prepare themselves for various events?

- In what way does age affect athletic performance?
- How is injury most effectively avoided?
- And finally—perhaps the most tantalizing question of all—in what ways can the mind help the body?

That such questions can currently be answered with more certainty than ever before betokens a new era in sport, one markedly different from any previous period. For no matter how arduously and artfully earlier athletes may have trained, they could not, lacking our scientific insights, have been as purposeful or as precise as you and I can be.

Recent improvements in training methods have, naturally enough, most profoundly affected full-time professional athletes, those men and women whose careers stand or fall on millimeters, microseconds and eye blinks. What the scientists are learning can, however, be of considerable help as well to the business executive pumping iron in order to look good on the beach on Aruba in February, the housewife swimming laps in a YWCA pool, the senior citizen trying to break ninety on the golf course, the man or woman striving to qualify for a spot in the Boston Marathon, the high school or college athlete trying to earn a berth on a varsity team.

Scientific contributions are coming from all over the globe— from laboratories in France, Britain, Spain, Italy, the two Germanys, the United States, the Soviet Union* and elsewhere. Peter Jokl, a physician who has long been a diligent student of international sport, cites, as an example of the efficacy of scientific research, the consistent success of East Germany's athletic efforts. "They have a population of seventeen million," he says. "That's only one-seventh the population of the United States. Yet their teams are every bit as good as our own. By itself, chance can't possibly explain what they're accomplishing. It's almost entirely the result of what they're finding out in the laboratories."

If the United States is not in all respects in the forefront of sports research, it is hardly for want of trying. Exercise physiology and sportsmedicine have become major industries, and on university campuses research projects involving sport are nearly as common

---

* In addition to the usual inquiries into physiology, kinesiology and the like, investigators in the U.S.S.R. have been looking into the athletic efficacy of a stimulant derived from a thorny creeping plant, *Eleutherococcus senticosus*, which in one test is said to have reduced running time in a ten-mile race by some five minutes. Virtually unknown among athletes of the West and not included in any Western pharmacopoeia, *Eleutherococcus* is thus far not among the drugs banned in international competition.

as Frisbees. Not long ago, at an international symposium, Dr. Richard C. Nelson, director of Penn State's highly regarded biomechanics laboratory, observed that "biomechanics is playing an increasingly important role in many aspects of sports in the United States. National and Olympic teams are utilizing biomechanical input in the training and development of athletes. . . . This science is also being applied in sports equipment design." Dr. Nelson further suggested that what we have witnessed so far is only a beginning: "Certainly the field of sport biomechanics is now recognized as a respected scientific discipline and will make increasingly important contributions to the performance and safety of not only elite athletes but the millions of recreational sport participants."

Even in many purportedly amateur sports, so much prestige and money is commonly at stake that marginal advantages are unprecedentedly important. To many athletes it is therefore no unreasonable sacrifice to devote a year's worth of California afternoons to modifying a perfectly effective backhand or to spend five thousand arduous miles on roads and trails teaching oneself to hold pace on Heartbreak Hill. Few athletes these days, professional or amateur, would disagree with the stark warning once expressed by the Boston Celtics' Ed Macauley: "When you are not practicing, remember, someone somewhere *is* practicing, and when you meet him he will win."

Sport is certainly central to our lives today. A recent poll showed that 44 percent of our population participates daily in one or another sports activity, and that only 3.7 percent of us admit to being (or, it may be, brag about being) entirely uninvolved in athletics.

ATHLETIC PARTICIPATION IN THE UNITED STATES

	DAILY OR ALMOST DAILY	ABOUT ONCE OR TWICE A WEEK	ABOUT ONCE OR TWICE A MONTH	LESS THAN ONCE A MONTH	NEVER	DON'T KNOW
	(percent)	*(percent)*	*(percent)*	*(percent)*	*(percent)*	*(percent)*
Swimming	13	20	16	9	40	2
Calisthenics	15	14	6	4	53	8
Jogging	12	17	13	7	49	2
Bicycling	13	15	11	8	51	2
Softball/baseball	7	14	13	9	54	3
Weightlifting	6	9	7	5	69	4
Basketball	6	8	10	8	65	3
Football/rugby	4	8	8	6	71	3
Tennis, squash, etc.	3	9	14	13	58	3
Pool/billiards	3	8	11	13	62	3
Boating	3	8	13	15	58	3
Aerobic dancing	3	7	4	3	80	3
Bowling	1	9	12	15	60	3
Table tennis	2	6	9	16	64	3
Skating	2	5	12	10	68	3
Volleyball	2	5	10	12	68	3
Skiing	1	5	7	8	76	3
Golf	1	5	6	9	76	3
Soccer	3	2	4	5	83	3
Gymnastics	2	3	3	4	85	3
Wrestling	2	2	2	3	88	3
Horseback riding	1	2	5	10	79	3
Archery	1	2	2	5	87	3
Other team sports	1	2	3	3	85	6
Handball	1	1	2	4	88	4
Hockey	1	1	2	2	91	3
Fencing	–	1	1	2	93	3
Lacrosse	–	–	–	2	94	4
Jai alai	–	–	–	2	94	4
Other	12	13	9	2	64	–

SOURCE: *The Miller Lite Report on American Attitudes Toward Sport*

Furthermore, we look upon sports as no idle pastime but as an activity of transcendent importance. Allen Guttman, a professor of American studies at Amherst College and the author of a perceptive book on sports history, *From Ritual to Record*, says, "In the United

States today, sports are more important to most people than the work they do." Guttman recalls that Louisiana State University, financially pressed some years ago, had to choose between continuing to publish its highly regarded literary magazine and providing fresh meat for the football team's mascot, a live tiger. The university folded the magazine.

This turn of events would have been no surprise to Walter Umminger, a distinguished sports historian, who wrote in his book *Supermen, Heroes, and Gods* that "sport commands greater devotion from the human race than any other uncompulsory activity." Nor, presumably, would it have startled Norman Vincent Peale, who once declared, "If Jesus were alive today, he would be at the Super Bowl."*

Whether the Super Bowl is in fact where Jesus would choose to be is open to speculation, but there is little doubt that that is where practically everyone else, at least in the United States, would like

AMERICANS' PASSION FOR SPORTS

SPORT	PERCENT
Super Bowl	18
World Series	17
Olympics	16
Kentucky Derby	7
Indianapolis 500	6
Heavyweight title fight	5
World figure skating	5
Bowl game	4
N.C.A.A basketball	4
U.S. Open (tennis) or Wimbledon	3
National gymnastics	3
U.S. Open (golf)	3
N.B.A. final playoff final	2
Stanley Cup final	2
Soccer World Cup	1
National track and field	1
Other	3
Don't know	1

SOURCE: *The Miller Lite Report on American Attitudes Toward Sport*

* The identification of sport and religion is not uncommon. Avery Brundage, long-time president of the International Olympic Committee, once declared: "The Olympic movement is a twentieth-century religion, a religion with universal appeal which incorporates all the basic values of other religions, a modern, exciting, virile, dynamic religion." And an even more celebrated commentator, Saul of Tarsus (later Saint Paul), characteristically wrote in sports metaphors: "All the runners run the race, though only one wins the prize. . . . I press toward the goal to win the prize. . . . Keep yourself in training for the practice of religion," and so forth.

to be on Super Bowl Sunday. In 1983 the Miller Brewing Company, which has long sought to identify itself with sport, issued a report on Americans' passion for athletics. Twenty-five percent of us, the Miller document revealed, attend more than twenty sporting events each year, 51 percent of us rate our interest in watching sports as either "very high" or "somewhat high," and 70 percent of us have some involvement with sport—watching athletic contests, reading about them or discussing them—every single day of our adult lives.

Nor is sport a preoccupation only for the stereotypical blue-collar beer drinker. Recalling his student days, Albert Camus once remarked, "Sport was the main occupation of all of us, and continued to be mine for a long time. That is where I had my only lessons in ethics." And Nikos Kazantzakis writes in *Report to Greco*: "When life has succeeded in conquering the enemies—hunger, thirst, sickness—sometimes it is lucky enough to have abundant strength left over. This strength it squanders in sports. Civilization begins at the moment sport begins."

CHAPTER 2

The Invention of Excellence

It's very hard to predict where the limits are.

—GRETE WAITZ

ONE DAY a pole vaulter named Dave Volz was, in accordance with his custom, more or less perched in space, a hand's breadth less than nineteen feet above the earth's surface, waiting to discover whether the energy with which he had a moment earlier stressed his fiberglass pole would prove sufficient to lift 185 pounds of painstakingly trained bone and muscle over the crossbar.

As not infrequently happens in Volz's intricately complex sport, it did not. With a familiar sense of disappointment, he felt his body dislodge the bar. In the normal course of events it would now tumble to the ground, signaling a failed vault.

Having at the moment nothing important to do except wait to plop into the foam-rubber pit below, Volz found himself entertaining a thought. With his left hand he reached out, seized the tottering crossbar and, quicker than a cat, set it back on the standards.

It was all perfectly legal and, it scarcely need be said, a paradigm of athletic innovation.

Marvelous occurrences, whether Volz's midair machinations or Rod Carew as he examines an approaching pitch or you or I trying to conquer twenty-six miles on foot or swat a careening ball with a racquet, are fundamentally what sport is all about; it is this that causes it to tug so powerfully at our imaginations. For through sport, as surely as through science, philosophy or the arts, we discover and define what the scope of humankind and its limits are. "World records," the psychologist Austin Gontang has written, "are human records. They record the goals that humans, alone and in association with fellow humans, have achieved. . . . They show us what men have accomplished when mind and body are put to the test of excellence."

For sport in its modern sense to emerge, however, something more than merely spectacular achievements was necessary. Modern sport requires the codification of unvarying rules, the maintenance of precise records and the standardization of playing conditions. (The distance between bases in baseball, we can be fairly sure, will remain exactly ninety feet for some time to come.) How else, after all, could accomplishments be compared and all-time champions celebrated? "Modern sport began," says Amherst's Allen Guttman, "when rules were laid down so people could try to do the same things other people had done."

The need for record-keeping is so evident to us that it requires an effort of mind to understand how the ancient Greeks could have maintained practically no records of speed or distance. A Greek discus or javelin thrower competed only against athletes who were present at the time, not, as athletes do today, against all others who had ever performed the event. For us, as Richard Mandell writes, "the record exists apart from chronological time, geography and any social distinctions of the person or persons who establish it." It was quite the opposite for the Greeks. It did not, apparently, occur to them to standardize the discus or to speculate about whether the winner in a particular Olympic event would have defeated the victor in the same event four years earlier. Could Bill Tilden have defeated John McEnroe? Might Tom Seaver have struck out Babe Ruth? To an ancient Greek, questions of this kind would have seemed incomprehensible.

Our preoccupation with records—with the tape measure and the stopwatch—is in one sense a burden, depriving us of the uncomplicated joy of the here and now. Yet in another it is an undeniable blessing. It means, for one thing, that even the likes of you and I are able to compete not just against those who are present but also against others we have never known and will never know. The record, Allen Guttman writes, "is a marvelous abstraction that permits competition not only among those gathered together on the field of sport but also among them and others distant in time and space. Through the strange abstraction of the quantified record, the Australian can compete with the Finn who died a decade before the Australian was born."

This marvelous abstraction also means that if we wish we can choose whom we will compete against, ignoring those we consider to be either above or below our class. In the Boston Marathon I do not imagine myself running against Salazar, Meyer or Benoit but against others of my own age, sex and relative ineptitude.

Athletic advances in our own era are particularly remarkable in light of sport's long history, which would seem on the face of it to have provided an abundance of time in which to reach full athletic potential. Archery, after all, was known as long ago as circa 8000 B.C. Ball games, depicted on murals at Beni Hasan on the Nile, date to circa 2050 B.C. Ancient Egyptians also enjoyed acrobatics, bullfighting, wrestling and a forerunner of what we know as juggling. Such feats, however, were only remotely related to contemporary athletics, with their unremitting emphasis on improvement. "Primitive peoples practiced," observes Professor Guttmann. "Modern athletes train."

Training in its modern sense seems to have begun with the Greeks, who held a view of sport not unlike our own. Among earlier peoples, grace, form and style were striven after; to the Greeks, winning alone mattered. Accordingly, coaches devised training regimens that are entirely sound, even if somewhat rudimentary, by current standards. The physician Galen, who at one time served as medical officer of a school for gladiators, described exercises for various parts of the body, subclassifying them according to their effects on the several muscle groups. "There is indeed little in our modern systems that we do not find anticipated in Greek medical writings," says E. Norman Gardiner, author of *Athletics of the Ancient World.*

To the Greeks as to modern Western culture, athletics were more than merely recreation. On the contrary, athletic ability was regarded as an indispensable facet of the harmoniously educated citizen. Greek society thus took athletics seriously, just as we do— sometimes, also like us, too seriously. On one occasion a chariot racer, Oebotar of Achaia, felt he had not received sufficient honor from his fellow Achaians. Not content with ordinary sulking or grousing, the sort of behavior for which so many present-day athletes are celebrated, he arranged that a full-scale curse be inflicted on his city. Its chief provision was that no Achaian would win an Olympic medal for the next three hundred years, and none did.

Despite the homage paid to the most admired Greek athletes, professionals were not held in universally high regard. In an essay entitled "Exhortation on the Choice of a Profession," no less an authority than Galen himself expresses a dim view of those who earn their living by athletics: "In the blessings of the mind athletes have no share. Beneath their mass of flesh and blood their souls are stifled as in a sea of mud."

Despite such cranky appraisals, it was these same professionals, with their training camps, municipal gymnasiums and full-time coaches, who advanced athletics far beyond anything previously witnessed. In the long jump, the javelin and discus throw, wrestling, boxing and foot racing, Greek athletes were without historical peer. They not only trained arduously but knew what ultimate effect might be anticipated from their exertions. The results were not infrequently spectacular. It is claimed, for example, that a Greek athlete covered fifty-five feet in the long jump—the current record is little more than half that distance—although historians assume that a confusion of some sort has found its way into the report. (The feat may in fact have been a triple jump.)

However beclouded by time the record has become, there can be no doubt that ancient Greece boasted more than a few impressively accomplished athletes. But exactly how accomplished? By our standards, perhaps not very. Were a top Greek athlete to find

himself reincarnated in the late twentieth century, Professor Guttman argues, he would probably not be considered outstanding. "I
doubt that he'd be very good," says Guttman. "First, we're more
scientific than the Greeks were able to be. From our point of view
most peoples previous to our own time were quite lackadaisical in
their training. Second, our athletes specialize more than Greek
athletes did."

Whatever their shortcomings, Greek athletes made a far more
significant and lasting mark than that of the ancient Romans, who
should logically have been able to build on their predecessors'
achievements. No such sequence occurred, however. For all their
fascination with gladiatorial contests and other razzle-dazzle events,
the Romans did little to advance athletic performance. What they
craved was pageantry, the bloodier the better, and whenever the
prospect of mayhem was at hand they had little difficulty in filling
the Circus Maximus (which held enough people to populate mod-
ern-day Montgomery, Alabama). It is little wonder that sport as
we know it did not flourish in such a setting.

Nor did Roman heads of state consistently lend their support to
the noblest of athletic principles. In A.D. 67 it occurred to Nero that
as emperor he was entitled, if he wished, to compete in the Olympic
Games. Although he weighed, according to one account, some 360
pounds and was not celebrated for his agility, he entered several
events (some of which he himself had invented) and won them all.
Nero's crowning athletic achievement may have come in a chariot
race. Although at one point he toppled inelegantly from his vehicle
and had to be restored to the reins by attendants, he scored a
comeback victory.

Roman sport did, on the other hand, have at least one distinction
worthy of commemoration, for it was here that women were first
welcomed to organized athletics. Except for the all-female Herean
games and a handful of other events, the Greeks had allowed women
no role in sports. Roman women, however, routinely engaged in
gladiatorial combat, chariot racing and gymnastics.

Sport in the contemporary sense, with its purposeful and egalitarian striving for improvement, languished for centuries.* Its
resurgence had to await the arrival of widespread free time, a
recent luxury in human history. "The idea that time for leisure

---

* As a pastime solely for the privileged, however, it never ceased to flourish.
According to Professor Mandell's reckoning, Paris in 1596 boasted no fewer than
250 tennis courts, and some 7,000 citizens earned their livings from the game.

would be available to the common man," writes Ernst Jokl, a perceptive chronicler of sports history, "sounded revolutionary not so long ago. . . . The boys and girls who slaved in coal mines and textile mills around the middle of the nineteenth century had neither the time nor the strength to play."

For the same reason early America was little occupied with athletics, having more urgent business on its mind. By the mid-nineteenth century, however, the lack was being intermittently redressed. "The game of football," declared an iconoclastic *Harper's Weekly* article in 1857, "ought to be of as much concern as the Greek or mathematical prize. Indeed, of the two it is the more useful exercise. . . . We had rather chronicle a great boat-race at Harvard or Yale, or a cricket match with the United States Eleven, than all the prize poems or the orations on Lafayette that are produced in half a century."

As our own century approached, a passionate interest in athletes was becoming increasingly common. Sports fans were legion, and in the early 1860's one enthusiast wrote as follows to the editor of the *Police Gazette*, an assiduous chronicler of sport: "Have been on the move so much lately that I have not received the *Police Gazette* regularly. Please send copy here and oblige, Jesse James."

During this period, surviving records show, serious training was undertaken in preparation for the numerous walking and running races that enjoyed widespread popularity. In Philadelphia, Joshua Newsam walked a thousand miles in eighteen days—an astonishing average of fifty-five miles per day—and on Long Island, Henry Stannard ran ten miles in less than an hour. It does not require an expert to know that such accomplishments are scarcely those of dilettantes.

The modern era of sport began with the spree of record-breaking in the 1950's, when Roger Bannister finally breached the four-minute-mile barrier, Gregory Bell long-jumped more than twenty-six feet, Bob Mathias became history's first two-time Olympic decathlon winner, Johnny Unitas helped the Baltimore Colts by passing for more than 40,000 yards, Pancho Gonzales enjoyed an almost decade-long reign as king of the courts, and swimmers, most of them mere teenagers, broke virtually every existing record. "Remember Johnny Weismuller's world record of fifty-one seconds for a hundred yards?" Bob Kiphuth, Yale's longtime swim coach and a member of four Olympic teams, said some years ago. "It was good enough to stay on the books for seventeen years. Why, Johnny couldn't even qualify these days for the National Collegiate Championships."* And today Weismuller's time wouldn't qualify for the finals of a schoolboy championship.

The record-breaking spree that began more than three decades ago has flourished with undiminished energy, fueled by the physiological and psychological findings that science so tirelessly pours forth. "The era since 1950 is a sort of golden age of sport," observes the sports physiologist E. C. Frederick. The seemingly endless bettering of past performance constitutes, for most of us, a continuing source of marvels. Just at the moment when we are ready to conclude that man or woman cannot possibly run faster, jump higher, or throw farther, someone invariably comes along to confound us. Until just recently, for example, Olympic officials insisted, with perfectly straight faces and apparent sincerity, that women could not, and certainly should not, compete in full-length 26.2-mile marathons. Women, it was argued, were plainly too frail for such wearying and problematical enterprises. In the ensuing debate, the most telling arguments proved to be not words at all but the marathon performances of such women as Grete Waitz, Allison Roe and the redoubtable Joan Benoit. A women's marathon is now, of course, part of the Olympic agenda.

Such sports progress ennobles us all. When a Jesse Owens, a Roger Bannister or a Bob Beamon does what no human being has ever before been able to do, a portion of that achievement is radiated to you and me, enhancing, if we care to let it, our own athletic potential. To the extent that we, like them, are human beings striving to surpass current limitations, we share in what the most distinguished athletes are able to accomplish.

* This is not to imply that records were not regularly broken in the years preceding the 1950's. No one, to cite perhaps the most salient example of irrepressible athletic achievement, has ever accomplished more in a single day than the late Jesse Owens did on May 25, 1935, at Ann Arbor, Michigan. In forty-five minutes he set or equaled six world records.

CHAPTER 3

The Path to Peak Performance

> If you're great at something you can never be
> stopped, so it's worth working at that one thing
> over and over until you get it exactly right.
>
> —HERSCHEL WALKER

SANDY MAYER, who for the past several years has been ranked well toward the top of the world's tennis players, is probably as analytical about his sport as it is possible to be. The son of a tennis coach, he was raised, he says, "in a very theoretical, technique-oriented environment." For years he has read about tennis, discussed it and, during his days and nights on the game's perpetual transglobal tour, been exposed to every conceivable approach to strokes, strategies and training techniques.

What is the chief lesson Mayer has derived from all his readings, conversations and ruminations? On the eve of the 1983 U.S. Open, Mayer addressed himself to that question. "What I've found out," he told the author, "is that tennis training is not yet at a very scientific level." From time to time, he went on, he has experimented with just about every alteration in his strokes that he or anyone else could think of. "I've concluded that I've fooled around too much with my game without knowing exactly why I was changing it," he said. "Right now I'm trying to collate a lot of information from different sources in an effort to find out what kind of training makes sense. After all these years I still don't know."

If an athlete of Mayer's experience and ability finds himself bewildered about exactly how to train, what about the rest of us? Training has, after all, been integral to sport since the days of ancient Sparta. When, after so many centuries of painstaking trial and error, our most accomplished athletes remain uncertain about how to train, what hope is there that you and I will discover a regimen suited to our needs?

The question is complicated by the diversity of human abilities. Thus the training that is precisely right for you may be utterly inappropriate for me. For excellent reasons Alberto Salazar sometimes chooses to run 130 miles in a single week. If, however, most other people were to try to imitate him, they would quickly collapse into a pile of exhausted bones. And Herschel Walker likes to do three hundred sit-ups and three hundred push-ups every day. What might happen if, inspired by his example, we set out to do the same?

Even athletes and coaches who take pains to stay informed about the principles underlying training can easily fall into error. Not long ago Joe Henderson, a conscientious student of running and author of several perceptive books on the sport, described some of the ways in which his views have changed. Where once, Henderson wrote, he believed a weekly run of fifteen or twenty miles to be essential, he now avoids running for more than an hour at a time. Where once he alternated hard and easy days, he now takes a single hard day and then an entire easy *week*. Where once he thought a person couldn't finish a marathon unless he devoted at least sixty miles a week to training, he is now persuaded that half that distance is plenty.

If experience can so radically change the mind of as knowledgeable an observer as Joe Henderson, how can you and I hope to arrive at a training program that is not only right for us now but will still be right a decade or more hence? Truth to tell, we will probably not be able to come even close to such a program—one so timeless in all its details that it could appropriately be chiseled in granite. Scientific knowledge is accumulating too rapidly to support any reasonable hope of such satisfying permanence.

The situation is not, however, as hopeless as it might seem. We have, after all, come a long way since the Greeks, and despite our multitude of remaining ignorances we possess knowledge that they could not have imagined. In future chapters, therefore, we will look into what is currently known about how men and women of all ages can most effectively develop such primary athletic attributes as speed, endurance, coordination, agility and, equally or even more important, the proper mental outlook. First, however, as preparation for that more detailed study, it will be worthwhile to look at some of the underlying principles of training—the practices and attitudes that, no matter what the sport or the sophistication with which it is played, characteristically distinguish champions from less able participants.

Set goals. Training is not an end in itself but an activity with a purpose—to learn to win more games and sets than the player just above you on the club ladder, to qualify for the Boston Marathon, or to help your team win the Super Bowl. In the absence of a goal, either modest or ambitious, it is virtually impossible to persevere long enough to see a training program bring results. For what is the point in exerting yourself, after all, if you are unable to evaluate what you accomplish? One person's goal may be to press 150 pounds by next month, another's to run ten kilometers in less than thirty minutes by 1986. "For motivation," says Edward Mather, a consistently successful high school track coach, "you can't let yourself get satisfied. You have to keep raising your goals."

The example of innumerable top athletes testifies to the soundness of this principle. *Sports Illustrated* reports that Evelyn Ashford, the American record holder in the women's 100-meter and 200-meter dashes and a 1984 Olympic gold medalist, once pointed to her head and said, "I fully believe it's here, this is where it is. . . . I told myself I wanted to do it and I was willing to work for it—and it came about."

Make your goals realistic. Edward Mather, head coach of the highly successful St. Bernard track and field team, likes to plan an entire year's training in advance. "I can't believe the coaches who work from week to week, or from meet to meet," he says. "We work on a whole year's program, looking far ahead to races that we want a boy to do well in." Some coaches and athletes look even farther ahead than that. Eugeny Shakuatov, a former distance runner who now directs a Soviet sports club, told Phil Shinnick, a writer for *Runner's World*, that in his opinion it takes four years to develop a top distance runner; his training regimens are therefore based on that timetable.

Whatever your personal program, however, it will not bear fruit unless its goals are likely to be attainable. Among West Point cadets, both men and women, 100 percent increases in strength are not uncommon, yet many of us would be profoundly disappointed if we were to hope for improvement of that magnitude. Or consider, at another tantalizing extreme, Alberto Salazar's aspirations in the marathon. "I think I can improve for another five or six years," he told the author recently. "I might run 2:05 on a fast course." For Salazar, such a goal may be entirely realistic; for almost any other runner it would be pointless.

Understand what training can and cannot accomplish. Even athletes with little theoretical knowledge of their sport are usually aware that training brings about a variety of physical changes. Within a few weeks of starting to work out, they notice that their muscles have greater girth and their breathing is less labored. Not all athletes, however, know why these phenomena occur. And why, many of them reason, should they? If they're getting results, why look further?

One reason for looking further is that the more we know about the adaptations our bodies are able to make, the better we can tune those adaptations to our needs. Practically everyone knows, for example, that training lowers the heart rate, allowing us to do more work with less effort. It is apparent, furthermore, that changes in heart rate occur quite readily when a person first starts to train but become more difficult to achieve as one becomes increasingly fit. Top marathon runner Tom Fleming once told the author that when he increases the intensity of his training it takes about three months for any effect to become noticeable. Some accomplished athletes might conclude, therefore, that harder training can scarcely be worth the effort. Not long ago, however, when researchers at the University of Montreal studied elite swimmers, both men and women, they found that even at their high level of performance a vigorous six-month training program produced distinct physiological improvements.

One might argue that, valuable as such self-knowledge may be, it is hardly necessary to be conversant with the minute cellular changes that occur in training. Yet this may not be entirely true. If a runner aspiring to distinction in the 100-yard dash understands that most of his energy must be derived not from atmospheric oxygen—from breathing, that is—but from chemicals lodged in the muscle cells, primarily adenosine triphosphate and creatine phosphate, he is more likely to be more content in enduring the repeated agonizing sprints that are essential if he is to unlock those elusive energy sources.

Or if a beginning athlete understands that each gasping breath means that his respiratory muscles themselves are being strengthened (along with much else), and that today's discomforts will inevitably mean more tolerable workouts tomorrow, might that knowledge not help make his rigors seem less pointlessly unpleasant?

Choose training methods suited to your needs. Recently Jody Jacobs, writing in the *Minneapolis Star and Tribune,* reported on how actresses, socialites and the like stay fit. "These days," she said, "whenever the Beautiful People, the young tycoons, the just plain rich and successful gather, the main topic is fitness and health. It rates far above politics, the stock market, the latest best seller and even the most recent scandal as the way to keep a dinner companion fascinated." Cheryl Ladd, she revealed, works out at a fitness center, Magda Gabor does yoga and something described as advanced body dynamics, Bo Derek uses Nautilus equipment, and Eva Gabor walks four miles a day.

An athletic elitist might be inclined to look down on such workouts, since they fall somewhat short of a typical top athlete's regimen. Yet the Gabor clan and the sleekly gorgeous company it keeps are doing what they have decided they need to do for their own purposes.

This is exactly what you and I should do for *our* purposes. Suppose, for example, you want to develop cardiovascular endurance for bicycling. You might want to work out every day, as many serious cyclists do. On the other hand, you might find that daily workouts, particularly when they are arduous, leave you more tired than you prefer to be—research shows that exhausted muscles require some forty-eight hours to recover—and you may therefore want to work out only every other day. In the commonly cited phrase, we must listen to our own bodies, not try to imitate professional athletes just because their training programs work for them. When Paul Slovic, a research scientist, analyzed questionnaires from 359 finishers in the Trail's End Marathon in Oregon, he found little consensus on preparation. On the contrary, the competitors' longest training runs ranged from three to forty miles, and the distance covered in the week before competition ranged from nothing at all to 120 miles. Rightly or wrongly, these runners were clearly training their own way.

Don't worry about being the "weaker sex." Western society has traditionally been assiduous in its insistence that women are less suited for sports than men. Brooks Johnson, coach of the women's 1984 Olympic track and field team, attributes this prejudice to a "white, male chauvinistic attitude." Until only recently, he says, self-appointed authorities "had a very clear idea of what women could do and could not do with their bodies: you can't do this, you can't do that, you might get hurt." But future achievements will depend almost entirely on the effectiveness of training and will in no way be inhibited by the kinds of artificially imposed limitations that have hitherto impeded women's progress. Says Gayle Godwin, women's tennis coach at UCLA: "There's no reason why men's and women's training should differ. Training should be on an individual basis, depending on what a particular athlete needs."

Before the admission of women to West Point, army researchers recruited sixty-three high school women and subjected them to a rigorous ten-week physical evaluation. The purpose of the ordeal was to find out, in advance of the first female cadets' arrival, exactly what women could and could not do. The researchers' chief conclusion: "Without question, women are far better physical performers than the literature suggests. Their physical potential will become more obvious as the social barriers which have traditionally inhibited their participating in sports . . . are overcome."

Given your goals and abilities, train as hard as you can. On the eve of Carl Yastrzemski's retirement from his twenty-three-year baseball career, his father was asked how Carl had managed to stretch his playing days so far beyond the customarily alloted span. "Real hard work," replied the senior Yastrzemski. "A lot of players with talent don't work at it, and they're gone before you know it. Carl worked at it."

In many of its particulars Yastrzemski's career was unusual; at age forty-four he still had fast reflexes, good coordination and 20/20 vision. His attitude toward training, however, was typical of what is invariably encountered among top athletes, no matter what their age. As Herschel Walker told the author, "I like to work on one thing until I'm great at it. If you're great at something you can never be stopped, so it's worth working at that one thing over and over until you get it exactly right." And Peter Fleming, a perennial tennis winner with his doubles partner John McEnroe, describes his attitude toward training: "The important thing for me is intense practice. I play points as I would in a match." Vitas Gerulaitis, who for the past decade has been ranked among the top players in tennis, adheres to a similar philosophy. "In practice I play exactly as hard as I would in a match," he says. "I don't play social tennis. Either I practice or I don't play at all."

Accounts of athletes who claim they never train, or who would have us believe their training is perfunctory, are legion. Even in his football prime Joe Namath was widely imagined to be such an athlete, yet he once wrote, "I try to keep myself trim. At the start of training camp each season, I do about fifty sit-ups at a time— hell, I can always do fifty, even in the middle of the off-season— and, gradually, I get up to two hundred at a time. I could do more." Jim Thorpe, who won both the pentathlon and decathlon in the 1912 Olympic Games, was by reputation a roisterer who, in the words of one account, "found training a drudgery and rarely bothered to get in shape."

Perhaps so. Still, for every athlete with the reputation (deserved or not) of a Namath or a Thorpe, one can cite hundreds who train with relentless diligence and who, moreover, unabashedly admit to their sometimes inhuman exertions. The Czech distance runner Emil Zatopek, who won three gold medals in the 1952 Olympics, trained so hard that fellow athletes told him he was crazy (on at least one occasion he fainted as he practiced holding his breath). Figure-skating champion Scott Hamilton is frequently on the ice six or seven hours a day. Moses Malone, the Philadelphia 76ers' center, often continues to train long after his teammates have left practice. And sprinter Evelyn Ashford, quoted earlier in this chapter, follows a training regimen that, according to one observer, "looks like the kind of torture that only a masochist would attempt."

Such athletes have sound reasons for their persistence.

First, the human body not only adapts continuously as training proceeds but responds most markedly if intensity is steadily increased. Not long ago researchers at the Institute for Aerobics Research in Dallas, having studied a group of marathon runners, confirmed that long runs and workouts every day contribute more reliably to racing success than shorter and less frequent efforts. The same has been demonstrated in a variety of other activities as well, and there is no reason to suppose that any sports might be cited in which this principle would not hold true.

Second, hard workouts prepare the mind. No athlete could withstand the rigors of an 82-game basketball season, 162 games of baseball spread over six months, or the year-round professional

tennis tour were it not for season after season of the mental preparation that persistent training provides. As it is with top athletes,
so it is with you and me. We may not wish to train with equal
effort, but if we are reluctant to push ourselves, at least on occasion,
our improvement will be distinctly limited.

Don't overtrain. If inadequate training limits performance, too
much training can prove equally harmful by causing injury that
may mean lost weeks or even months. Achieving peak condition is
a balancing act. When you are approaching maximum ability, you
may be perilously close to injury. In *The Sportsmedicine Book* Dr.
Gabe Mirkin warns that overtraining can affect athletes of all abilities. "Beginners," he says, "usually do too much for their out-of-
shape bodies to handle, become injured or fatigued, and quit their
program. Seasoned amateur or professional athletes who overwork
are frequently injured and always dragging." Not long ago Alberto
Salazar, world record holder in the marathon, finally yielded to
his coach, Bill Dellinger, and decided to spend two weeks resting.
Although he was aware that some deconditioning would take place
during his layoff, he felt even more severely threatened by the
opposite danger: fatigue and mental staleness.

Overtraining is avoidable if we are alert to its warning signs.
Furthermore, our caution may benefit us in other ways as well.
More than one competitor, having undergone an enforced layoff,
has turned up for competition worried that he has trained inadequately. As often as not, however, it is at such times that he does
better than he expects. On one occasion, while preparing for a track
meet, Emil Zatopek developed a stomach ailment and spent two
weeks in bed. Getting up just before the meet, he put on his uniform
and won both the 5,000 and 10,000. And in 1964 Abebe Bikila won
the Olympic marathon after spending much of the preceding six
weeks recovering from an appendectomy. These apparent misfor-
tunes were in fact opportunities for some beneficial rest.

Train twelve months a year. A generation or so ago the typical
athlete got into condition only for the season during which his
sport was played. Baseball players arrived at spring training bearing a winter's accretion of fat, tennis players lay fallow most of
the winter, and basketball players scarcely stirred so long as leaves
were on the trees. Today, across the entire spectrum of sport, training has become a year-round activity. Intensity may, it is true,
lessen temporarily in the off-season, but workouts rarely cease.

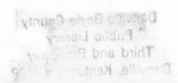
Danville Boyle County
Public Library
Third and Br
Danville, Kentu

Not long ago Alpine ski coach Bob Beattie speculated on the reasons for our country's growing success on the slopes. One of the important changes, he said, is "a program of year-round training, both on and off skis." And Gene Monahan, trainer for the New York Yankees, urges his players to make good use of the winter months. "The job over the winter," he says in a booklet which he provides to Yankee players every autumn, "is basically geared to the maintenance of physical condition. For most players this is the time to improve total fitness as well as work on problem areas they experienced during the recent baseball season. . . . You will improve your skills and become a better player, free from nagging injuries, by developing as many of the fitness components as you can."

Practice overall conditioning. Until not very long ago the typical athlete pursued only his own sport. Today most conditioning authorities have concluded that an athlete can derive significant benefits from working out in other sports as well. For this reason Herschel Walker augments his football skills with karate, Pittsburgh Steelers wide receiver Lynn Swann practices ballet, Tim Gullikson builds endurance for tennis by running two and a half miles a day, New York Yankees pitcher Jay Howell does aerobic dancing, Rosie Casals seeks to improve her tennis skills through Nautilus workouts, and several members of the Denver Nuggets are trying to increase their quickness for basketball by playing tennis.

The usefulness of such supplementary workouts was demonstrated recently when researchers at Lenox Hill Hospital in New York City monitored the heart rates of six professional football players in a practice session preceding tryouts. Of the group, three exceeded a heart rate of 140 beats per minute only 39 percent of the time, while the other three surpassed it half again as often. Because they were able to tolerate effort more easily, those with the lower heart rates made the team while the others did not. Additional conditioning would almost certainly have lowered the heart rates of the three unsuccessful players and might have contributed to more satisfactory tryouts. "Football teams should place more emphasis on cardiovascular conditioning in training sessions," suggested a report on the study.

Overall conditioning has recently been brought into prominence by widespread interest in the triathlon, an event that combines swimming, bicycling and running. While an athlete preparing for a single sport may suffer no overwhelming penalty if he confines training to that sport alone, in the triathlon it is essential to develop all-around fitness. Even an extremely skillful swimmer, cyclist or runner cannot hope to do well in combined scoring without a good performance in all three sports.

Use stress to improve performance. Stress is one of the more frequently heard words of our age. It is no doubt true that we live in a time of considerable—perhaps, some would argue, unprecedented—emotional pressure. Haste, competitiveness and society's vexatious complexities all serve to produce a more or less constant sense of frustration in many of us. The result is that stress is an inevitable accompaniment of our lives. Continually bedeviled by its annoyances, we come to think of it as having little redeeming merit.

Where athletics are concerned, however, this is not altogether the case; we too easily forget that stress can be both physical and psychological. Physical stress, judiciously applied, is one of the chief means of enhancing sports performance. Dr. Van Rensselaer Potter, a biochemistry researcher at the University of Wisconsin Medical School, points out that just one training technique—high-altitude workouts—can confer numerous benefits. For all their undeniable stress, workouts above 5,000 feet bring such welcome changes as an increase in blood volume and hemoglobin concentration, a proliferation of new capillaries, and the development of fresh sites in the cells for energy production. (Studies show that chest volume and lung size may be favorably affected as well.)

The search for beneficial stress is what prompts Benji Durden, one of the world's most accomplished marathoners, to train in sweat clothes even in the hot weather of his native Atlanta. Most guides to athletics recommend staying as cool as possible while working out, but Durden thinks otherwise. And, for him at least, his contrariness clearly works. Never underestimate the varieties of confusion and ambiguity in sport.

Stay at your proper weight. For almost everyone but shot-putters, weightlifters and football linemen, the right athletic weight is less than that suggested in the charts issued by life insurance companies. When first seen by the uninitiated, such athletes as marathon runners and gymnasts appear to be startlingly thin; to shake hands with such a person is to be aware that you are grasping bones as much as flesh. Yet it is only when the human body is at its lightest that it functions with maximum speed and agility. This is why athletes work so tirelessly to avoid gaining excess weight. In the summer of 1983 Rosemary Casals told the author she had recently lost several pounds and felt herself to be quicker on the court than she had been in some time. Steve Denton, whose serve is among the fastest in the game, improved markedly when, under the prodding of his coach, Warren Jacques, he went on a crash diet and lost twenty-five pounds. In 1981, after Henry Rono took off thirty pounds, he lowered his 5,000-meter time by two minutes.

Weight can, of course, come off too quickly and, if one is over-zealous, in excessive amounts. Peter Fleming, who has had as good an opportunity as anyone to observe John McEnroe's career, said recently that he thought his doubles partner's strength declined somewhat a few years ago after he lost weight. Now that McEnroe has regained a few pounds, he went on, he is playing better tennis.

A recent study at the University of Waterloo in Ontario showed that rapid weight loss, the kind commonly practiced by wrestlers before a meet, can reduce muscle glycogen—the body's primary source of energy—by more than half; a sense of fatigue and diminished performance are the common results.

In early 1983 the *New England Journal of Medicine* raised a related issue when it published an article under the title "Running—An Analogue of Anorexia?" Wrote the authors: "We noted that the character, style, and background of certain runners, whom we shall designate 'obligatory' runners, were similar to the character, style, and background of the typical obsessive patient with anorexia." The article raised unsettling questions in the minds of runners as well as other athletes. After all, if sport and anorexia are provably related, might we not have to reassess some of our athletic values? As it turned out, the article's validity was called into question in the weeks following publication by a variety of knowledgeable critics. Its case histories, it was discovered, were not those of bona fide individuals but, as one of the authors told writer Amby Burfoot, composites "of traits and qualities found in a number of the runners we interviewed." Furthermore, according to Burfoot, who explored the issue in a thorough and penetrating article for *Runner's World*, the authors "didn't use tape recorders or keep precise notes, nor did they ask the subjects they interviewed to complete standardized psychological tests. Instead, they asked open-ended questions about their backgrounds and motivations for running."

The most damaging criticism of the article, however, lay not in matters of detail but in the fact that whatever truth it contained was stretched considerably further than the facts seem to have warranted. Like other people, athletes experience emotional problems from time to time, and a compulsive concern with weight is not infrequently among them. But anorexia, even in long-distance runners, is extremely low on the list of such problems.

Avoid injury. This may sound like a quixotic undertaking. After all, injuries are by their very nature accidental, since no athlete sets out deliberately to hurt himself. True enough; for the most part injuries catch us by surprise. In every sport, however, measures can be taken that will minimize the risks—such steps as increasing strength and flexibility, relaxing one's effort when fatigue becomes pronounced and, above all, learning to decipher the warning signs that precede most if not all injuries. (Traumatic injuries, such as might be caused by finding yourself trying to occupy a patch of Astro-Turf where Ed "Too Tall" Jones felt that he and not you belonged, are an obvious exception.)

A fuller discussion of this subject, one of the most important to athletes of all abilities, will be found in Chapter 12.

Warm up before you work out. Stretching is a more effective way to promote suppleness than competing varieties of warmup. This is not to say, however, that other warmup techniques, including massage, should be avoided. On the contrary, as simple a procedure as gently moving around—shooting a few baskets, jogging, hitting ground strokes and volleys for a few minutes—can serve at least two important purposes.

First, such activities prepare the various physiological systems for more strenuous activity by elevating metabolism, improving the range of motion of joints, and increasing blood flow and the speed with which nerve impulses travel.

Second, they reduce the possibility of injury. Jeff Galloway, a member of the U.S. 10,000-meter Olympic team in 1972, says that in his sport "the muscles, tendons, ligaments and other connections need to be gradually introduced to top performance. One of the leading causes of injury is pushing these primary running components too far beyond their capacity too soon."

The same is true of other sports, particularly those involving sudden movement or forceful physical contact. Most top tennis players, wanting to start matches at full effort, warm up for at least thirty minutes. Bob Russo, a widely respected trainer, says,

"Tennis uses almost every muscle in the body, so it's very important to do a complete warmup before stepping onto the court to hit." He suggests a brisk walk or jog for ten or twelve minutes, followed by stretching.

If your muscles are sore, rest. Athletes have long believed that after a hard effort, whether in training or competition, the quickest way to recover is by working out the next day. The common understanding has been that this practice loosens up the muscles, stimulates blood flow, and in these and other ways speeds the recovery process.

Recent research casts doubts on this ancient belief. Investigators at Ohio and Ball State universities recruited a group of marathon runners and, after a race, divided them into two groups. Members of the first group ran for twenty minutes the day after competition and for somewhat longer periods on each subsequent day. Meanwhile, the runners in the second group simply rested. After seven days, when the investigators tested the volunteers, the resting group turned out to have recovered more fully.*

The problem of recovery from athletic effort is complicated by the persistence of the physical damage that occurs. In 1980 researchers reported in the *Yale Journal of Biology and Medicine* on an investigation in which the blood of Boston Marathon participants was tested for the presence of creatine kinase, a chemical that accompanies muscle injury. Four weeks after the race, a significant number of the runners still displayed elevated creatine kinase levels, indicating that they had not yet returned to prerace condition. Muscle damage would not, presumably, be as persistent following less stressful activities, yet neither would it disappear at once.

Get enough sleep. When we lack time for all the things we need to do, it's tempting to cut corners by sleeping less. For athletes this is not a good idea, however. Although instances are on record

---

* This is yet another instance of a myth that might have been laid to rest much earlier, thereby sparing countless athletes the needless discomforts of postcompetition workouts. The author has in his files a portion of a thesis written at the University of California by St. John Francis Smith. Mr. Smith describes a study in which muscle soreness was shown to be prolonged rather than relieved by exercise. "After having performed an exercise which produces muscle soreness of the delayed type," he writes, "later performance of moderate exercise results in a tendency to perpetuate the soreness. . . . Coaches and trainers whose primary objective is immediate relief of this type of soreness had best forgo moderate exercise as a remedy." Mr. Smith's thesis was written more than forty years ago, in 1942.

of outstanding performances following surprisingly little sleep, it is well established that such deprivation usually has an adverse effect. In 1981 a group of researchers in Prague, Czechoslovakia, announced results of a study in which volunteers were prevented from sleeping for five days while levels of key muscular enzymes were monitored. Sleep loss was found to lessen enzyme activity, a sign that oxidation—and therefore the capacity to perform work— had diminished. Although five sleepless days are more than most of us ever experience, the same phenomena no doubt occur, although presumably with diminished severity, when sleep loss is less severe.

Drink enough water. Loss of body fluids, such as occurs in all high-intensity sports through sweating, not only reduces performance capacity but can also contribute to heat illness. It is therefore important that fluids continually be replaced. In a study at the University of Alabama, W. Donald Myers and Kennon T. Francis administered a commercial replacement fluid to football players as they worked out in temperatures as high as 95 degrees. They found that a surprisingly large amount of the fluid—about a pint every fifteen minutes—was necessary in order to maintain proper hydration.

On the basis of what is known about such commercial fluids— Gatorade is perhaps the best-known preparation—there is no reason to suppose that the results would have been any different had plain water been used. Commenting on the University of Alabama study, Dr. Roy J. Shephard, director of the University of Toronto's School of Physical and Health Education, said, "There is little need to buy expensive commercial fluids under the climate conditions specified—water is as effective as any other replacement fluid."

Stay as cool as possible. The human body functions best when its temperature remains close to normal; any substantial deviation brings a loss of efficiency and can even be dangerous. In warm weather, therefore, an athlete should drink cool fluids, dress lightly, train in the shade or during the cool of the day, and work out less vigorously than usual.

Select proper equipment. As Chapter 13 will show, we are currently in the midst of a revolution in sports equipment. So much that is new—and in some cases genuinely more useful than was previously available—is currently being offered that choosing what is suited to our needs can be a bafflingly complicated undertaking. Even the ratings published by sports magazines are not necessarily reliable guides, since individual variations are so pronounced. Should I buy a tennis racquet as big as a snowshoe? I can hardly hope to decide without considerable experimentation and perhaps the advice of experts.

The selection dilemma is compounded by the fact that the usefulness of much of the newly available equipment has yet to be convincingly demonstrated. Would I be wise to suspend myself upside down by special boots? Wear a beeping watch to set the proper pace as I jog? Breathe through a plastic mouthpiece to ward off the cold? Until the equipment revolution abates enough to afford us time to catch up, our befuddlement is unlikely to vanish.

After a layoff, resume cautiously. It is not entirely clear how much conditioning is lost when for one reason or another we interrupt or reduce the intensity of a training program. Dr. Steven Subotnick, a widely consulted sportsmedicine authority, declares, "Injured runners lose three weeks for every week they are off. The body deconditions very fast." Other authorities, however, have arrived at different conclusions. Recent research at the University of Illinois, for example, suggests that even a two-thirds reduction in training over a period of fifteen weeks does not adversely influence endurance. The physiologist E. C. Frederick comments: "The fact that this could be done for up to fifteen weeks with little or no change in endurance capacity should assuage the fears of most of us who have believed, up until now, that even a slight drop in mileage should mean a significant loss of fitness."

Consider the psychological aspects of athletics. The world of sport would be considerably less puzzling than it is if games were won solely by muscular skill, without the complicating intervention of the mind. Increasingly, however, athletes and their coaches are coming to suspect that the mind may be the single most important element in training as well as in competition.

A growing number of scientific studies confirm the crucial role of both the emotions and the intellect. In 1982 Susan G. Ziegler, James Klinzing and Kirk Williamson of Cleveland State University reported in the *Journal of Sports Psychology* on an investigation into the effects of psychological stress not on subjectively perceived feelings, which by their nature tend to elude accurate measurement, but on such verifiable physiological functions as heart rate and oxygen consumption. Applying standard stress-management techniques to one group of cross-country runners but not to a corresponding control group, the researchers found that mental training had a consistently beneficial effect on physical performance.

In early 1983 Martina Navratilova told a reporter, "No one can beat me psychologically. Those days are gone." Her optimism, described by the *New York Times* as "invincible," lasted during the ensuing months, and Miss Navratilova was seldom seriously pressed. There can be little doubt that attitude had much to do with her succession of victories.

An exploration of this increasingly important subject, with a number of suggestions for improving performance by the use of recently discovered psychological techniques, will be found in the next chapter.

Relax. An odd paradox exists in athletics: To do one's best, one is ill advised to try too hard; a sense of philosophical distance almost always yields the best results. It is in fact a commonplace among athletes that remarkable performances, including many that are entirely out of the ordinary, most often taken place when they are unanticipated. Marathon runners frequently report that their fastest races are their least taxing, and almost any participant in a sport that requires a number of complex skills—basketball or lacrosse or hockey—can recall miraculous days on which, with less than normal effort, everything went wonderfully right. Edwin Moses, the world record holder in the 400-meter hurdles, says he runs his best races when he can bring himself to avoid what he calls "over-concentrating." And every tennis player knows the hazards of choking, which is nothing more than an inability to relax when we take a match too seriously.

Sharpen for competition. Months or years of practice, no matter how faithfully pursued, serve little purpose if an athlete is not at a peak on the day of competition. Conditioning consists of two principal phases: first, the acquisition of basic strength and fundamental skills; second, fine-tuning, in which training is intensified. Mary Decker has called peaking "being in the best shape of your life." Her definition, though entirely true, is for most of us more easily said than done. Miss Decker's coach, Dick Brown, says of peaking, "It's a mysterious thing. Coaches fret about that more than anything else. I think peaking can be a science, but at this point it's an art." The high jumper Dwight Stones, who has cleared 7 feet 8 inches, works hard to peak for an important track meet

Edwin Moses

such as the Olympic Trials. "Three weeks after the trials," he says, "I'll be flat as a pancake. I won't be able to clear seven feet then if my life depends on it."

Tom Osler, an authority on running, suggests in *The Conditioning of Distance Runners* that "great and astonishing improvement can be observed in just six weeks." The sharpening period will vary from sport to sport and from athlete to athlete, but there is no doubt that, used judiciously, it can produce performances that would otherwise be unattainable. Told his record-setting time after the 1975 Boston Marathon, Bill Rodgers exclaimed, "It can't be true. I can't run that fast." Years of training had made him a first-rate marathoner; sharpening had turned him into the best who had ever run the course.

CHAPTER 4

Mind Over Muscle

At least 50 percent of the process of playing well
is the result of mental and psychological factors.

—JAMES E. LOEHR, *sports psychologist*

IN EARLY 1983, following a layoff from the game that he had once
played with masterful wizardry, Bjorn Borg was attempting a
comeback. Although he appeared to be purposeful enough in his
efforts, and beyond question still possessed, at age twenty-six, the
requisite physical abilities, several of his traditional rivals expressed doubts about whether he would manage to recapture the
form that had earned him five consecutive Wimbledon victories,
an achievement unprecedented in the history of tennis. "I don't
know if he's mentally got the desire," said John McEnroe, echoing
the thoughts of other players who, like him, had experienced the
relentless struggle necessary to remain at or near the summit of
an intricate and demanding sport.

Although Borg tried diligently, in the end he abandoned his
comeback attempt, acknowledging that he had lost the necessary
desire. "I cannot give 100 percent," he said. "If I cannot do that,
it would not be fair to myself to go on."

No one could doubt that Borg, had he thoroughly wanted to
regain his championship form, would have been able to do so. Few
players, after all, had so decisively dominated the game or done
so for as long. No, in the end it was not any diminishment of

physical capacities that conquered Borg but a slackening of will. Paradoxically, although he had relied throughout his career on an apparently emotionless game, it was mind and not muscle that ultimately failed him.

The mind's importance in athletics is well known. In Greek antiquity, training was undertaken at least in part to accustom the mind to the rigors of competition. And in our own century Paavo Nurmi, who won Olympic medals in distance running during the 1920's, once declared, "Mind is everything, muscles pieces of rubber." Only during the past several years, however, have athletes and their coaches begun to perceive that the mental component of sport may be not merely important but paramount, that strength, speed, agility and the other athletic skills are not in themselves enough, ever, to produce a champion. The champion invariably has something more—a special way of looking upon competition that permits him to elevate his game when he most needs to perform at his best.

The difference was described with uncommon clarity by the Soviet weightlifter Yuri Vlasov, who in an interview with a *New York Times* writer said, "At the peak of tremendous and victorious effort, while the blood is pounding in your head, all suddenly becomes quiet within you. Everything seems clearer and whiter than ever before, as if great spotlights had been turned on you. At that moment you have the conviction that you contain all the power in the world, that you are capable of everything, that you have wings." Not every athlete, even in his or her finest moments, will experience Vlasov's poetic sense of peaceful power. Still, it is an athletic commonplace that one's best competitive experiences—peak performances, in the customary language of sports psychology—are likely to be those from which strain is startlingly absent and in which the chief feeling is of limitless ability.

The current emphasis on mental strengths and weaknesses, and on their application to performance on the playing field, has come about partly because scientific researchers, in increasing numbers, have found themselves fascinated by the role of the mind in the games we play. The North American Society for the Psychology of Sport and Physical Activity, which listed scarcely more than a dozen members at its founding in 1966, today has a membership of some 500. A quarterly publication, *The Journal of Sport Psychology*, chronicles discoveries in the field. And sports psychology is rapidly becoming a staple of university curricula. Springfield

College, for example, where basketball had its origins and where sport has always been taken seriously, offers a graduate major in "psychophysical movement," the study of how the mind interacts with the active body.

Despite such attention, however, sports psychology remains a science in its infancy. (Other parts of the world, most notably the Soviet Union, have been at it considerably longer than we have and have applied their psychological findings more assiduously.) Furthermore, it is at best an inexact science. Bruce C. Ogilvie of San Jose State University, a respected clinical psychologist who has been at work in the field for many years, says, "In spite of everything we've accomplished, sports psychology remains not so much science as an art form. The research is meager, and we know that 65 to 70 percent of what we do is placebo." He adds, on the other hand, "Let's not knock it; medicine is 80 percent placebo."

Nonetheless, a recognition of the crucial role the mind plays in athletes is increasingly visible across a broad range of sports. Some cases in point:

- In the 1982–83 season the University of Illinois basketball team compiled a strikingly successful record after it undertook a psychological training program. One player, Derek Harper, increased his field goal average by more than 35 percent.
- As a rookie on the PGA tour, Dick Zokol turned to a psychologist, Dr. Richard Lenetto of Toronto, who helped him learn how to relax, to discover the natural rhythms of his game and, not incidentally, to increase his earnings severalfold.
- Tom Gullikson, a ranking tennis pro referred to earlier, was having difficulties with his confidence a few years ago. He turned to a sports psychologist, Dr. James E. Loehr, and within a short time regained much of his earlier form. Tennis was, in fact, forever altered by Timothy Gallwey's 1974 best-seller, *The Inner Game of Tennis*, with its emphasis on the game's psychological complexities and how a player can most effectively turn them to his advantage.
- Finally, in a variety of other sports, an increasing number of athletes have become convinced that what happens in the mind is fully as important as what takes place in the rest of the body. Rick McKinney, one of the nation's most consistently accurate archers, says, "Anyone can buy the equipment I use, but only the person with the strongest mind can make it really work." And Joe Fields, center for the New York Jets, said recently, "Any

sport is 95 percent mental, and anyone who tells you differently doesn't know what he's talking about."

The reason for the current emphasis on the psychological aspects of athletics is not at all obscure. At the topmost levels of a sport, differences in skill itself are likely to be slight. Given the right day and reasonable luck, countless baseball players might hit a home run, innumerable wide receivers make a difficult sideline catch, a dozen or more marathon participants outrun Alberto Salazar or Rod Dixon. That for the most part they do not ordinarily do these things is largely attributable to the fact that such characteristics as tenacity, concentration, resistance to fatigue and a fondness for either individual or team sports differ much more markedly among athletes than does pure playing ability. "At least 50 percent of the process of playing well," says James Loehr, "is the result of mental and psychological factors." Writes Steven J. Danish, a Penn State sports psychologist: "The difference between an outstanding athletic performance and a good athletic performance really has very little to do with physical skills. It is mostly related to mental skills." In the same vein, Gayle Godwin, UCLA's women's tennis coach, told the author, "A player's attitude is the most important factor in competition. The farther toward the top you get, the more important it becomes. Everyone's game is good at that level, so it's psychological factors that make most of the difference."

Sports psychology appears to some observers to have so much promise that one writer on the subject, Rod K. Dishman, has called it "the last frontier in the exercise and sport sciences." In the eyes of its proponents it has two distinct and enormously valuable uses: helping individual athletes reach their potential and identifying, in some cases far in advance of actual achievement, those men and women who are eventually likely to excel.

The latter function derives from the fact that athletic excellence appears to go hand in hand with distinct personality traits. As long ago as 1954 a researcher named W. R. Johnson, having tested a number of athletes who were either all-Americans or top national competitors, found them to be more self-assured, more aggressive and more anxious than less gifted people. A few years later E. G. Booth, Jr., reported that no fewer than twenty-two items on the widely used Minnesota Multiphasic Personality Inventory were able to discriminate fairly reliably between good and poor competitors. (Among other incidental findings, he revealed that participants in individual sports, such as swimming and running, were charac-

teristically more depressed than those involved in team sports.)
And for many years Soviet researchers have been testing for ideal
physical, psychological and emotional traits among the young. Those
deemed capable of unusual athletic achievement are customarily
placed in special sports schools.

Sports psychologists in the West are currently turning to increasingly discriminating varieties of analysis, including many that
could not have been accomplished, or for that matter even con-
templated, before the computer era. Not long ago, for example,
three researchers examined some fifty wrestlers who were competing in a Big Ten championship and compared their performances with replies to a long list of psychological inquiries (e.g.,
"How much do you think about the quality of your performance?"
"To what extent do you use visual imagery in your training?").
The investigators—Daniel Gould, Maureen Weiss and Robert
Weinberg—found that success in wrestling was closely correlated with three qualities: self-confidence, the ability to focus one's
concentration, and a feeling that one is close to maximum potential.

The first two, it is apparent, are largely independent of specific
physical abilities. It is this fascinating aspect of such tests that
leads some sports psychologists to speculate that one day it may
be possible, with striking reliability, to identify a successful athlete
long before he or she has picked up a racquet or thrown a ball. "At
the University of Wisconsin," a leading sports psychologist named
William P. Morgan wrote in *Psychology Today*, "we have given the
MMPI [the psychological test referred to above] to freshman wrestlers and rowers during their first week at school for five successive
seasons. When we correlated the results with their careers over the
next four years, the successful athletes—those who later made the
varsity teams—showed significantly better mental health . . . than
their less successful classmates."

In another investigation, involving candidates for an Olympic
wrestling team, those selected to represent the United States proved
to be well below average in such measures as tension, depression,
confusion and fatigue, and well above average in vigor. Unsuccessful candidates, by contrast, were comparable in outlook to the
general population.

Psychological studies, it has also been shown, are able to help
predict the likelihood of injury. They accomplish this by pinpoint-
ing the varieties of emotional stress, such as might be caused by

a parent's death, that typically precede a mishap. Since injury so often means lost training time and a consequent decline in skills, such studies can serve to improve athletic performance.

Some athletes, of course, have no need for a sports psychologist. These are the naturals, those men and women who experience no apparent difficulty in doing with ease and precision what the rest of us struggle so mightily to achieve. Asked about what a sports psychologist might do for such athletes, Bruce Ogilvie shrugged and said, "How can you improve on perfection?" The rest of us, as representatives of a lesser species, might well benefit from the ministrations of the right sports psychologist. But how much benefit could we expect to derive?

Thus far, no one can be sure. For one thing, sports psychology is not yet a settled discipline. "There's a lot of quackery going on," says Ogilvie. "Then, too, in many respects we don't really know what we're doing. We haven't improved much on what the yoga masters were teaching three thousand years ago." Jon Spaventa, a sports psychologist at the University of California at Santa Barbara, shares Ogilvie's view. "We don't have many statistics or experiments to show that sports psychology works," he says.

Furthermore, for a variety of reasons many athletes themselves are skeptical of overanalyzing performance problems. "You can't explain slumps," says Jay Howell, a pitcher for the New York Yankees. "Everyone gets them, but practically nobody knows what to do about them. You finally leave a slump when you don't pay any attention to your body. You just throw the ball and you know it's going to go where you want it to go."

Sports psychology, moreover, practically never confers instantaneous relief. The typical sports psychologist works with athletes over an entire season or longer, and even then no one can be entirely certain whether improvement, if any, is the result of psychology or merely of time. "I do not know of any quick and easy method from psychology that will increase performance," writes Dorcas Susan Butt, an associate professor of psychology at the University of British Columbia (and formerly Canada's top-ranking women's tennis player), in *Coach, Athlete, and the Sport Psychologist*.

One reason the techniques of sports psychology are so slow to bring identifiable results is that, as few of us need to be reminded, the human mind is forbiddingly complex. An apparently simple problem, such as an inability to concentrate sufficiently for the purposes of a particular sport, may in fact be far more complicated than it seems, reflecting motives, goals and anxieties that lie buried so deeply as to be all but inaccessible.

Any athlete, for example, may be presumed to be interested in winning. What other purpose, after all, is there in competing? Yet it has repeatedly been demonstrated that many athletes harbor a distinct fear of doing well. Writing recently in the *American Journal of Sports Medicine*, Stephen Rosenblum observed that some athletes win minor contests aplenty but rarely win important ones, while others repeatedly injure themselves and in that way avoid outstanding performances.

One reason is that outstanding performances exact a price, as George Sauer, Jr., the former New York Jet, observed not long ago. "You stick out too much," he said feelingly in an article written for the *New York Times*, "the world enlarges around you to dangerous proportions, and you are too evident to too many others. There is a vulnerability in this and, oddly enough, some guilt involved in standing out. It is a subtle, inescapable facet of public people and is rarely understood."

Yannick Noah, who won the French Open in 1983, acknowledged a few months later that his life had been greatly changed by his victory. "Afterward," he said, "I felt here I was, still the same person with the same feelings and attitudes, but the people around me, my surroundings, were changed. People look at you differently, expect something else from you."

The success problem may be even more severe for women than for men. At the University of North Carolina, John M. Silva III recently asked some 200 undergraduates, both athletes and nonathletes, a series of questions intended to assess their fear of doing well. When the results were analyzed, they revealed that women, perhaps wary of losing their femininity, were significantly more uneasy about achieving success than were men.

A growing number of scientific studies suggest, in fact, that even in our purportedly liberated age athletics are quite a different matter for women than for men. True, male and female athletes have been found to be more similar in personality than are, for example, athletes and nonathletes of the same sex. Nonetheless, distinct differences remain. Personality tests show that, compared with men, women are inclined to be less dominant and less self-sufficient. In athletics, therefore, where dominance and self-sufficiency are valuable traits, a woman who wants to become successful may have to modify her natural inclinations. Studies suggest not only that such modification regularly takes place but that no exorbitant price need be paid for it. Several years ago J. F. Kane and J. L. Callaghan, having studied the personalities of world-class women tennis players, concluded that they demonstrated high emotional stability and great ego strength—just as a male player would be expected to—but that they nonetheless retained "markedly feminine personalities."

Perhaps the most reliable antidote to the conflicts so many women experience is simply self-confidence. The problem, of course, is that self-confidence, directly sought, is stubbornly elusive. Rather, self-confidence is a characteristic that tends to manifest itself as a by-product of achievement. Here again, distance running offers a relevant example. Lynn McCutcheon, a psychologist who has spent the past several years looking into effects of the sport, reports as follows on an investigation into runners' attitudes: "Long-distance-running females were . . . more likely to endorse the notion that human beings have control over their own fate (at least as compared with nonrunners). They agreed that the average person is largely the master of her own fate, and disagreed that success in life is determined by forces outside of her own control."

Experience itself is the most effective confidence builder. A few years ago Charles B. Corbin, a professor of health, physical education and recreation at Kansas State University, tested elementary school children as they played electronic Ping-Pong, pedaled a stationary bicycle and sought to outdo each other in a balancing game. Before the activities began, Corbin reported, the girls were markedly less self-confident than the boys. Immediately afterward, however, no difference was discernible. "Because of their inexperience and because they perceive some sports as 'male' activities," he explained, "they tend to assume they can't do well. . . . Even single experiences of success can be important for preadolescents in developing self-confident behavior in competitive situations."

Corbin's argument is as true for adults as for children. In 1976, when women were first admitted to the United States Military Academy at West Point, many were unable to accomplish the institution's standard obstacle-course tasks. Colonel James L. Anderson, the academy's physical fitness director, recalls seeing new cadets standing at the bottom of a rope, crying because of their inability to climb it. Instructors set about teaching rope climbing to the women. "The following year," says Anderson, "the incoming women *knew* women could climb a rope. So they didn't waste time crying—they just went ahead and learned how to do it, difficult as it may have been. It was a fascinating sociological lesson."

Such accomplishments exert a powerful effect on women's self-esteem. In 1982 the *Journal of Sport Psychology* described a revealing study conducted by Elizabeth Y. Brown, James R. Morrow, Jr., and Stephen M. Livingston. The researchers' purpose was to discover what effect, if any, a fourteen-week program of jogging, weightlifting and flexibility training might have on the way young women view themselves. By the use of a standard measure, the Tennessee Self-Concept Scale, fifty college students were tested both before and after the program. Following the fourteen weeks of exercise the women were found to be distinctly more satisfied with their lives.

This could, of course, be nothing more than a scientific way of expressing what most of us have already found out for ourselves: that achievement, especially when hard-won, begets satisfaction. Nonetheless, it is a crucial lesson for women who hope to become more skillful in athletics. For each success provides sustenance and encouragement for further effort. The cycle is endless, and endlessly satisfying.*

When a woman, or for that matter a man, consults a sports psychologist, an inherent contradiction is inevitably part of the encounter. Presumably whatever psychological efforts are applied are being directed toward enhancing one's chances of winning, yet winning itself is not at all a customary event. In his book *Winning Isn't Normal* Dr. Keith Bell points out that winning is in fact a significant deviation from the expected course of events. "Winning is unusual," he writes. "In order to win you must do extraordinary things. You can't just be one of the crowd. The crowd doesn't win. You have to be willing to stand out and act differently. . . . You can't train like everyone else. You have to train more and train better."

Part of training more and training better—the most important part, some would insist—consists of giving proper attention to the advantages that can be gained through appropriate psychological techniques. Much has been written, and continues to be written, about this vast and vastly complex subject, and anyone foolhardy

---

* It has only one apparent drawback. According to a study by D. A. Cohen and M. L. Young, women with the highest self-concepts are more subject to injury than those who think less well of themselves. The reason, presumably, is that self-confident people, both men and women, are more inclined to take chances.

enough to set out to stay abreast of its intricacies would soon discover that he had undertaken a lifetime's labor. Nonetheless, most sports psychologists would subscribe to the principles and practices that will occupy our attention for the remainder of this chapter. For if conscientiously followed they should, among other effects, accomplish the following:

- Increase an athlete's self-image and self-confidence.
- Make athletic performances more consistent.
- Enhance relaxation and decrease tension before, after and during competition.
- Improve concentration.
- Reduce sensitivity to pain.

Here, then, is a distillation of much of the recent research into significant facets of sports psychology:

Set specific goals. An athlete whose goals are vague, who wants merely to "do better," will probably always be dissatisfied. Under such circumstances, after all, who is to judge success? Is scoring 12 points in a basketball game a good performance or not? What about a game lost to a favored team, but more narrowly than was expected?

What are needed, as a corrective to ambiguities like these, are clearly recognizable goals: to avoid careless errors, to demonstrate better teamwork, to run farther than you are now able. The attainment of such goals is largely within your own control, rather than subject to what an opponent does or does not do. As Chris Brooks, former women's track coach at Penn State, writes, in *Coaching Women's Athletics*, "The athlete must have concrete goals that are totally within her control and not dependent on other factors in order to measure her success or failure."

Success under such circumstances is nothing less than progress toward one's goals; it does not necessarily consist of winning. Bill Dellinger, Alberto Salazar's coach, insists on establishing specific goals for the athletes under his direction. "Every runner, no matter at what level, should have a goal," he told the author. "A goal gives you something to work toward." (His own goal, he said, is to "run forty minutes a day and have it be enjoyable." Salazar's, as you might suppose, is somewhat different.)

Develop confidence. At the University of Adelaide in Australia not long ago, Christina Lee, a researcher, conducted a revealing experiment. She asked a group of gymnasts to predict their scores in a meet to be held a few days later. These competitors' predictions, which might so easily have been flawed by wishful thinking, turned out to be more accurate indicators than any other measure, including the gymnasts' performances in previous competitions.

Miss Lee's study was of modest size—it included only fourteen gymnasts—and was, moreover, confined to only one sport. Nonetheless, it reminds us of an important truth about competition: that we accomplish largely what we expect to accomplish. This is the chief reason an outstanding performance rarely comes in the absence of self-confidence. Olympic gold medalist Greg Louganis, who spins and twists with such stratospheric agility from his thirty-three-foot-high platform, once joked, "With the new dives I'm doing, just for survival's sake I *have* to be confident." The gymnast Mario McCutcheon has said, "I feel the most at ease on the high bar. There's a lot of fear in the high bar, and I guess I'm the type of person that likes to challenge myself. I like the high bar because it's dangerous and elegant at the same time."

Just after he had won a Masters golf tournament in the mid-1960's, Jack Nicklaus was described in this way by a British golf writer, P. J. Ward-Thomas: "There is an impregnable confidence, an almost overpowering belief in himself, the like of which I have never known in any other player of games. It is alive in every move of his solid frame, in the urgency of his walk, the crisp unhesitating speech, the direct regard of the clear blue eyes that see life in pure straight lines with none of the doubts, inhibitions and fears that sabotage others. There is no material for the analyst's couch in Jack. Faith in one's own ability is perhaps the greatest single gift a golfer can have."

Such a faith can, of course, rationally be developed only to the extent that one's abilities allow it. (It would do me little good, and would in fact render me a prime candidate for psychiatric aid, were I to let myself imagine that I might appear in the next NBA playoffs.) The essential task is to have as much confidence as is justified by the facts. In 1983, after Eamonn Coghlan ran his first sub-3:50 indoor mile, he said, "I never doubted it at all. At least I *tried* not to doubt it in my mental preparations." There was no hint of braggadocio in this candid observation; Coghlan simply knew what he might accomplish on a good day, just as Babe Ruth, pointing at the bleachers, did. The same is true of Rod Dixon, winner of the 1983 New York City Marathon. Long before he had even thought of entering the marathon, he told John Hawley, a researcher, "My whole aim was to make my presence felt and to shoot for number one. That's always been my attitude in athletics— that you must be number one. I've trained exclusively to be the best."

Confidence of this magnitude is by no means rare among top competitors. An accomplished triathlete, Mark MacIntyre of Greenwich, Connecticut, said recently, "My attitude toward training and racing is that in my triathlons it's either winning or nothing at all. I go for the win. And I feel that I should win every single time I go out." MacIntyre does not, of course, win every time, just as no other athlete does. All the same, his confidence serves him well. In Hawaii's 1983 Iron Man Triathlon he finished sixth out of nearly a thousand competitors, and in his mid-twenties he is continuing to improve.

Confidence is so essential to superior sports performance that professional athletes monitor their moods as assiduously as any airline pilot studies his instrument panel. The Pittsburgh Steelers' quarterback, David Woodley, once commented on the difference between playing well and playing poorly: "What accounts for the difference? I don't know. We're not doing anything different. I'm not doing anything different. I think a lot of it has to do with confidence. When things are working well, you have a different

PSYCHOLOGICAL VS PHYSICAL FITNESS

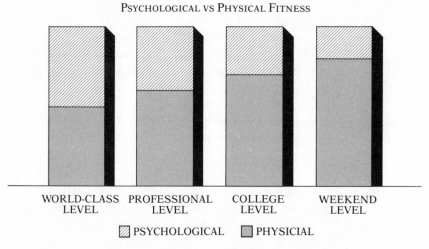

SOURCE: From James L. Anderson and Martin Cohen, *The Competitive Edge*. New York: William Morrow, 1981.

type of attitude. You *expect* things to happen rather than *hope* things will happen." Finally, professional golfer Rex Caldwell said not long ago, "My mental attitude is very strong. Every time I walk up to a shot I feel like it's going to go where I'm aiming it."

Can the weekend athlete develop such supercharged confidence? Perhaps not. Confidence of that sort comes only from repeatedly executing an action flawlessly. When John McEnroe decides to attempt an ace, he can afford to be confident; he has, after all, served more than a few during his tennis career. The average athlete can, however, work to develop a confidence commensurate with his abilities. As James G. Bennett and James E. Pravitz put it in *The Miracle of Sports Psychology,* "Your thoughts can give you confidence, hope and determination. You cannot think fearfully and build confidence. You cannot think of losing and expect to win. You cannot think indecisively and be quick to act. Nor can you think of failure and expect success."

Try to enhance team spirit. Team spirit—or cohesiveness, as it is commonly called in scholarly circles—is a concept much beloved by coaches that few athletes thoroughly understand because of its inherent vagueness. Some time ago a researcher proposed, as a definition, "the desire for group success." Such a desire is complex. It not only varies from team to team but from moment to moment and is, furthermore, subject to such influences as friendships between a team's members and the value attached to membership in the group. Since a cohesive team is likely to share the same competitive goals, a group that exhibits strong team spirit will typically be more successful than one that for some reason is weaker in team spirit. Whatever a coach or player can do, therefore, to build a sense of unity among team members is likely to pay off in points earned on the court or playing field.

Mentally rehearse what you hope to accomplish in competition. On the night before a game, Glen Hanlon of the New York Rangers customarily visualizes an entire hypothetical game play by play. Some might think this an odd way of occupying himself, when he might more contentedly be watching television or getting some extra sleep, but in fact it accords precisely with recent findings in sports psychology. For researchers have discovered that when practice occurs solely in the mind, it is more effective in at least some respects than when it takes place on the playing field.

This is why so many coaches urge their athletes to use the techniques of mental rehearsal, and why so many top competitors have adopted them. Robert Wipfler, head baseball coach at the Landon School in Bethesda, Maryland, is a proponent of what he calls "mental batting practice"—asking players to imagine themselves at bat, to visualize a variety of pitches, and to picture themselves connecting solidly with each. The runner John Gregoreck, a 3:51 miler and Olympic steeplechaser, says, "I like to plan out my big races well in advance. I start about a week before a race, imagining where I'll be at certain stages." The sports psychologist Robert M. Nideffer reports in *The Inner Athlete* that Pete Maravich used to replay entire basketball games in his mind. A recent study revealed that well over half of world-class gymnasts visualize their entire routine prior to competition.

Mental rehearsal is no Johnny-come-lately in sports. Its theoretical antecedents are traceable to the late nineteenth century, when W. B. Carpenter, author of *Principles of Mental Physiology*, postulated what he called an "ideo-motor principle." According to this principle, whatever idea occupies our minds finds expression in our muscles. Since Carpenter's time, the ideo-motor principle has been augmented in a number of ways, but psychologists of nearly a century later have no important quarrel with it. "Mental imagery is one of the most important areas in sports today," says Dr. Patricia Mihevic, a psychologist at the University of California at Santa Barbara.

There is no doubt that mental rehearsal is well worth an athlete's attention. James Loehr, who currently provides psychological counsel for a number of professional athletes, calls it "one of the most powerful mental training strategies available to performing athletes," and Peter Klavora and Juri Daniel, editors of *Coach, Athlete and the Sport Psychologist*, cite an instance in which its value was displayed in perhaps the purest possible form. Robert Foster, a rifle champion, was called into military service and was unable to train for a full year. During that time his practice consisted of ten minutes a day devoted to mental rehearsal. At the end of the year he entered a meet and broke his own world record.

Strive for consistency. All other things being equal, it is apparent that an athlete who trains 365 days a year will probably perform more ably than one who works out only every other day or so. This is so evident that it would hardly be worth mentioning if it were not for the fact that regular training is a principle that is elusively difficult to follow. Any runner who, on a winter morning foul with sleet and icy gales, has ever debated whether to venture forth that day knows at first hand the magnetic lure of slothful inconsistency. Yet regular workouts, no matter how severe the temptations to skip more days than we should, are the backbone of successful performance. Mere aptitude, and for that matter even brilliance, cannot serve as a substitute.

Consistency in competition is a different matter, since it is partly dependent on unavoidable periodic fluctuations in physical and psychological functioning. It is nonetheless possible to train oneself to be more consistent, particularly if an athlete is aware of the various contrary pressures. "In baseball," says the New York Yankees trainer, Gene Monahan, "you need to develop a psychological endurance. Let's say you've been pitching over a long period. The manager has been screaming at you, the catcher has been giving you all those signs, the fans have been yelling, the trainer has been telling you not to break down. Through all this you still have to concentrate, to keep your head together. It can be done, but it's not easy."

Rich "Goose" Gossage, one of baseball's most reliable pitchers, said recently, "My goal is to be as consistent as possible." Bill Russell, who led the Boston Celtics to eleven NBA titles and was a five-time recipient of the Most Valuable Player award, expressed much the same view in *Go Up for Glory*. "I am paid because people pay to see me play," he wrote. "Therefore I must give them forty-eight minutes' worth of the best game I have, regardless of whether we are playing for the world championship, or just playing out the string in early March, after we've already won the regular season title."

In his book *Athletic Excellence* James Loehr writes, "Consistency is the ultimate measure of mental toughness in an athlete. It is also the earmark of any real champion."

Be up for competition. Most athletes follow their own procedures, often unique to their special competitive style, in order to establish a proper frame of mind for competition. Geoff Smith, winner of the 1984 Boston Marathon, says, "If I can go into a race without thinking about running, I'll run well. Before competition I like to get away from everybody. I prefer to sit by myself and relax." So does Hubert Birkenmeier of the New York Cosmos, but he adds his own idiosyncrasies. "When I go to the stadium," he says, "I always go the same way. And when I go onto the field I always go past the right side of the goal, never the left." Kelly Tripucka of the Detroit Pistons, describing himself as "very superstitious," says, "I always drive to the game by the same route and put on my uniform in the same order." Rusty Staub of the New York Mets recently described a technique he followed at one time in his twenty-one-year baseball career: "If I didn't feel good I would have people slap me in the face to get the adrenaline going. Just have someone give *you* a good slap and see how *your* body reacts." (Effective as it no doubt was, Staub's procedure never gained wide acceptance among fellow players.)

Some athletes question the value of such ritualistic techniques. "I used to have a favorite uniform," says the runner Matt Centrowitz. "In college I had a special pair of spikes and a special T-shirt to warm up in. Once when my T-shirt was dirty on a day we were having a meet, I had to rummage around in the laundry for it. Now I try not to fall into doing that kind of thing. What if I lose my bag, or I go to the Olympics and I have to wear a special uniform?" Franco Harris of the Pittsburgh Steelers shares Centrowitz's mistrust of pregame rituals. "I don't have a set routine before a game," he says. "If we're winning, I guess I keep doing the same things, but I can't recall what those things are."

For many athletes, being up for competition depends not on mental techniques but on thorough preparation. "If you know you're in shape and have hit enough tennis balls in practice," says Tim Gullikson, "you have confidence. For me, there's no other way to have that confidence." Another tennis player, Vitas Gerulaitis, also stresses the importance of being ready for competition. "You've got to figure out a plan of what you want to do," he says. "If I'm scheduled to play Ivan Lendl, all I'm going to be doing is sprinting to the net and hitting a lot of balls to his backhand, so I'll practice those things, along with plenty of serves and overheads. With McEnroe it would be different. I'd get somebody left-handed to serve to me and charge the net so I could get used to what McEnroe does. Then I'd feel prepared."

Lee Roy Selmon, defensive end for the Tampa Bay Buccaneers, likes to spend several days in mental preparation for a game. "Motivation for me begins early in the week, at practice," he says. "From watching game films and reading reports, I learn what to expect from an opponent. You have to go into a game prepared for whatever your opposition might do." Gary Fencik, free safety for the Chicago Bears, is another believer in thorough preparation. "Before a game," he says, "I try to feel ready but not anxious. I don't get excited unless I haven't done everything I should do."

Whatever specific psych-up techniques athletes turn to before competition, they are all intended to achieve what sports psychologists refer to as "arousal"—a state of eager readiness to play. Is one method inherently better than others? Thus far there is no evidence that this is the case. Not long ago three researchers, Robert S. Weinberg, Daniel Gould and Allen Jackson, recruited eighty volunteers, equally divided between men and women, and subjected them to psych-up intervals ranging from fifteen seconds to as much time as they thought necessary to ensure maximum performance. When the volunteers' strength was tested after the varying preparation periods, the time spent proved to have had no discernible effect. What works best, it seems, is the psych-up techniques you yourself find most comfortable, including whatever rituals and routines you have discovered to be effective. (Investigators at Moscow's Sport Research Institute have found, for example, that listening to music increases strength in some athletes.)

Based on his experience as a sports psychologist, James Loehr suggests several psych-up techniques:

• Before competition, don't deviate from your usual practices.
• Spend a few minutes each day thinking about how you want to perform. Don't wait until the night before competition.
• Do whatever works for you in order to achieve a physical, emotional and intellectual high. Avoid depressing or upsetting thoughts.
• Limit personal conflicts. Try not to quarrel on the day of a game.
• Look forward to competition. Plan to enjoy it.

Relax. By their nature, athletics contain an almost impossible contradiction: To win, we must try hard. At the same time, we should try to keep ourselves entirely relaxed. The reason is that nervousness and anxiety, the result of the pressure of competition, invariably interfere with performance. It was no accident that in his final season with the Boston Red Sox, Carl Yastrzemski had a handwritten reminder taped to the inside of his locker. "Relax," it read.

According to sports psychologists, the relaxation problem can be stubbornly difficult to eradicate because it is likely to be rooted in early experiences, when adult expectations often ask of a child more than he or she is able, physically or emotionally, to give. Bud Winter, San Jose State University's longtime track coach, says most athletes who react unfavorably to pressure are simply trying too hard, possibly as a result of a coach's repeated admonitions to "give 150 percent." At San Jose State, Winter's inventive antidote was to ask his athletes to give only 90 percent, in order to free them from undue pressure. This might be viewed as no more than a coaching eccentricity, were it not for the fact that over the years, under Winter's tutelage, San Jose State's sprinters broke no fewer than thirty-seven world records.

A feeling of pressure is so common that probably no athlete is entirely immune to it. In *The Education of a Tennis Player* Rod Laver, one of the game's most consistent winners during the 1960's, wrote, "Maybe it won't be much consolation, but you ought to know I've choked, still do sometimes, and most likely always will. And I haven't met anybody who hasn't." John McEnroe, explaining his loss to Mats Wilander in the quarterfinals of the 1983 French Open, said simply, "I choked. There's no excuse for it. I was terrible in the last set and a half." Even Wilt Chamberlain, as sports psychologist Robert Nideffer describes him in *The Inner Athlete*, was so beset by anxieties at the foul line toward the end of his career that his record there was far worse than his field goal record (51 percent vs. 73 percent during one season).

Physiologically, nervousness has a number of adverse effects. It increases heart rate, blood pressure, muscle tension and the flow of perspiration. It also causes rapid breathing, insomnia, nausea, blurred vision and a need to urinate frequently. Psychologically, it produces sensations of panic and confusion and can cause dizziness, depression, lack of coordination and a feeling of fatigue.

Studies documenting the effects of anxiety on golfers, basketball players, swimmers and other athletes suggest that nervousness never improves performance, whatever the sport. In soccer, for example, Hubert Birkenmeier of the Cosmos says, "When I was younger I was always nervous before games. Then I found that nervousness causes you to make mistakes. As soon as you start thinking about those mistakes, you make *more* mistakes and lose your concentration."

Sports psychologists have found that much can be done to diminish even severe cases of anxiety. Clearly, pregame nervousness is not a malady that can attacked head-on, since the harder we try to suppress it the more anxious we ordinarily become. Rather, it must be dealt with indirectly, by changing our attitudes toward competition. In his practical book *The Nuts and Bolts of Psychology for Swimmers*, Dr. Keith Bell describes several useful techniques:

- Don't demand perfection from yourself.
- Keep competition in perspective; a poor performance is not the end of the world.
- Focus on the event, not the results.
- Try to enjoy competition. (Compare James Loehr's advice above.)

The last, because it so powerfully enhances relaxation, is perhaps the most important of all. One of the secrets of Babe Ruth's success, by all accounts, was that he genuinely enjoyed hitting a baseball. He may, for all we know, have felt nervous before a big game, but the anticipation of the pleasure he would soon enjoy outweighed his anxiety. "The crack of his bat, the sight of the ball soaring against the sky—these thrilled him as much as they did the fans," wrote Frank Graham in *The New York Yankees*.

Concentrate. Not long ago *Runner's World* asked Joan Benoit, the woman's marathon record holder and winner of the 1984 women's Olympic marathon, to explain her athletic successes. Her answer was simplicity itself: "My mental concentration. My mental toughness." And when Reggie Jackson was asked what makes a player perform well in the clutch, he replied, "It's an ability to concentrate, and it entails a certain strength of character. I really think that strength of character is the most important aspect, and it's something you've got to *have*, something you can't make or fabricate."

A few years ago William P. Morgan, a well-known sports psychologist, found himself curious to know in what ways marathon runners occupy their minds during their 26.2-mile races, which can require anything from slightly over two hours to five or six hours, depending on skill, physical condition and weather. As he questioned runners of various abilities, from novice to world class, he began to notice a consistent distinction. Almost without exception, top athletes spent their time attentively monitoring what they were doing and how they felt at each stage of the race. By contrast, less accomplished athletes, presumably hoping to escape tedium and discomfort, tended to dwell on unrelated matters—friends, school, career and the like.

Keeping one's mind from wandering during competition is no easy task. "It's tough to concentrate for a whole match," said Jose-Luis Clerc in early 1983 after losing a set to Mats Wilander and then coming back to win the next two. Franz Beckenbauer, long-time star of the New York Cosmos, points out that maintaining concentration is particularly difficult over a sustained competitive season. "I find it hard to concentrate for an entire season," he says. "This is especially true with the easy games. When I find I'm not paying attention during those games I talk to myself." And Grete Waitz told the author, "It's hard to concentrate for the two and a half hours of a marathon. That's the big thing for me—to keep my mind on what I'm doing. I have to tell myself that I'm going to run for two and a half hours. I tell my mind: *two and a half hours, two and a half hours.* Even if I do that, I have to work hard to concentrate. During the race I'm so busy concentrating that I don't see the people along the course. Sometimes I lose my concentration, but not for a long time. If you lose your concentration you have a tendency to slow down."

Improved concentration invariably raises the level of play. Even John McEnroe, who seems to thrive on disruptions, told Ira Berkow of the *New York Times*, "I don't play my best tennis when I get involved like that. I'm trying to tone it down. I know it'll be better for me in the long run."

Psych out your opponent. Suppose you're having one of those days when nothing seems to go right. Your shots aren't working, your opponent is having his way with you, and a partisan crowd is jeering your most valiant efforts. You're tired and anxious and you lack confidence.

Before you decide to give up sports for good, one possibility remains: psyching out your opponent. A fine line exists, needless to say, between what's fair and foul in the use of athletic mind games, but you are perfectly free to look fierce or to swagger as if to suggest that your confidence is boundless. A word of warning, however: Sometimes one good psych-out is answered by another. Once, years ago, the English chess champion Sir George Thomas faced a young opponent who, no doubt seeking to evoke the older man's merciful instincts, complained of a headache. Sir George was not to be lulled into easing up, however. Instead he replied, "Young man, in forty years of tournament playing I do not believe that I have ever defeated a wholly well man."

A final aspect of the psychological element in sports deserves discussion, and this is hypnosis. For years a subject of controversy on the grounds that it constitutes an unnatural tampering with God-given talents, hypnosis today is being employed with increasing frequency as an aid to perfecting skills, enhancing concentration and overcoming anxieties that interfere with performance.

There is little doubt that hypnosis works, at least in many cases. Dr. J. Arthur Jackson, an Australian physician and longtime student of sport, cites the instance of an international cricketer who, despite considerable achievements, had never entirely lived up to his potential. In particular, whenever he found himself doing well in a game he would characteristically go into a slump and finish poorly. His problem was diagnosed as an overeagerness to excel. This caused him to become anxious, which in turn interfered with concentration.

The cricketer was treated by hypnosis. Says Jackson: "The player was given suggestions that he would maintain a here-and-now approach, treating each ball on its merits and not dwelling on previous shots or innings. He was told to remind himself of this by focusing on one key thought: *this ball*." The player's performance promptly improved.

A second case in point occurred recently when a researcher brought about marked improvements in video-game scores by asking hypnotized volunteers to imagine that a ball on the screen was moving more slowly than it actually was.

And when Jim Eisenreich of the Minnesota Twins found himself so incapacitated by panic attacks that he was forced to abandon his career, he turned to a hypnotist, Harvey Misel. After working with Misel for several months, he had improved enough to report for spring training. "It was a miracle," said Misel. (Unfortunately, it was only a temporary miracle. During the 1984 season the Twins released the ailing Eisenreich.)

One could, however, cite hundreds of other examples in which practicing athletes, both amateur and professional, have been helped by hypnosis. Nonetheless, many authorities, though no longer skeptical about the technique's efficacy, feel it is of limited usefulness in sport and can, in certain circumstances, actually be dangerous. Bruce Ogilvie, for example, used hypnosis at one time but stopped when he realized that it too often created an undesirable dependency; athletes were relying on his treatments rather than on their own mental abilities.

Finally, knowledgeable observers point out that there is no need to turn to hypnosis until an athlete has made all possible nonhypnotic efforts to correct mental habits that are inhibiting performance. For many athletes, the benefits of hypnosis are unlikely ever to equal those that result from nothing more esoteric than sustained conscientious training and an effort to control the mind in the usual conventional ways.

CHAPTER 5

Becoming Strong

Among elite athletes, and all the rest of us for
that matter, strength can make all the difference.

—E. C. FREDERICK, *physiologist*

GENE MONAHAN, the New York Yankees' trainer, sits in the sub-
terranean catacombs of Yankee Stadium, musing about some
of the oddities of baseball. Nearby, arrayed around the perimeter
of a good-sized room as if they were so many monks' cells, are
forty-five or so doorless cubicles, each of them identified by a label
over its portal: GUIDRY, RANDOLPH, MATTINGLY, WINFIELD, NIEKRO,
RIGHETTI . . . Monahan, who is in his late thirties and has served
as a Yankee trainer since the glory days of Mantle and Maris, is
responsible, among a multitude of other duties, for keeping the
members of the team free of injury, or at least as free of injury as
is humanly possible in a sport that so determinedly courts physical
mishap. "The running that's done in baseball is all blast sprinting,"
Monahan says. "One minute a player is sitting around, doing practically nothing, and the next he's running ninety feet at top speed.
Knowing this, you might think speed would be the big thing in
baseball, but no, the fundamental quality turns out to be strength.
If you want to be a major-league baseball player, you have to have
agility, good reaction time and a highly accurate kinesthetic sense.
But if all those things are equal, the stronger man is going to be
a better ball player."

Monahan's convictions are borne out not only by his own observations in the Yankees' training room but by the experience of other baseball teams as well. In 1982 Sparky Anderson, manager of the Detroit Tigers, was taken aback when his first-string catcher, Lance Parrish, turned up for spring training weighing a bearlike 240 pounds, the result of an off-season weightlifting regimen. Quite justifiably, Anderson feared that Parrish's prodigious muscularity—teammates took to calling him the Incredible Hulk—might diminish his speed and flexibility. When Parrish proceeded to enjoy the best season he had ever experienced, Anderson was finally persuaded to abandon his antimuscle prejudice.

In another era it would no doubt have seemed contradictory, particularly when one's sport is so heavily reliant on speed, agility and coordination, that such stress should be laid on strength. In the past several years, however, an accumulating body of evidence has come to suggest that strength—the ability to apply force against a resistance—is the linchpin of a multitude of sports, if not in fact of all of them. The reason is that nearly every movement in sport is carried out in opposition to a resistance. Thus an increase in strength means an improvement in performance.

WEIGHTLIFTING PROGRAM

Unless you want to gain strength for a specific action, such as punting a football or high jumping, your weight program should at least involve the major muscle groups: shoulders, upper arms, back, abdomen and thighs. The following sample program will give you a framework for designing a program of your own.

WEIGHTLIFTING GUIDELINES
• Warm up before working out. Flexibility is important if you are going to train a muscle's full range.
• Always work with a companion or spotter when lifting free weights. Your spotter should be in a position to take the weight away from you if you can no longer lift it.
• For muscular strength: Lift six to eight repetitions maximum, one to three sets, every other day.
• For muscular endurance: Lift twelve to fifteen repetitions minimum, one to three sets, every other day.
• Exhale during the pressing part of the lift and inhale as you return the weight to its starting position. Never hold your breath.

• Use different muscle groups during training. Avoid, for example, several shoulder exercises in a row.
• Remember that improvement will take place only in those muscle groups trained.

Bench Press
For chest (pectorals) and arm extensor muscles (triceps)
Lie flat on your back with your feet on the floor astride the bench. Grasp the bar at points slightly wider than shoulder width. Lift bar to starting position; arms fully extended, perpendicular to the floor. Lower the weight until it nearly touches your chest, then return it to its starting position.

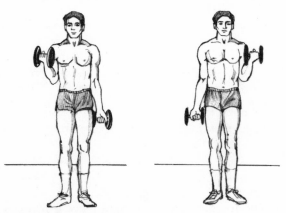

Alternating Dumbbell Curls
For upper arms (biceps)
Stand with your back straight and arms extended, resting at your sides. Hold the dumbbells so that your palms are facing out. Bring one arm up by flexing the bicep. Keep your elbows in and be

careful not to arch your back. Raise the dumbbell until your arm is nearly vertical, then slowly lower the weight to its starting position. Repeat with the other dumbbell.

Squats
For front of thighs (quadriceps) and buttocks
Stand with your feet 12 to 14 inches apart and place the barbell on your upper back. Help stabilize the bar with a comfortable grip. Keep your head up, back straight, and feet stable. Squat down until your thighs are parallel to the floor, then slowly return to the starting position. Because of the stress placed on the tendons and ligaments that surround your knees, it is dangerous to go any lower. If you feel yourself moving backward when squatting, elevate your heels with a solid base of one to two inches.

Pull-ups
For biceps and shoulders (deltoids)
Stand facing a pull-up bar. Grasp the bar with an overhand grip—palms facing away from you. Begin with your arms fully extended

and your feet off the floor. Pull yourself upward as high as possible or until your chin is over the bar. Inhale as you pull. Lower yourself to the starting position and repeat.

Calf Raises
For calves (gastrocnemius)
Stand with a barbell resting on your upper back and the balls of your feet on a two-inch stable base. Your heels should be on the floor. Raise your heels off the floor as high as possible and then return them to the starting position.

Push-ups
For pectorals and deltoids
With hands just outside of your shoulders and your body straight, slowly lower yourself until your chest is nearly touching the floor. Always keep your head up, eyes looking forward, so that your body remains straight. Exhale as you return to the starting position.

Tricep Extension
For triceps
Sit on bench with your back straight. Grasp bar with an overhand grip with hands about two inches apart. Bring the bar to a full arm extension overhead. Lower the bar behind your head, keeping your elbows still, and then return it to starting position.

Sit-ups
For abdomen
Sit with your knees bent and your chin tucked toward your chest. To start, place a 5- to 10-pound dumbbell behind your neck and hold it at both ends. Lift your chin to your knees using your stomach muscles—do not pull with your arms. Return to the starting position and repeat.

Shoulder Shrugs
For upper back and neck (trapezius)
Grasp the barbell with your arms fully extended at your sides—palms facing in. Keep your back straight and attempt to shrug your shoulders to your ears. Lower your shoulders to the starting position and repeat.

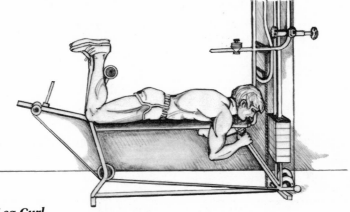

Leg Curl
For back of thigh (bicep femoris)
Lie in a prone position while your spotter holds your ankles or use leg curl machine. Curl your lower legs upward while your spotter offers resistance. Resistance should also be given when lowering your legs to the starting point.

A decade ago, for example, few distance runners saw any value in strength training. Most, including many of the leading 10,000-meter and marathon runners, felt that the best training for running was simply to do as much running as possible. Wasn't it logical, after all, to spend your time practicing whatever it was you wanted to improve? Recent experience has changed that view, with the result that most distance runners today do at least modest amounts of training with weights (including, in an increasing number of cases, weighted gloves or weights such as Heavyhands that are grasped during a workout). "Strength is an important component of endurance," says the physiologist E. C. Frederick. "Animals use their front paws to control their gait. The pattern in the forelimbs generates patterns in the hind limbs. It's the same with people. When their front legs and paws—their arms and hands—aren't strong enough, something goes awry in their legs."

Jeff Johnson, a colleague of Frederick's at Nike, Inc., tells of coaching a girls' track team that lacked depth and thus could ill afford to lose any members to injury. Accordingly, he decided to build strength first and leave speed and endurance for later. "We did badly at the start of the season," says Johnson, "but we didn't lose one girl and finally went on to win the state meet."

Competitive gymnasts, too, have come to place an increasingly high value on strength despite the fact that agility, quickness and coordination are paramount skills in their sport. Abraham Grossfeld, a former Olympic gymnast who as a coach has helped produce twenty-nine NCAA champions and 125 all-Americans, says, "In gymnastics you're never strong enough. The stronger you are, the more you're able to do."

Before the start of the football season Archie Manning, quarterback for the Houston Oilers, does weight training three days a week. "I lift both to prevent injury and to maintain strength," he says. "As a result of the triceps exercises I started last year, I feel that even in my mid-thirties I've increased the strength in my arm. I can throw the ball harder and I'm putting more rpm's on it."

Another quarterback, Jim Hart of the St. Louis Cardinals, is similarly a believer in weight training. "I do both Nautilus and free-weight workouts," he says. "Ever since I started lifting weights, seven or eight years ago, I've had fewer sore arms, and overall better health. Maybe I can't throw the ball as far or as hard as I once could, but I haven't lost as much as I would have if I hadn't been using weights."

The names of football players who do weight training are legion. Franco Harris, who was quoted earlier, told the author, "All through high school and college, and even after I got into the pros, I felt I lacked strength. In my rookie year I got into a weightlifting program, and it really helped me. One way it helped was mentally; I found that I had a lot more confidence."*

In increasing numbers, coaches and players in nearly all sports are coming to feel that without a good deal of strength—sometimes considerably more than one would suppose might be required—an athlete is incapable of approaching his or her best performance. Dr. Ellington Darden of the Athletic Center in Atlanta, Georgia, recently wrote: "Stronger muscles . . . give the athlete greater movement potential. If everything else is equal, the stronger athlete will be bigger, faster, more flexible, more enduring, and less prone to injury."

The last point is significant. When two athletes are of roughly equal skill, the ability to continue training without lost days can make the difference between winning and losing. "One of the benefits of strength is that it acts as a shock absorber for a muscle," says the fitness authority Michael Quinn. "Most injuries, such as tennis elbow, are caused by a force or a succession of forces that cause the muscle to exceed its tensile strength. When that happens, the muscle tears. The stronger you are, the less likely that is to happen."

Peter Fleming, who is not only John McEnroe's doubles partner but also a top-ranked singles player (he was thirteenth in the world in one recent year), agrees. "I lift weights because of all the injuries I've had," he told the author. "I feel I was weak to begin with, and then I let myself get into really decrepit shape. Since I've been doing weight training I'm about twice as coordinated as I used to be. When I go up for overheads, I can sense that it's a more graceful movement."

Developing a weight-training program of your own, however, can appear to be a formidable task. Visit any scientific library and examine, even cursorily, the volumes devoted to muscular power. Unless you are a physician or hold a Ph.D. degree in human physiology, you will come away with your brain numbed not only by the mountains of material available on the subject but by the impenetrable complexity of much of it. For most of us, a Ouija board would yield more readily digestible information.

* Part of the apparent benefit may, however, be psychological and therefore essentially indirect. One authority on weights, Joe Little, recently wrote that "weight training can add to your mental well-being by allowing you to rationalize: 'I work harder than he or she does.' Just this amount of arrogance can possibly get you past that sticking point to better your personal record."

Does a weekend athlete, or for that matter a professional earning a million or more dollars a year for his exertions, need to be conversant with such complexities? The answer, fortunately, is: Not at all. All he needs to know are the three principal methods of developing strength and which of those methods is most effective for his athletic purposes.

The three methods can be simply described:

Isometric (constant measure) conditioning requires that a muscle remain essentially motionless while it flexes in opposition to an immovable object—a wall, for example, or another muscle. Charles Atlas's "dynamic tension," so useful as a repellent for beach bullies who kick sand at ninety-eight-pound weaklings, is of this variety.

Isotonic (constant tension) conditioning employs a movable weight, such as a barbell, that remains the same throughout an exercise but, because of changes in angular forces, provides varying resistances.

Isokinetic (constant motion) conditioning, like isotonic, requires that the muscle be moved, but in this case the exercise is carried out with the use of a weight that provides an unvarying resistance no matter what the angle. Nautilus equipment, which is designed around a system of cams and chains, offers this variety of workout (though at a markedly higher price than either of the other methods).

Each of these varieties of strength development has its proper uses, and no single variety is ideal for every athletic purpose. Because strength training is fundamental to so vast a range of sports it is worth looking more closely at each system.

Isometric training enjoyed a considerable vogue in the 1960's. Based on research carried out in Germany a generation or more ago and made public in 1953, it seemed at first to promise unprecedented gains in return for strikingly little work. Furthermore, it required no special equipment—just something solid to push or pull against. Many professional sports teams became enthusiasts of isometrics, and it was the rare businessman who failed to do isometrics from time to time at his desk.

Curious about the apparently effortless magic of isometrics, other researchers, some of them of a skeptical bent, began to look at the system more closely. When they did, some drawbacks came to light. For one thing, the increase in strength produced by isometrics was measurable chiefly at the precise muscle length and joint angle at which the exercise had been done; it manifested itself scarcely at all at other positions. If, for example, you were repeatedly to practice pressing your hand against a wall, you would become adept at applying pressure to walls, but not at much else. Isometrics, researchers have found, have some legitimate uses—among them building strength in order to get past a sticking point in a lift or becoming stronger for static exertions such as occur in wrestling or in the tasks of an offensive lineman in football. In general, however, other forms of exercise are now thought to be more effective for most purposes.

Isotonic exercise, the oldest variety of all, is the type practiced by anyone who has ever moved progressively greater resistances— weights, for example—in order to build strength. A person who undertakes to lift a calf on the day of its birth and every day thereafter until at length it has grown to full heiferhood is a prototypical adherent of isotonics. So, too, is the ordinary basement weightlifter. Although this method has long been known and, at least in an intuitive way, practiced, it was not until the 1940's that two researchers, T. L. DeLorme and A. L. Watkins, finally outlined the most effective method of employing isotonics.

If isotonic exercise has a drawback, it is that the force opposing a muscle's effort is not of uniform intensity but varies from extremely strong at some times to uselessly weak at others. Consider a weightlifter doing a curl—that is, using his biceps muscles to raise a barbell from its lowest position, near his thighs, to its highest, near his chest. At the beginning of his lift, when the weight in effect merely hangs from his arms, the muscular force required is slight. By the time the barbell has been raised about halfway and the forearms are at an angle of ninety degrees to the body, force is at its maximum. Thereafter, as the barbell continues to be raised, it diminishes toward its starting value.

This would present no particular problem if it were not for one of the inescapable characteristics of muscle: that it exerts maximum force when it is fully rather than only partly extended. This means that the weight's maximum force and the muscle's do not coincide but arrive at different points in the curl, making it impossible to derive optimum benefit from the resistance exerted by the weight. Exercise would be more effective, theoreticians have long argued, if a method of providing a uniform resistance throughout an exercise could somehow be devised. In this way maximum muscle hypertrophy, or enlargement, would presumably take place. (Since a muscle's strength varies directly with its cross-sectional area, a larger muscle is invariably a stronger muscle.)

This is where isokinetic conditioning comes in. Isokinetics, it is said, combine the best features of isometrics—a strong resistance against which muscles can exert themselves—and of isotonics—a wide range of motion. In theory, therefore, isokinetic exercises, such as those provided by Nautilus equipment, should be more effective than isotonic.

Many authorities believe this to be the case. For example, Brian J. Sharkey of the University of Montana's Human Performance Laboratory is something of an isokinetics enthusiast. In his book *Physiology of Fitness* Dr. Sharkey writes, "Theoretically, this method should lead to greater overall strength of the muscle." Yet in 1978, when Sharkey himself, in company with three associates, evaluated groups of young women who had volunteered to train by means of weights, isokinetic devices and calisthenics, isokinetics proved to be the least effective method.

A widespread sense prevails among exercise physiologists and other experts that, where isokinetics are concerned, all the evidence is not yet in. Nautilus and Universal equipment certainly *looks* as if it should be incomparably effective, but is it any better than other devices that are considerably less elaborate and costly? Not long ago Michael T. Sanders of the University of Wisconsin compared the use of Nautilus and traditional equipment in college-age men enrolled in a five-week training program. Commenting on Sanders' investigation, Frank George, Brown University's head athletic trainer, said, "The two types of training appeared to be equally effective in developing muscle strength and endurance. . . . It has always been my opinion that the type of equipment used is the least important factor in any strength-building program. The motivation of the individual is by far the most important factor. It has often been stated that the motivated athlete using inexpensive weights will far surpass the less motivated athlete using the most expensive training equipment available." Another authority puts the matter even more simply: "The muscle doesn't know, and certainly doesn't care, what anyone hangs on the end of it."

Whether in response to using Nautilus equipment or hefting a sack of cement, human skeletal muscle—the variety that constitutes the body's guy wires and other rigging—reacts to effort in much the same way. As muscle fibers are contracted repeatedly under tension, they become fatigued at first. If, thereafter, the exercise is repeated on successive days, several characteristics of the fibers begin to change. The concentration of certain enzymes increases, making possible the more efficient production of the muscle's chief energy source, adenosine triphosphate (usually abbreviated ATP). The capacity for oxidizing fat to produce mechanical energy is enhanced. The mitochondria—the microscopic sites where energy is ultimately produced—become both larger and more numerous and their protein content increases. Finally, myoglobin, an oxygen-carrying substance, becomes more efficient at transporting that vital element from cell walls to the mitochondria at the cells' interior.

Athletes, and for that matter most nonathletes, have always been aware that training increases strength by enlarging muscles and improving their capacity for performing work. It has only been since the 1960's, however, that researchers have begun to discover exactly why the so-called training effect occurs. The fundamental reason, it appears, is that profoundly significant changes take place within the cells themselves. This new knowledge has vastly increased our ability to fine-tune a training program in order to bring about precisely the results required for a particular sport. If your goal is to run the 100-yard dash, there is no point, after all, in putting all your effort into acquiring the endurance of a marathoner, or of trying to look like Arnold Schwarzenegger if the greatest exertion you plan is wielding a billiard cue.

From what is known about the cellular alterations that take place as a result of conditioning, it is possible to derive a single all-encompassing training principle that, if correctly applied, will cover all cases and provide reliable guidance for any conceivable sport. This principle can be briefly stated: *We improve at exactly what we practice.*

This apparently simple principle is as central to sports as $E = mc^2$ is to physics. Often referred to as the principle of specificity, it contains four main subprinciples:

1. *The pattern of movement during training should precisely duplicate the pattern you hope to improve.* This aspect of specificity was first announced in 1957, when two investigators, P. J. Rasch and C. E. Morehouse, revealed the curious results of an experiment they had done. The two researchers had set out to strengthen the arm muscles of volunteers by asking them to flex their elbows

repeatedly while standing up. After a period of training, Rasch and Morehouse conducted tests to determine exactly how strong the volunteers' arms had become. The results were startling. When the volunteers' strength was measured while they were in their accustomed standing position, it turned out that it had greatly increased. When measured while they were lying on their backs, however, the improvement was markedly less—despite the fact that exactly the same muscles were being evaluated in each case.

Specificity of movement also applies to the angle at which a muscle and its related joints are exercised. If, for example, you were to practice half-push-ups, raising your body only partway off the floor, this would do little to increase your strength at the top of a fully extended push-up. Similarly, while arm strength is useful to runners, they will not benefit much from pressing weights over their heads. "It won't help them," writes Dr. Gabe Mirkin in *The Sportsmedicine Book*, "because they don't run with their hands over their heads."

2. *Movement during training should be at exactly the speed you plan to use during competition.* This principle was first enunciated in 1970, when researchers asked volunteers to exercise at slow speeds. When tests were conducted, strength had increased at the familiar slow speeds but not—or at least not much—at higher speeds. (High-velocity training, on the other hand, confers something of an improvement at slow speeds as well.)

You should, therefore, work out at a speed that as closely as possible approximates that of competition. "If you wish to throw a baseball faster," writes Brian J. Sharkey in *Physiology of Fitness*, "use light weights at a fast speed. If you are a shot putter, throw heavier weights as fast as possible."

3. *Muscle contractions during training should be of the type used in competition.* Contractions are of three varieties: concentric, when a muscle shortens; eccentric, when a muscle lengthens; and isometric, when no change in length takes place. It is important that the contraction during training duplicate, insofar as possible, the type of contraction that will take place in competition. If, for example, you want to strengthen shoulder muscles in order to develop a more effective tennis backhand, you might consider doing bench presses in order to strengthen the triceps muscle by shortening it. You would, however, derive far less benefit from doing an exercise in which the triceps was lengthened.

There is one exception to this principle, based on the recently discovered fact that eccentric contractions build strength more effectively than either of the other types. If you want to develop as much strength as possible, therefore, you may want to do some eccentric weight training even though your particular sport might not seem to call for it.

In order to stimulate maximum strength development, you should, incidentally, lower a weight more slowly than you raise it. A ratio of about two to one is recommended. That is, if it takes two seconds to raise a weight, spend four seconds lowering it.

4. *Strength training should be of fairly high intensity.* You will not build strength by the mere repetition of movements that are easy. "The athlete must constantly attempt the momentarily impossible," says Ellington Darden. "Attempting the momentarily impossible causes the body to resort to its reserve ability. Forcing the body to use this reserve ability is an important factor in stimulating a muscle to get stronger."

In practice, this means choosing a resistance that can be overcome not more than six to eight times at first. Once you find that you can overcome it twelve times, you should increase the resistance by about 5 percent. "To increase muscular strength and endurance," says West Point's James Anderson, "the muscles must be worked a little harder than normal."

Not all authorities agree that six to eight repetitions is an ideal number for everyone. Dr. Leroy Getchell of Ball State University argues, "For the average adult, such effort could be dangerous. The very nature of the exercise—short bursts of exertion against a heavy resistance—creates large increases in blood pressure, causing a heavy strain on the heart. Therefore, if you are beginning a strength-development program, I suggest a milder approach." For such people, Getchell recommends three sets of fifteen to twenty repetitions each, performed three times a week. What it comes down to is that you will no doubt find that you have to do some experimenting to arrive at a workout that suits your particular needs.

Many women, incidentally, hesitate to undertake weight-training programs because of anxiety that they will develop unwanted bulges. Because of the presence of the hormone estrogen in their systems, however, most women are incapable of achieving the sharply defined muscularity attainable by most men. "I gained five pounds but my clothes got looser," said a Connecticut woman,

Sandra Swan, after six months on a Nautilus program. Mrs. Swan, who runs some fifty miles a week and has entered three marathons, says she knows a number of women who avoid lifting weights because of fears that they will become too obviously muscular. She points out, however, "That doesn't happen. What does happen is that your clothes start fitting better and you have an overall feeling of fitness that doesn't come just from running or any other single sport. Since I started at Nautilus no one has told me I look muscular. What people *do* tell me is that I look great."

In addition to its application to specific sports, increased strength brings other benefits as well.

It makes you feel better. Robert S. Loeb, who serves as sales manager for a New York office supply company, worked for a heating and air conditioning firm when he was younger. "I lifted air conditioners, moved boilers and did hard manual labor," he recalls. "I was always in good shape. When I changed jobs, I found that I quickly got out of condition." Loeb took up weightlifting and has acquired some $4,000 worth of equipment. "Now I feel terrific again," he says. "The weightlifting is a habit I wouldn't want to give up."

Ted Arcidi, a Massachusetts power lifter who in 1972 bench-pressed a record 630 pounds, made much the same point recently in an interview with the *Boston Globe*. "I like to lift big weights," he said. "It's something that's very hard for some people to do. I like to do it. I like to be very strong. I'm not bragging. I just like to be strong."

Women who take up weight training frequently report that they feel much the same way. "I never knew what it was to be really strong," said Lillis O. Palmer of Monument Beach, Massachusetts, after several months of lifting weights. "I've never felt as good as I feel after a good workout. I had been running for several years, and I had even won a few medals, but this is entirely different."

Research shows that strength can also retard the aging process. Not long ago a scientific investigator in Stockholm, Lars Larsson, studied eighteen sedentary men, some of them in their sixties, in order to see what might happen as a result of a weight-training program. Muscle biopsies, performed before training began, showed the atrophy and decline in strength typically associated with aging. After a four-month training program, however, the effects of growing old had in effect been reversed. "The age-related decline in

muscle-fiber area previously seen did not exist after training,"
Larsson concluded.

Michael Quinn, who has trained men and women of all ages,
comments, "You reach your peak at about twenty-two and go
downhill from then on. You can't entirely stop the decline, but you
can slow it down. There are plenty of people in their eighties who
are playing golf and even running marathons, and there are other
people the same age who are almost crippled. I'm convinced that
most of us don't have to be that way."

Research supports Quinn's observations. After age twenty-five
we lose a mere 1 percent of our remaining strength each year. At
age sixty-five, therefore, we are fully 65 to 70 percent as strong as
we were at age twenty-five or thirty—strong enough, certainly, to
do much of what anyone might reasonably want to do.

Thus far we have been discussing strength largely in isolation from
other capacities, as if it could be developed by itself. Needless to
say, it cannot. Chief among the capacities with which it is inevitably associated is endurance. There wouldn't be much point, after
all, in increasing your strength for swimming if you had so little
endurance you could take only a stroke or two.

Fortunately, anyone, no matter how unathletic or sedentary, can
increase his or her endurance. Not all of us, however, can develop
this valuable capacity to the same degree. Earlier we discussed the
two principal types of motor units found in human muscle: slow
twitch and fast twitch. From birth, each individual has a fixed
ratio of fast twitch to slow twitch. Because of the different metabolic characteristics of the two types, men and women who are
heavily endowed with slow-twitch motor units characteristically
display greater endurance than those whose muscles are made up
predominantly of fast-twitch motor units.

Moreover, there appears to be little we can do to alter the ratio.
More than a decade ago a Washington State University researcher,
P. D. Gollnick, conducted a now-celebrated study intended to find
out whether one type of muscle could be converted to another.
Using sedentary volunteers possessing a high percentage of fast-
twitch fibers (which contract about two and a half times as rapidly
as slow twitch), Gollnick put his subjects on a six-month bicycling
program designed to develop endurance. At the end of the training
period he took biopsies of the quadriceps muscle. There was no

change in the ratio of fiber types. Training had done nothing to change the volunteers' fast-twitch motor units to slow twitch.*

No matter how diligently we work at becoming strong, some of us are bound to develop more strength than others. There are several reasons for the variations that occur from person to person. Age and sex affect one's response to training. And so does our condition when we begin; out-of-shape muscles gain strength more readily than well-conditioned ones.

Suppose, however, that you are finally as strong as you are capable of becoming. Every muscle cell that can be affected by training has acquired its fullest possible complement of energy-producing mitochondria. Cellular enzyme activity has been pushed to its limit. Are you now at maximum strength, or is there still something you can do to become even stronger?

As it happens, there are at least two steps that you can take.

First, you can increase a muscle's contracting force by forcing it to stretch just before calling upon it to deliver its power. A baseball pitcher does exactly this as the final phase of a windup, and so does a high jumper before attempting a jump.

Second, as outlined in the preceding chapter, you can increase strength by preparing yourself mentally before an exertion. Not long ago three investigators, Robert S. Weinberg, Daniel Gould and Allen Jackson, compared the performance of weightlifters who had been urged to become as psyched up as possible with other weightlifters who were instructed merely to count backwards quietly before attempting a lift. Reported the scientists: "The lifters who were instructed to 'psych up' showed dramatic increases in performance."

Although much is known about the psychological element in the use of strength, much remains to be discovered. Scarcely a week passes without a report of new (and not infrequently tantalizing) findings. Not long ago, to cite only one curious example, a group of researchers decided to see whether looking at various colors before an athlete effort might make a difference in performance.

* What training may do, according to experiments conducted by Dr. William J. Gonyea of the Department of Cell Biology at the University of Texas Health Science Center, is to prompt muscle fibers to multiply by a process he calls "splitting." Before the Gonyea investigations, which involved specially trained weightlifting cats, it was supposed that the number of fibers in a given muscle is unalterable. In cats, at any rate, this now appears not to be the case. Training of sufficient intensity can increase the number of muscle fibers by 20 percent or so. The same splitting process probably occurs in human beings.

Volunteers first viewed areas of red, blue or pink on a wall and afterward were asked to attempt various tasks, including one in which strength was evaluated. The volunteers, it turned out, demonstrated markedly greater strength after gazing at the red area than after being exposed to either blue or pink. No one, thus far, has any idea why.

CHAPTER 6

The Forever Factor

W HENEVER WE INCREASE either speed or distance, our bodies unavoidably expend more energy and therefore use more than ordinary amounts of oxygen. As fuel stores become depleted, we grow tired and athletic performance suffers.

That improvements can be made in our ability to endure is apparent even to those with no great experience in athletics. An untrained man or woman who undertakes to jog a quarter of a mile each day will find within two or three weeks that the effort has become markedly easier and that increasingly great distances are attainable. Furthermore, a few among us have managed to accomplish such extraordinary feats that many authorities insist we have not begun to plumb, or for that matter even imagine, the ultimate in human capacities.

Consider, for example, what occurred in the summer of 1983 on Randalls Island in New York City. There, twenty-four runners, both men and women, ran for six days without letup. Although most paused only for nourishment and occasional minor repairs during their ordeal, at the end they were in surprisingly energetic condition and had no difficulty answering onlookers' questions and commenting intelligently on the grueling experience they had undergone. ("It would hurt to keep running," said Stu Mittleman, who finished in second place, "but it's going to hurt to leave.") The forty-one-year-old winner of the event, Siegfried Bauer, covered 511 miles, an average pace of three and a half miles per hour during the 144 hours of the race.

Perhaps the greatest endurance feat of all time, however, was the 623¾ miles covered during six days in 1888 by an Englishman named George Littlewood. B. B. Lloyd, an Oxford University physiologist, has called the century-old record "something like the limit of . . . sustainable human effort."*

Few of us will ever run for six uninterrupted days, or for that matter pursue any other physical activity for so long a time. Yet the accomplishments of such athletes as Bauer and Littlewood suggest that we are capable of far more than we suppose. These days thousands of perfectly ordinary citizens regularly compete not just in 26.2-mile marathons but in so-called ultramarathons and triathlons such as the Ironman. Held in Hawaii each year, this triathlon requires participants to swim 2.4 miles, bicycle 112 miles

and run a full-length marathon. Commenting on the race, a writer named Paul Perry said, "Most of the people who train for the Ironman belong to the School of Aerobic Excess." There is no denying

* Littlewood's record held up until the summer of 1984, when Yiannis Kouros of Greece reset the six-day mark by covering 635 miles, 1,023 yards on the Randalls Island track in New York City.

that he had a point, but the fact that scores of men and women enter the event each year, and that most manage somehow to stumble to the finish line, 140.6 sweaty, hard-breathing miles from the start, reveals something marvelous about human capacities.

Among other facts, it tells us that to possess extraordinary endurance does not necessarily require that one be an inherently extraordinary man or woman. In 1981 the *Journal of the American Medical Association* published a report on Stan Cottrell, then thirty-seven years old, who not only averaged some eighty miles per day in running across the State of Georgia but on another occasion set a twenty-four-hour record of 167 miles, 440 yards (about seven miles per hour). The authors of the report, Drs. S. Robert Lathan and John D. Cantwell, remarked with surprise that despite Cottrell's unusual endurance he was not endowed with any discernible physical or biochemical advantages. His blood pressure, weight, body fat, cholesterol level, and other commonly accepted indicators of health and fitness were entirely within normal ranges. Lathan and Cantwell wrote, "This person is not extraordinary in his physical or biochemical makeup. . . . He exemplifies the specificity of training in that he is geared, both physically and mentally, to run ultralong distances." You and I, that is to say, might be able to do exactly what Cottrell did if we were willing to train as diligently as he trains. (Training intensity, and how to determine what is appropriate for you, are discussed more fully a few pages farther on.)

Nor are older athletes exempt from attaining unusual endurance. Not long ago a sixty-one-year-old Australian potato farmer, Cliff Young, took first place in a 535-mile Sydney-to-Melbourne race. The achievement required more than five and a half days of unremitting effort.

Unusual feats of endurance do, it is true, frequently require not just good genes but unusual perseverance as well. When Joan Benoit took the lead in the 1984 women's Olympic marathon, the remainder of the field, the most auspicious collection of female distance runners ever assembled, aware of the enormous difficulty of being the focal point of a two-and-a-half-hour race, assumed she would soon drift back to the pursuing pack. To their surprise, however, Benoit was undaunted by such seemingly overwhelming pressure and for the next twenty miles continued to build a lead, giving pause only once, at the thirteen-mile mark, when she smiled at a group of boisterous fans from Bowdoin College, her alma mater. In the end, even the redoubtable Norwegian Grete Waitz could make only the slightest dent in what Benoit had built into a nearly quarter-mile gap.

Such instances are, of course, extremes. Most of us have no wish or need to imitate them and, in fact, shudder at the thought. What we hope to achieve, chances are, is the endurance necessary to play three vigorous sets of tennis or a brisk, aggressive game of basketball or squash. We want endurance not for mere endurance's sake—to demonstrate how far a human being can travel in six days or sixty—but in order to perform some activity more proficiently and pleasurably than we are now able to do.

Whatever accomplishments we achieve, therefore, will come about primarily through hard work. Fortunately, where endurance is concerned, the types of hard work that need to be done are more fully understood today than ever before.

An important reason is the running boom of the past decade, which has attracted the interest of great numbers of scientific researchers. For one thing, many of the scientists themselves are runners and therefore have a natural interest in the sport's effects. For another, as noted in the opening pages of this book, running is one of the most easily studied of endurance activities. Because of all the scientific scrutiny, a person who sets out to improve his or her endurance has readily available a body of principles that will almost surely bring the desired results.

In order to understand these principles, let us look first at some of the effects of endurance training on the human body.

Training has its primary effects on three physiological systems, those involved in blood circulation, breathing and muscular activity. (There are other effects as well, but for the moment they may be ignored.) The organ chiefly responsible for blood circulation is, of course, the heart. When the heart is repeatedly made to perform more work than usual, as at the beginning of a training program, it responds by manifesting several important changes. Perhaps most significantly, its left ventricle, the chamber that squeezes blood into the aorta and thence throughout the body, becomes larger and stronger. It is thus able to pump more blood with each beat—nearly twice as much, in fact—than in an untrained person. Since athletes and nonathletes require essentially the same blood supply at rest, the heart of a trained man or woman beats more slowly. A recent study of athletes of several varieties, conducted at the University of Melbourne in Australia, revealed a

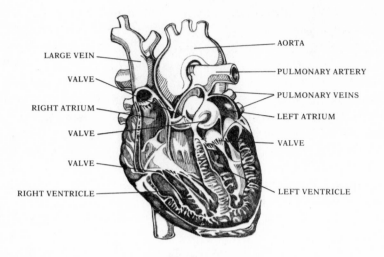

LARGE VEIN

VALVE

RIGHT ATRIUM

VALVE

VALVE

RIGHT VENTRICLE

AORTA

PULMONARY ARTERY

PULMONARY VEINS

LEFT ATRIUM

VALVE

LEFT VENTRICLE

The heart

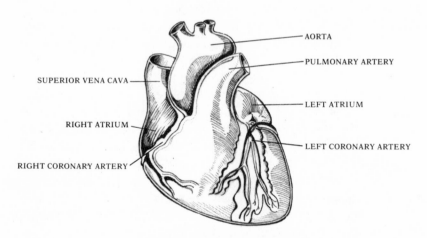

SUPERIOR VENA CAVA

RIGHT ATRIUM

RIGHT CORONARY ARTERY

AORTA

PULMONARY ARTERY

LEFT ATRIUM

LEFT CORONARY ARTERY

The heart with coronary arteries

mean heart rate of fifty-seven. Nonathletes average well over seventy.

Some people, incidentally, are concerned that the cardiac enlargement that comes with athletic training may be harmful. It has long since been demonstrated that it is not. As long ago as 1960 it was shown that, as one medical report expressed it, "the heart, enlarged as a result of endurance training, was not damaged but was an indication of a particularly efficient heart."

The practical significance of a heart rate that has been slowed through training is that physical performance is markedly improved. Numerous studies have shown a correlation between heart rate and endurance.

When one trains, the muscles used in the breathing process also develop greater endurance. For the past several years Bruce J. Martin of Indiana University has been studying the physiology of respiration. His research shows, first, that the respiratory endurance of athletes is likely to be three or four times that of nonathletes and, second, that this advantage appears not to be of genetic origin but to be produced solely by training.

Finally, the skeletal muscles—those responsible for most of the body's movements—undergo numerous alterations during training. The cells' energy-producing sites, the mitochondria, become more numerous. The density of the capillaries that supply oxygen to the muscles becomes greater. The muscles' fuel, glycogen, is consumed more slowly. All these changes mean that the trained muscle functions more efficiently.

An athlete's purpose in training for endurance is to bring about precisely these physiological alterations. Chief among the principles to be followed is that sustained activity rather than the development of strength should be stressed. Strength and endurance are, not surprisingly, inescapably related, and a person who sets out to develop one capacity invariably develops the other to some degree as well. For example, a man or woman who repeatedly raises a five-pound weight will eventually be able to lift it with less effort (because of increased strength) and will also find it possible to perform more repetitions (because of increased endurance). Strength and endurance are thus inescapably related. Even so, if desired, it is possible to train in such a way that endurance and not strength is emphasized.

The secret of achieving this result is to work out for a fairly long time with relatively little effort. In one study, two groups of volunteers were asked to exercise using, in the first instance, high resistance with a small number of repetitions and, in the second, low resistance with a large number of repetitions. Those in the first group increased endurance by 24 percent, those in the second by 41 percent.

In seeking to improve endurance by lifting weights, incidentally, it does not matter greatly what kind of resistance is selected. Not long ago Michael T. Sanders of the University of Wisconsin compared the use of Nautilus equipment with that of conventional barbells. The two types of training turned out to be equally effective. You can gain just as much endurance by hoisting a piece of cordwood as by working out with a chrome-covered marvel made of cams, chains and pulleys.

A second key principle is that we must train hard enough to produce the results we hope for. Although this may seem so self-evident as to be scarcely worth mentioning, it is often overlooked. The chief reason for its neglect is that the training load that brings impressive improvement during the first few weeks in a sport will after a while produce no further improvement but will serve only to maintain the present level of conditioning. Accustomed to improvement, an athlete may not at first realize that he is no longer gaining endurance.

The importance of adequate training for endurance sports is illustrated by a comparison, made not long ago in Melbourne, Australia, of weekly training mileage with performance in marathon running. As the graph below shows, a distinct corre-

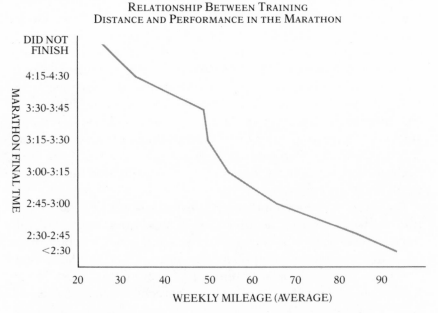

RELATIONSHIP BETWEEN TRAINING
DISTANCE AND PERFORMANCE IN THE MARATHON

SOURCE: From J. L. Sumner, "The Effect of Training and Pre-Race Diet on Performance in the Marathon," in *Modern Athlete and Coach*.

lation exists between finishing times and the number of miles athletes had covered in preparation for the event. Participants who averaged above ninety miles per week did extremely well, while those who averaged less than thirty miles failed to reach the finish line.

In a related study, carried out at the Institute for Aerobics Research in Dallas, the training regimens of fifty runners were analyzed during the nine weeks preceding a local marathon. Having correlated their data with performance in the race, the investigators concluded: "Success in distance running is related to the frequency, intensity and duration of the training program which precedes the competitive event."

The training programs of top athletes, in running as well as in other sports, invariably conform to this principle. The Japanese runner Toshiko Seko, who is among the world's most gifted marathoners, covers from six to nine miles every morning and another twelve to eighteen every afternoon. Ron Tabb, one of America's most accomplished distance runners and the second-place finisher in 1983's Boston Marathon, logs more than 100 miles a week and once ran a 10-kilometer race in an impressive 29:30 after a 114-mile training week. And when Mike Haffner played wide receiver for the Denver Broncos, he told the author, he never felt he had acquired adequate endurance until twice-daily workouts, so-called two-a-days, were well under way. Two-a-days are intensive morning and afternoon sessions that leave an athlete so exhausted he can scarcely distinguish one primary color from another.

Some athletes, most notably those involved in the increasingly popular sport of triathlons, train even more strenuously than Seko and Tabb do. Mark MacIntyre, who finished sixth in the 1983 Ironman Triathlon in Hawaii, typically works out from nine in the morning until six at night. Not long ago Todd Benoit, this book's research associate, talked with MacIntyre, who told him, "For the endurance athlete, consistency is of the utmost importance. For me, it's crucial that I do all three events every day. Today was an average training day. I ran ten miles, swam four thousand yards, and bicycled forty miles. I also do push-ups, sit-ups, pull-ups and flexibility exercises, and I practice yoga."

A person's capacity for developing endurance is governed not just by his or her willingness to train but also by genetic influences. "Natural endowment . . . probably plays a major role in a person's performance capacity," write Per-Olof Åstrand and Kaare Rodahl in their *Textbook of Work Physiology*, the most widely consulted guide to the subject. We have already seen, for example, that muscle fibers can be classified into two varieties, fast twitch and slow, and that slow-twitch fibers, because of their rich oxygen supply, are able to continue working considerably longer than fast twitch.

A few years ago three researchers, David L. Costill, William J. Fink and Michael L. Pollock, decided to investigate this phenomenon in order to determine, if they could, its relationship to the performance of endurance athletes. From laboratory studies they knew that in the general population some 58 percent of muscle fibers are of the slow-twitch type. They therefore assembled fourteen accomplished distance runners (among them Frank Shorter), performed biopsies of their calf muscles, and examined the samples with a microscope. Slow-twitch fibers, it turned out, averaged 79 percent in this group—more than 36 percent higher than would normally be expected—and in one case reached 98 percent.

A study conducted recently at Karolinska Hospital in Stockholm, Sweden, suggests why slow-twitch fibers are so important in endurance sports. One common reason for fatigue is the accumulation of lactic acid in muscle. The Karolinska study, which used as its subjects eighteen participants in the 1979 Stockholm Marathon, found, first, that the buildup of lactic acid varies considerably from person to person and, second, that the greater the percentage of slow-twitch fibers the less lactic acid is present. This fact has an important application to endurance athletes. Specifically, the more slow-twitch muscle they have, the less tired they are likely to feel.

There is at least one other important piece of evidence buttressing the case for a strong genetic influence in endurance sports. In 1980 Michael L. Pollock, Andrew S. Jackson and Russell R. Pate reported on an investigation in which top middle-distance and marathon runners and a group consisting of merely "good" runners were compared. Evaluating such aspects of athletic performance as the ability to use oxygen, lactic acid buildup, and percentage of body fat, the researchers found that top athletes and their less gifted brethren are distinguished by "a general physiological efficiency factor." The various internal mechanisms of the best athletes, it seems, are simply better suited for sports.*

* A related study, conducted by Douglas L. Conley and Gary S. Krahenbuhl at Arizona State University's Human Performance Laboratory found that 65 percent of variations in racing performance are explainable by nothing more than differ-

Endurance, though commonly thought of as providing only a single benefit, enabling an athlete to play longer without becoming tired, offers several other benefits as well, however.

It is well established, for example, that proper form is important in all sports. Fatigue, the onset of which is hastened by lack of endurance, is the archenemy of good form. Baseball pitchers invariably lose accuracy as they tire. Wayne Harer, whose assignment it is to use an electronic device to time the pitches of the New York Yankees, says, "Pitchers don't lose a whole lot of speed as they get tired. What they lose is accuracy, and their pitches don't move around as much." And when B. C. Elliott and A. D. Roberts, two Australian researchers, used high-speed photography to analyze the biomechanics of middle-distance running, they found that tired athletes not only shorten their strides but also angle their legs in inefficient ways, use their thighs less effectively, and keep their feet on the ground longer than when they are rested.

For many athletes, a lack of endurance merely means they will play less effectively than they otherwise might. For those involved in contact sports, however, it can significantly increase the dangers to which they are exposed. Statistics show, for example, that most football injuries occur during the second and fourth quarters of a game, after the benefits of rest have worn off. In other sports as well, risk is augmented as fatigue increases.

Still another benefit of good endurance is that it delays the transition from aerobic to anaerobic activity. This is of paramount importance in athletics because, while aerobic exercise can be carried on almost indefinitely (recall the six-day runners mentioned earlier in this chapter), anaerobic exercise must halt as soon as the muscles' lactic acid concentration reaches a critical concentration.

The occurrence of this phenomenon depends, first, on what physiologists call VO_2 max—that is, the body's capacity for making use of oxygen. (The higher one's VO_2 max, the more intensely one can work out without becoming out of breath or feeling tired.) It depends equally, however, on the endurance that has been developed through training. Although the best male marathon performances have remained about the same for some time now, apparently

---

ences in running economy. Many aspects of the way a man or woman runs are, of course, inherited rather than learned.

indicating an imminent approach to an intrinsic limit, a vast and growing number of runners are recording times under 2:20, a reflection of their improving ability to perform at close to maximum capacity without experiencing intolerable levels of lactic acid. It is primarily more enlightened endurance training that has made this widespread change possible.

One aspect of such training has yet to be mentioned. This is diet. Under normal circumstances muscle glycogen, the fuel that makes work possible, is exhausted after about twenty miles of running. A carbohydrate-rich diet for three days before a marathon, however, can greatly increase glycogen stores and thereby prolong effective performance. This technique, commonly called carbohydrate loading, has been shown to be particularly effective in distance running, cross-country skiing, bicycling, mountain climbing, canoeing, soccer and ice hockey. (Most other sports are not so sustained that carbohydrate loading is helpful.)

Recent research has added a second dietary procedure to those commonly followed by endurance athletes. This is the ingestion of caffeine before exercise. The physiologist David L. Costill and his associates reported not long ago that 250 milligrams of caffeine—the equivalent of slightly less than two cups of coffee—taken an hour before the start of exercise and then another 250 milligrams immediately preceding exercise can increase work capacity by more than 7.4 percent. Apparently the caffeine hastens the use of fat for energy production, thus preserving muscle glycogen.*

Athletic nutrition is discussed in detail in Chapter 11. For now, it will perhaps be enough to bear in mind that important as diet may be, it is unlikely ever to replace diligent training. Though some athletes are reluctant to concede the point, no pill or potion has thus far been discovered that can serve as a substitute for a workout.

---

* Knowing what to do in sports can be a complex matter. Eager to put Costill's findings to a personal test, the author decided not long ago to try drinking two cups of coffee just before a 20-kilometer race. The caffeine may have increased his energy, but the fluid brought a second, unsought result as well. After an hour's running he found he had to relieve himself behind a tree, thus losing whatever advantage he might otherwise have gained.

CHAPTER 7

Searching for Speed

I don't expect a whole lot of improvement out of anyone until a year has gone by.

—BILL DELLINGER, *coach*

COMMENTING ON Nolan Ryan's celebrated 100-mile-an-hour fastball, Peter Alfano of the *New York Times* once wrote, "No one can be taught to throw that hard. It comes naturally." Alfano's observation reflects two truths about speed in athletics—first, that limits exist to the velocities that our bodies and their component parts can attain and, second, that those limits vary markedly from athlete to athlete.

These truths are of fundamental significance, for in most of our games speed is an essential component. It serves not only to move our bodies swiftly, thereby giving us an advantage over opponents, but also to accelerate the various implements of sport—footballs, baseballs, tennis racquets, lacrosse sticks and so forth. Furthermore, it contributes to the development of power (a combination of force and velocity), which is self-evidently of critical importance in such activities as weightlifting and football but which plays a role to one degree or another in almost all other sports as well.

Some aspects of speed are beyond an athlete's control. If, for example, you were to compete on Harvard University's indoor track, which has been scientifically "tuned" to enhance runners' speed, you could expect to run roughly 1.5 percent faster than on an ordinary cinder track. In this case, the running surface is an inescapable determinant of speed.

Or suppose you were to run a marathon when the temperature was in the low thirties or the mid-seventies. Under either of those circumstances, according to calculations by E. C. Frederick, you would require approximately ten minutes more to cover the 26.2-mile course than you would need if the temperature were an ideal 55 degrees. (Records for the sixty-one marathons Frederick studied show that temperatures in the mid-fifties yield the fastest marathon times.)

Such influences as playing surface and ambient temperature are external. They affect all athletes more or less equally, conferring many of the same advantages and disadvantages. Others, however, are internal, reflecting who we are as individuals and how efficiently our bodies are able to perform various tasks. Internal determinants of performance are of two types: those we are unable to change and those we can improve through training.

Influences in the first category are those that produce the so-called natural athlete, or that—if we suffer an all too common misfortune—prevent us from being such an athlete. Body build, for example, exerts a considerable influence on speed. A researcher at the Free University of Amsterdam, G. J. van Ingen Schenau, recently asked several speed skaters to work out in a wind tunnel at his country's National Aerospace Laboratory. While they did so, he measured various components of the effort they were making. Bodily proportions, analysis showed, had an important effect on wind resistance and therefore on maximum attainable speed. The same is true, of course, of athletes in other sports. To a significant degree, your shape governs how fast you are able to move.

Body build, however, is only one of several genetic influences that determine our capacity for rapid movement. Another such influence is muscle type. As we have already seen, muscles are classifiable into two varieties, fast twitch and slow twitch. Top marathon runners typically have a preponderance of slow-twitch fibers, which contribute to endurance, while world-class sprinters tend to have more fast-twitch fibers, which suggest speed.

Even in the absence of scientific scrutiny, most athletes come to know through experience roughly what their muscle composition is. In a conversation with the author, Vitas Gerulaitis acknowledged—he was not bragging but merely reporting a plain fact—that he possesses better speed on a tennis court than many of his rivals. Similarly, Stanley Floyd, a world record holder at several indoor sprint distances, was quoted in *Sports Illustrated* as saying, "I was a 9.3 sprinter coming out of high school. I had a gift of speed from God."

In addition to muscle speed—what physiologists refer to as movement time—each of us has a distinct reaction time, the interval that elapses from the instant we decide to execute a movement until we are able to start doing so. In many sports, particularly those in which quick responses are important, reaction time is the overriding element in overall speed. For this reason, a vast amount of research has been done, and continues to be done, on the subject.

The physiological mechanism that governs reaction time involves motor neurons, muscle fibers and a chemical called acetylcholine. A reaction requires two-tenths of a second or more—*considerably* more when complex information must first be interpreted or when an initial response turns out to be mistaken and one's intentions must therefore be altered. A diligent student of the subject, Robert W. Christina of The Pennsylvania State University, has found in his laboratory that when volunteers are tricked into executing an incorrect movement, they require not the customary two-tenths of a second to change a response but some 50 percent longer than that. This is precisely what happens when a basketball or football player fakes an opponent. Christina's research suggests why such moves, which cost a rival so much time, are effective tactics in high-speed sports.

An athlete's reaction time, while governed principally by genetic endowment, can be significantly enhanced by practice. Through repeated efforts, we can improve our anticipation—the ability either to guess or to foresee what will happen and to decide what response is likely to be appropriate. Anticipation, Christina points out, is of two principal types. One is the sort used by a skier who, looking down a slope he has never before skied, makes a mental inventory of moves that may be required. The other is the sort used by a batter in baseball. While the batter cannot know exactly what pitch will come his way next, experience has taught him to expect certain patterns based on a particular pitcher's strengths and weaknesses, the game situation, and his own ability to handle curve balls, sliders and so forth. By reviewing all the information we possess about a forthcoming play, or even an entire game, we may be able to effect a noticeable improvement in our anticipation.

Still another influence on speed over which we have little control is age. Until we are about thirty-five years old little if any decline in speed is detectable. (Until he reached his mid-thirties Bill Rodgers was still setting personal records.) Thereafter, however, speed begins to fall off. As the graph below shows, at distances of 100 meters a steady decline occurs with increasing age, and starting at about age sixty the decline steepens. John A. Kelley, a two-time Boston Marathon winner who in his late seventies continues to compete in marathons and other races, noticed only a slight decrease in his running speed until he reached his late fifties. "I suddenly lost a lot of my speed at about that time, and it happened suddenly," he says. "In endurance, I was still a tiger. But I was like a transmission that had lost high gear."

MASTERS' 100 METERS

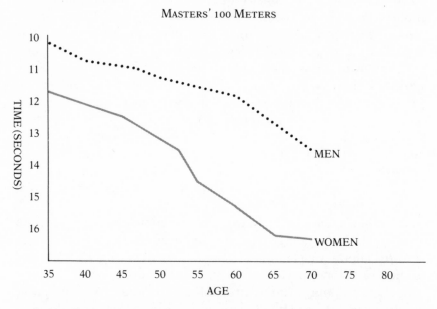

The techniques of training for speed—either for rapid movement of the body as a whole, as in sprinting, or of its individual parts, as in batting a baseball or passing a basketball—are not at all obscure; they merely require sustained, painstaking application. The following are some key principles:

Work out vigorously. The physiologist David L. Costill, a leading authority on sports training, points out that high-intensity workouts not only stress those physiological systems that are used in competition but also increase the oxidative capacity of the muscles, enabling them to function more effectively than when they are less adequately conditioned.

Even if the muscles contain a preponderance of slow-twitch rather than fast-twitch fibers, most people can markedly increase their speed. By fully exercising whatever fast-twitch fibers they possess, they can train their bodies to get the most out of them. An inherently slow person who works out with maximum effectiveness will often have more speed than a man or woman who has greater potential but has not yet mobilized it.

A word of warning, however: Unless an athlete is in excellent condition, moving at maximum speed can easily strain or even tear a muscle, possibly necessitating a long period of inactivity while recovery takes place. It's safer to back off and run at 90 percent of top effort. You'll benefit almost as much and incur less risk.

Plan to devote at least a year to speed training. A measurable increase in the velocity of muscular contractions is usually observable within a few weeks after speed training begins. For speed to reach its maximum, however, as much as a year may be required. Bill Dellinger, one of the country's most consistently successful coaches, reports that he does not look for results until an athlete has been on a speed program for at least twelve months. Dellinger's observation is reflected in the experience of other observers who report that a man's or woman's best performance not infrequently follows twelve months or more of hard training.

Since present ability and potential speed vary so greatly from person to person, no single program of improvement is suitable for all athletes. Nonetheless, the fundamental principles are the same for beginning joggers and world-class athletes. The box on pages 92 and 93 offers guidelines and a sample eight-week program to help improve an athlete's leg speed without sacrificing the endurance work he has already done. A program such as this one is useful for anyone who is training to cover 10,000 meters in thirty-four to thirty-eight minutes or would like to run a sub-three-hour marathon. By modifying intensity and distance, one can readily adapt the programs to other goals.

SPEED-WORK GUIDELINES

• Before beginning a speed-work program you should first build a base of endurance and strength. Running 40 to 45 miles a week for six to eight weeks will help you prepare for the following program.

• Warming up prior to speed work is essential. Running a mile or two and doing a few stretches will help your muscles warm up before you try to extend them in your workout.

• A speed-work program should be limited to once a week. In addition to the buildup of lactic acid in your muscles from oxygen debt, your body must absorb more punishment because of your increased speed. As you pick up the pace, your feet will strike the ground harder and this jolt will be transmitted throughout your body. Rest is a must. Plan on easy exercise for the day before and for two days after speed work.

• To help reduce the pounding effects of speed work, try to exercise on a soft surface. A well-tended cinder or tartan track surface will negate some of the shock. So too will a smooth field or lawn.

• When you can, try to run on a slight downhill and with the wind at your back. Remember, one of the ideas behind speed work is to teach your leg muscles to move quickly. Anything you can do to help this cause without damaging your body will increase your speed.

Sample Program

WEEK ONE	2 × 220 yards @ :36
	6 × 440 yards @ 1:18
WEEK TWO	2 × 220 @ :36
	6 × 440 @ 1:18
	1 × 880 @ 2:40
WEEK THREE	8 × 440 @ 1:18
	1 × 880 @ 2:40
WEEK FOUR	8 × 440 @ 1:15
	2 × 880 @ 2:40
WEEK FIVE	10 × 440 @ 1:15
	1 × 880 @ 2:35

WEEK SIX	12 × 440 @ 1:15
	1 × 1320 @ 4:00
WEEK SEVEN	12 × 440 @ 1:15
	1 × 880 @ 2:40
	1 × 1320 @ 4:00
WEEK EIGHT	12 × 440 @ 1:15
	1 × 880 @ 3:35
	1 × 1320 @ 3:55

Let us assume that our preparation, or as much of it as we have had time or inclination for, is complete. Our present task, therefore, is to extract from our muscles as much speed as possible in order to score points or outrun an opponent.

The chief component of speed under pressure is not physical at all but mental. Whether in a marathon race lasting two or more hours, or a football or basketball play of a few seconds' duration, we rarely do our best when we neglect to focus our attention fully on what we hope to accomplish.

Concentrating is rarely easy. Distractions are abundant. Fatigue and our opponents threaten to take our minds off what we are trying to accomplish. Nonetheless, concentration is well worth whatever effort it requires to achieve.

Some athletes feel they concentrate best when they take the trouble to psych themselves up thoroughly beforehand. They may pace the locker room, think aggressive or even hostile thoughts about their opponents, try to foresee key moments of the forthcoming contest. When competition begins, it is as if these athletes were already in mid-game.

Other competitors concentrate most fully when they are able to achieve a calm, meditative frame of mind. Their preparation may consist of closing their eyes as if sleeping, envisioning tranquil scenes, perhaps reciting a silent prayer.

The specific technique scarcely matters. What does matter is that, given the individual athlete's interests and inclinations, it should help achieve his or her maximum concentration. That, after all, is the best way to keep from sacrificing momentum during the pressure of competition.

Nor can top speed be approached, in most sports at any rate, without a willingness to endure discomfort. This is most apparent in endurance events such as bicycle and marathon races, but it is also true in basketball, football, tennis, volleyball—any sport, in short, that requires a player to remain in motion for a sustained period.

A desire to continue functioning while experiencing pain is not, as we all know, an innate human characteristic; any sensible person, feeling discomfort, wants to slow down. Rather, it is an ability that must be learned and, if training is for some reason discontinued and later resumed, relearned.

It is only through repeated exposure that an athlete can learn the permutations of pain. To a beginner, pain appears to be a single sensation, beginning at some moment in a contest and, if effort is continued, worsening until work can no longer continue. Although there is an approximate truth in this interpretation, it is by no means the entire truth. For pain rarely worsens in a tidily linear manner. Rather, it does so in waves. We may feel dreadful at one moment, imagining that we will soon have to stagger off the field. A few seconds later, however, we are surprised to find ourselves almost totally restored. As we tire, the troughs between the waves become deeper and the peaks less high. Nonetheless, the process may continue for quite some time, allowing us to perform well for much longer than we thought possible.

Furthermore, it is by no means certain that pain, once having begun, will worsen. In some cases it reaches a certain intensity, one that is not at all intolerable, and simply stays that way. Alberto Salazar, world record holder in the marathon, recently told of his discovery that even when the discomforts of marathon running become fairly intense, it may be possible to withstand it for another hour or more because it does not necessarily grow more bothersome. In such a case the athlete's chief struggle is not physical at all but mental: How long can the mind overcome the natural impulse to slow down?

Sustaining maximum speed over a period of time depends, too, on the efficient use of energy stores. In some sports, such as rowing and running the mile, a fast start is customary. Although such starts may serve tactical purposes, they are physiologically unsound because fast movement prompts the muscles to produce lactic acid, a major cause of fatigue.

A more effective strategy is to move at an even pace throughout most of the race and finally to introduce a fast finish. (By the end of an event it doesn't matter whether or not the muscles accumulate lactic acid.) This is, however, more easily recommended than executed, since it is extremely difficult to calculate a proper pace for an event lasting an hour or more. A pace that is too fast, even by a single percentage point, will sooner or later force an athlete to slow down, while one that is too slow may put him at such a disadvantage that he never regains lost time.

This is true for events of all durations. Even in sprintlike efforts that last only a few seconds, it is rarely possible to move at top speed from start to finish; some energy must be held in reserve. At track meets it is not uncommon to see a runner stumble only a few feet from the finish line. What has happened is that he has reached exhaustion a second or two before he planned to.

Improvements in speed also depend, however, on exactly where the existing records stand. Analysis of record-breaking across the entire range of sports reveals that it is uncommon for a record to be broken by a great deal. Rather, records are typically broken by the smallest possible increments—mere tenths of a second or fractions of an inch. The reason is that breaking a record is in itself sufficient achievement. There is little point, and for that matter little added glory, in exceeding it by an overwhelming margin. Few athletes, therefore, either train for that purpose or attempt it in competition.

Most of us, needless to say, will never participate in the breaking of a world record (except perhaps, with luck, to be present when such an event occurs). This is not to say, however, that we are destined to have no involvement with records of any kind. For each of us, through training, perseverance and the application of principles like those described in this chapter, can strive to exceed his or her own previous limits. That, whenever it occurs, is an achievement worthy of celebration.

CHAPTER 8

Gracefulness Under Pressure

Is the beauty that is derived from ice skating
and dancing, from gymnastics, . . . hockey and
horseback riding categorically different from
that of, say, music and the stage?

—ERNST JOKL, M.D.

Tᴇᴅ Wɪʟʟɪᴀᴍs once called batting a baseball "the single most
difficult thing to do in sport." While this heartfelt opinion
may have reflected Williams' own frustrations as much as it did
the nature of objective reality, it is difficult to imagine a task more
diabolically calculated to induce self-doubt. Consider, first, the
mere speed of the oncoming ball—anywhere from 65 miles per
hour if it is a knuckleball to 100 miles per hour if it is an expertly
delivered fastball. Next, ponder the ball's flight, which, depending
upon the intentions and ability of the pitcher, may variously jump,
dance, dart or curve. Then there is the batter's reaction time—his
ability to assess the pitch and decide whether or not to swing
his bat and, if so, in what plane and with what force. Finally, if
his bat does meet the ball, consider that the two rounded surfaces
must collide at such an angle that the ball does not pop straight
up or slant toward home plate.

This is where coordination and agility, whether innate or learned,
come in. For between an excellent batter—a Stan Musial, a Mickey
Mantle, a Willie Mays—and a merely good one lies an enormous
difference. Analysis by James L. Breen, the author of a scholarly
report entitled "What Makes a Good Hitter?" and a diligent student

DECISION AND SWING TIMES IN BATTING

.26 SEC.		.28 SEC.		MAJOR LEAGUE HITTER (<300)
.31 SEC.		.23 SEC.		TED WILLIAMS
.32 SEC.		.22 SEC.		ERNIE BANKS, HANK AARON
.33 SEC.		.21 SEC.		MICKEY MANTLE, WILLIE MAYS
.35 SEC.		.19 SEC.		STAN MUSIAL

PITCHER   BATTER

·· ·56ft.· · ·····················►

| 60 | 50 | 40 | 30 | 20 | 10 | 0 |

DISTANCE FROM PLATE (ft.)

☐ DECISION TIME   ☐ SWING TIME

SOURCE: From James G. Hay, *The Biomechanics of Sports Techniques*. Englewood Cliffs, N.J.: Prentice-Hall, 1978.

of athletics, shows that the slower major-league batters require .28 sec to execute a swing and therefore—assuming the ball to be in flight for .54 sec—have only .26 sec to decide how best to do so. A quick hitter, by contrast, needs only .19 sec to swing and therefore has a comparatively leisurely period to contemplate the path of the ball. The untutored observer might not view this as much of a difference, since we are discussing mere hundredths of a second, yet it turns out that a good hitter's quickness in fact affords him nearly 17 percent more time in which to delay his swing and arrive at a more fully informed decision.

It is tempting to dwell solely on the practical advantages of agility, since it is those that win games and earn trophies. Yet, as Ernst Jokl has pointed out, agility also serves an esthetic purpose, adding beauty to the lives of athletes and onlookers alike. He writes, "Is the beauty that is derived from ice skating and dancing, from gymnastics and water diving, from soccer, hockey and horseback riding categorically different from that of, say, music and the stage? . . . The esthetic implications of the acts that engender beauty in sport are fundamentally the same as the arts that engender beauty in music and on the stage."

Howard Gardner goes even further. In *Frames of Mind: The Theory of Multiple Intelligences* he argues that an athlete's agility is nothing less than a form of intellect—what he calls "bodily kinesthetic intelligence." The athletic intelligence, Gardner suggests, does not produce thought of a conventional sort but, rather, yields a satisfaction obtainable in no other way: "The athlete's ability to excel in grace, power, speed, accuracy, and teamwork not only affords a source of pleasure to the athlete himself but also serves, for countless observers, as a means of entertainment, stimulation, and release."

However agility is ultimately interpreted, plainly it is partly a genetic trait. It does not, after all, require a sports expert to observe that the movements of some people are naturally faster than those of others, or that some men and women seem to be more inherently graceful than their fellows. (An average tennis player might strive for a lifetime yet never once move as swiftly or with such effortless efficiency as John McEnroe.)

To a significant degree, however, agility can also be learned, provided an athlete is willing to expend the necessary effort. The potential rewards make such an effort well worth while. During a game in the spring of 1983 Julio Cesar Romero, a New York Cosmos midfielder, received an exceptionally quick pass from a teammate. He was in scoring position, but was, unfortunately, facing his own rather than his opponents' goal and realized that he could not possibly turn around in time to try for a point. He could think of only one thing to do. While falling onto his back. Romero gave the ball an overhead scissors kick and, to the astonishment of spectators, scored the goal. Without his extraordinary agility, Romero could only have continued passing the ball.

Even men and women who appear to be irredeemably clumsy can, with enough practice, become reasonably graceful. At a seminar in Zurich some years ago Ernst Jokl pointed out that an untrained person gives few hints of his ultimate potential. The reason is that acquiring a high order of physical skill is a complex process, consisting as it does of a variety of components, among them clarifying the idea of the task to be performed, deciding how to set about learning it and, finally, practicing it long enough to perfect its technique.

While these tasks, by their nature, require much time, accomplishing them has become considerably more certain during the past few years than ever before. The chief reason is the existence of the science of biomechanics. An outgrowth of what was once known as kinesiology, biomechanics emerged in the mid-1960's with the establishment at several American universities of laboratories devoted to the minute and systematic analysis of human motion.

With the advent of biomechanics, however, lore and tradition were for the first time subjected to sustained scrutiny. Dr. Richard C. Nelson, director of Penn State University's biomechanics laboratory, tells of a top steeplechaser who, at training camp, was experiencing trouble in clearing the water jump. He was asked to make an attempt while several coaches and athletes tried to figure out what he was doing wrong. Although the experts all had an opportunity to scrutinize the athlete's technique at close range, there was little agreement on the cause of his problem. At length his performance was videotaped. Viewed in slow motion, the videotape revealed that, instead of leaving the barrier on one foot and landing on the other, as is customary, he was hopping off the barrier and landing on the same foot—an error analogous, as Nelson describes it, to batting cross-handed in baseball.

Not all of us are capable of developing the agility of a world-class athlete, with or without the benefit of biomechanical counsel. In tennis, for example, a large player is likely to be less well coordinated than a smaller man or woman, although among tennis players Chip Hooper and Andrea Temesvari prove that few sports axioms, including this one, hold true without exception. (Hooper's ballet lessons may be relevant here.) The chief reason coordination tends to decrease with size is that as people become larger their proportions change as well. In carrying out studies of athletic shoes for Nike, Inc., E. C. Frederick discovered that the feet of tall men and women are in most cases proportionately smaller than the feet of those who are shorter. Nor, because of Newton's laws of physical motion, are most large people able to move or change direction as quickly as smaller ones, any more than an elephant is as perkily energetic as a sandpiper. (It is no accident that the typical champion gymnast or marathon runner looks as if he needs nothing so much as a good meal.) True, an occasional athlete with the graceful skills of 222-pound Herschel Walker seems to suggest that we might profitably reexamine Newton's laws, yet for the most part the bigger a person is the more ponderously he moves and the more effort it requires to do so.

This fact is reflected in a story told about Jim Thorpe, winner of both the decathlon and pentathlon in the 1912 Olympic Games. According to legend, Thorpe was once asked to participate in an experiment. All he needed to do was spend a day imitating the actions of a baby. After a few hours, so the story goes, the great athlete gave up in exhaustion.

As this story is customarily told (usually by the overworked mothers and fathers of young children), it is intended to suggest that babies are so active that it is difficult, if not impossible, to keep up with them. Yet it contains another, unintended lesson as well. This is that a large person cannot in all respects imitate the actions of a smaller one, for in attempting to do so he must exert proportionately more force in order to overcome the inertia of his greater mass.

For this reason dieting alone can often increase agility. A 200-pound athlete who reduces his weight to 175 pounds will almost certainly be able to move more quickly and, provided he does not need the extra 25 pounds for putting the shot or penetrating a football line, will be a more effective athlete. Other than by dieting, however, and perhaps exercising to alter muscle girth, there is little we can do to change the proportions with which nature has provided us. Given these constraints, therefore, by what method can one set out to improve agility?

To some extent, the method chosen will depend upon the sport, since different athletic movements call for different forms of agility. Even within a single sport, it is not always possible to find agreement on what methods work best.

In football, Art Monk of the Washington Redskins favors racquetball and basketball workouts. Gary Fencik of the Chicago Bears plays tennis. Freeman McNeil of the New York Jets and Herschel Walker of the New Jersey Generals practice karate.

Among basketball players, Kelly Tripucka of the Detroit Pistons jumps rope. The Philadelphia 76ers work out with a ballet instructor prior to their daily practices. Carl Scheer, president and general manager of the Denver Nuggets and himself a former basketball player, recommends that team members improve their agility by playing tennis, volleyball and racquetball.

Not all sports authorities agree that such supplementary activities are helpful. Abraham Grossfeld, who won eight gold medals in international gymnastics competition during the 1950's and 1960's, says, "Probably the best way to increase coordination and agility is through repetition—by practicing a move over and over. I don't think activities like dance help an athlete much, although they certainly won't hurt him. True, dance might make an athlete *look* more graceful. When a wide receiver goes up for a pass, he might look better catching the ball. But I don't think he'd catch it any more often.''

Agility is not, of course, a matter of quickness alone. It also depends on flexibility. Fitness authorities point out that flexibility, which is most commonly induced by stretching, affords the joints a greater range of motion by giving muscles and tendons more limberness.

This view has numerous adherents, including the members of most professional sports teams, and has spawned a considerable library. (Among the best books on the subject is Bob Anderson's *Stretching.*) Not everyone agrees, however, that stretching is desirable. While the pro-stretching faction insists that flexible athletes are less frequently injured than those who are not so flexible, the opposition points to such contrary evidence as a survey conducted at the 1979 Honolulu Marathon. The results revealed that, in defiance of all reasonable expectations, runners accustomed to stretching were more subject to injury than those who never stretched at all.

An explanation may be that many athletes turn to stretching only when they have once become injured, hoping thereby to prevent a recurrence. Thus researchers, such as those who evaluated the Honolulu Marathon results, would observe a correlation, however misleading, between injury and stretching.

It may be, on the other hand, that stretching itself causes injury. It seems unlikely that stretching in what is generally regarded as the correct manner—slowly and without bouncing—causes any significant numbers of injuries. So-called ballistic stretching, however, of which bouncing is a part, not infrequently produces muscle and tendon damage.

Curiously, given the avidness with which researchers these days pursue most aspects of sport, no full-scale study of stretching has thus far been undertaken. Until someone settles the stretching controversy once and for all, perhaps all we can do is conduct our own personal experiments in hopes of finding out whether we, as individuals, perform better or worse when stretching is part of our regimen.

On one point, however, there is little disagreement. This is that whatever means of improving agility one selects, hard work is imperative. In his essay "The Acquisition of Skill" Ernst Jokl cites the Czech gymnastics champion Eva Bosakova's account of how her father trained her from the time she was fifteen years old: "He prescribed daily thirty-minute periods of work on the beam during which it was necessary to remain on the apparatus constantly in action, walking, hopping, turning, and again walking without rest. I spent hundreds of hours and uncounted kilometers walking and running on the beam. . . . In the process I gained complete confidence, accustomed myself to unfamiliar situations, and lost all fear of falling."

"It is thus," observes Jokl, "that skill is acquired."

CHAPTER 9
Natural Gifts

Athletes are born and *then* made.
—JOHN SPAVENTA, *sports psychologist*

I N AN EGALITARIAN WORLD, athletic endowment—speed, strength, agility and so forth—would be parceled out to each of us with evenhanded impartiality, and only our determination in training and our tenacity in competition would govern whether we did well or poorly. But as every athlete—and, perhaps more to the point, every would-be athlete—is aware, such gifts are bestowed not just parsimoniously but unpredictably.

As scientists give increasingly minute scrutiny to the sources of the athletic distinction found in top athletes, they are unearthing dozens of physiological and psychological influences that contribute to—and in some cases detract from—excellence on the playing field. What color are your eyes? (Dark-eyed people, in general, enjoy swifter reaction time than those with light-colored eyes.) And what color is your skin? (Dark skin seems to bring certain athletic benefits, light skin others.) It is plain, moreover, that little can be done about altering such traits. To become a top athlete, it has been widely declared, one must choose one's parents with care.

Consider, for example, the curious endowment of that enduring tennis player, Billie Jean King, who in her book *Billie Jean* attributes much of her success to her frequently ailing knees. "Athletically speaking," she writes, "my knees are a gift. . . . My knees swivel more than the average person's; that allows me quick starts not only to the left and right, but also up and back."

And what substitute could possibly exist for Kareem Abdul-Jabbar's seven feet two inches of height or the 420 pounds of Olympic wrestler Chris Taylor?

The influence of form on human function, so apparent in top athletes, is as old as our species itself. Neanderthal man was endowed with thick, sturdy bones whose mechanical leverages suggest enormous power and a considerable capacity to withstand stress. (*Homo neanderthalensis* was no doubt a fine wrestler but would have made an inept gymnast.) By the classical Greek era it was well established that some athletes are best suited for one sport, others for a quite different one. "The combination of prowess demonstrated by the pentathlon," writes Allen Guttman in *From Ritual to Record*, "was in itself an indication that there were different specialties to be combined in a single test of more general ability." In our own time, specialization may be approaching some sort of ultimate. It is, after all, significant that most football players rarely lay hands on a football and that no American League pitcher ever has occasion to wield one of the fundamental tools of his sport, the baseball bat.

The genetic factors that, over the centuries, have given rise to increasing athletic specialization are of numerous varieties and affect performance in different ways. Some are undetectable except

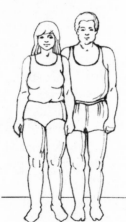

ENDOMORPHY
A very endomorphic person is stocky, with a large round body, a short thick neck, short arms and legs, and a tendency to considerable body fat.

MESOMORPHY
A very mesomorphic person is strongly built, with a broad muscular chest and shoulders, very muscular arms and legs, and little body fat.

ECTOMORPHY
A very ectomorphic person is tall and thin, with a narrow body, thin arms and legs, little body fat, and wiry muscles.

by abstruse scientific analysis. Cellular enzyme activity, which influences the production of muscular energy, falls into this category. So does the type of muscle cell—fast or slow in its contractile characteristics—that predominates in a particular man or woman. Other characteristics, however, can readily be observed with nothing more sophisticated than the naked eye and some crude measurements.

Perhaps most obviously, each of us displays distinct bodily proportions, ranging from the blocky endomorphy of the typical shot-putter to the fat-free ectomorphy of Kareem Abdul-Jabbar or, on a less stratospheric scale, Mary Decker. It is evident, innate athletic ability aside, that certain shapes—dictated chiefly by skeletal proportion—are best suited for certain tasks. The gymnast Mary Lou Retton is an athlete without equal, but who would ask her to do or die against Herschel Walker?*

A second important difference is that our muscles are of different diameter. Muscle cross-sectional area is the chief determinant of potential strength, since the wider the muscle the greater its maximum possible volume. If your muscles are thinner than average, the strength of which you are capable will on that account be less than average as well.

Third, the efficiency of nerve impulses varies from person to person. When signals from the brain activate a muscle group—the biceps, let us say, or the calf—a predetermined number of fibers is set in motion. Most men and women characteristically use about 30 percent of their muscle mass. The person who can activate 40 percent or, as occurs in an occasional rare instance, 50 percent enjoys an important advantage.

Fourth, body fat varies from person to person, apparently because of the number of fat cells that are unalterably present. The average person of normal proportions has perhaps 25 billion fat cells, while an extremely obese person may have more than 200 billion. (Researchers are increasingly convinced that some people may indeed be intrinsically fatter than others, and not merely self-indulgent.) Since low body fat confers an advantage in most sports, some men and women are better fitted than others to be athletes.

* This question serves to remind us that of all athletic differences, none is more pronounced or more crucial than sex. Unpopular as it may currently be to acknowledge such differences, it remains a fact that women in general run and swim more slowly than men, and that they also jump less high, throw less far, and are able to lift less weight. This is scarcely to argue that women are not achieving performances that only a few years ago would have been unthinkable or that in many sports they are not currently improving more rapidly than men.

These four characteristics—bodily proportions, muscle area, neurological efficiency, and degree of fatness—are bestowed on us in a manner that, if not entirely random, is far from predictable. If your father and mother are both over six feet tall, you are likely, it is true, to grow up to be fairly tall, but on the other hand you may not.

SOME DIFFERENCES BETWEEN THE SEXES

MEASURE	WOMEN	MEN
Weight of Brain		
Small	37.04 ozs.	38.8 ozs.
Average	44.98 ozs.	49.38 ozs.
Large	54.68 ozs.	60 ozs.
Weight of Heart	8 ozs.	10 ozs.
Quantity of Blood	.875 gal.	1.5 gals.
Surface Area of Skin	1.93 sq. yds.	2.21 sq. yds.
Water: % of Body Weight	54%	60%
Muscle: % of Body Weight	36%	42%
Fat: % of Body Weight	28%	18%
Bone: % of Body Weight	18%	18%
Average Length of Spine	24 ins.	28 ins.
Total Lung Capacity		
at Age 25		
Small	3.3 qts.	4.5 qts.
Average	4.4 qts.	6.8 qts.
Large	5.7 qts.	9.5 qts.
Number of Breaths		
Per Minute (at Rest)	20–22	14–18
Intake of Air Per Breath		
Resting	.36 qt.	.79 qt.
Light work	.91 qt.	1.77 qts.
Heavy work	.93 qt.	2.15 qts.
Deepest possible intake		
(vital capacity) at age 25	3.17 qts.	5.18 qts.
Number of Red Blood Cells		
Per Cubic Millimeter		
(Blood Count)–U.S. Average	4,200,000–5,400,000	4,600,000–6,200,000

SOURCE: Alan E. Nourse, *The Body*. New York: Time-Life Books, 1968. Courtesy of Time-Life Books Inc.

A fragment of evidence that supports the influence of heredity on sports performance, however, is the way uncommon gifts so often run in families. Carl and Carol Lewis in track and field, Tim and Tom Gullikson in tennis, and Eric and Beth Heiden in ice skating are all examples of nature's openhanded prodigality in this respect.* "Identical genetic endowment combined with identical

---

* During the 1984 season, the National Football League had some 22 pairs of brothers on its rosters.

design of training results in virtually identical athletic performances," writes Dr. Ernst Jokl.

To dwell overlong on the role of genetic factors in athletics could, for most of us, be a discouraging undertaking. By the very nature of the bell-shaped Gaussian curve, all but a few athletes are ipso facto not far from average—not notably inept but not particularly gifted either. So far as natural endowment is concerned, therefore, most of us would seem to be destined for mediocre athletic careers.

But are we really so destined? Some researchers wonder. For even if certain of our inborn traits tend to inhibit achievement, so much is known today about how to train effectively for various sports that it is frequently possible to overcome or at least partially nullify genetic influences. Not long ago, in the *Journal of the American Optometric Association*, C. Douglas Stine, Michael R. Arterburn and Norman S. Stern explored the relationship between visual acuity and athletic excellence. In virtually all sports, they reported, accomplished athletes enjoy better vision than those who are less able. Whichever visual qualities are tested—peripheral vision, depth perception, the ability to detect slight movements, or any of half a dozen or so others—good athletes see more, see it more clearly and see it more promptly. On the other hand, every one of the visual capacities cited by the authors can, it turns out, be improved through training. And so it is with other athletic capacities as well.

We shall return to this theme—the possibility of overcoming genetic shortcomings—later in this chapter. First, however, it will be useful to review a sampling of recent scientific findings concerning inborn traits and the role they play in some of the sports that have recently claimed the attention of researchers.

Running. Because scientists, as already noted, find the study of running so revealing, the information available on runners is more plentiful than for any other kind of athlete. In running, men and women of all ages respond quickly to alterations in training, and it is possible in the laboratory to gather data on volunteers—their heart rate, respiration, copiousness of sweating and so forth—more readily than in any other sport. Even though the present era of mass participation in running is not yet a decade old, much is known about the physiological characteristics that best equip us for running as well as those that tend to make us ill suited for the sport.

Researchers at the Institute of Health and Sport Science of the University of Tsukuba in Japan, for example, recently analyzed anthropometric data on well over a hundred runners and equated their findings with performance at distances ranging from 800 meters, or slightly less than half a mile, to 10,000 meters, or 6.2 miles. Anyone who has ever watched a major marathon knows that practically anyone, no matter how gargantuan, can learn to run long distances. Yet according to the new Japanese research, not everyone can anticipate equal success. The reason, the investigators found, is that excellence in distances from 800 to 5,000 meters is most closely equated with three measurements—chest girth, upper leg length, and subcutaneous fat—and in the 10,000 to but a single surprising factor—the circumference of the arms. (In all cases, smallness, lightness and linearity were found to contribute to success.)

John Gregorio, a 4:00.1 miler and a close student of the sport, has calculated that, other measurements being equal, 140 pounds is the dividing line between top distance runners and also-rans. Studies of Olympic and other runners not only confirm Gregorio's research but suggest that his conclusions may be understated. According to one investigation, the average weight of a male long-distance runner of championship caliber is 128 ¼ pounds, a weight that is, needless to say, well beyond the reach of most men.*

Other researchers have been investigating the relationship between heart rate and distance-running ability. In one study, conducted by Dr. Douglas L. Conley at Arizona State University's Human Performance Laboratory, experienced athletes were asked to run on a treadmill at three successive speeds, 6:40, 6:00 and 5:30 minutes per mile. When the heart rate elicited at each speed was recorded and analyzed, it was found that the slower the heartbeat the better the runner's performance in a 10,000-meter race. At a six-minute pace, for example, a runner whose heart was beating at about 90 percent of maximum had a time of nearly thirty-four minutes, while a runner whose heart was beating at only 80 percent of maximum during the test ran the 10,000 meters in just over thirty minutes.

---

* Requirements are markedly different in the 100-meter dash. Investigators at the Soviet Union's Research Institute of Physical Education have calculated that the ideal sprinter is twenty-three years old, stands five feet ten inches tall, and weighs 160 pounds. By 1990, according to their extrapolations, such an athlete should be able to run 100 meters in 9.75. The present record is 9.95.

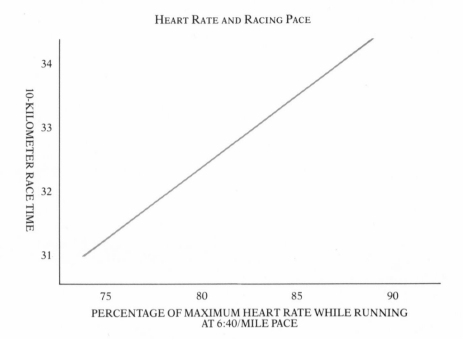

HEART RATE AND RACING PACE

PERCENTAGE OF MAXIMUM HEART RATE WHILE RUNNING
AT 6:40/MILE PACE

The reason for the difference in performance is not elusive. Each of us has what scientists term an anaerobic threshold—a point at which exercise ceases to be comfortable and turns instead into a laborious, hard-breathing effort in which searing accumulations of lactic acid prompt the muscles to give unmistakable complaint. "It's analogous to an engine," explains Dr. Robert Arnot, who serves as training advisor to a number of U.S. athletes. "Like a well-tuned car, the human body can go all out for short periods of time, but the body also has an optimum cruising level." If you try to exceed that level you will pay a severe price. Training itself inevitably slows the heart rate somewhat, and can thereby compensate in part for genetic deficiencies, but there is a limit to what even the most faithfully performed workouts are able to accomplish.

Tennis. Anyone who has ever watched John McEnroe, one of the most deftly agile players in tennis, stretch for an apparently unreachable volley and send it skidding crosscourt for a winner may have had reason to reflect that tennis players are not all cut from the same cloth. A recent study at Stanford University suggests that this is the case not only at the game's top level but among ordinary club players as well. In the Stanford study, fifty successful tennis players, equally divided between men and women, were tested for a variety of anthropometric and physiological measurements. Among the researchers' findings:

- The subjects demonstrated an oxygen-processing capacity—the chief measure of sports fitness—greater than that of roughly 90 percent of the population.
- Their resting heart rates were about ten beats per minute slower than would be expected in a population of comparable nonathletes.
- Their blood pressure was lower.
- Their grip strength was greater than average.

As far as genetic significance is concerned, a skeptic might dismiss these findings on grounds that the tennis players' superior characteristics could be the result of nothing more than their average of 4.7 practice days each week. While acknowledging that possibility, the Stanford researchers also suggest another, quite different theory—"that phenotypically and genotypically superior individuals choose to play tennis." If additional research should one day demonstrate this to be the case, such findings would tell us that many tennis players, like many other athletes, are born rather than made. A tantalizing corollary would be that some nonplayers, if they were once to lay hands on a racquet, might prove to be more adept than they have any reason to suspect.

Skiing. At the University of Colorado's Human Performance Laboratory, two researchers, Emily M. Haymes and Arthur L. Dickinson, recently studied fifty-four skiers who had competed in alpine, cross-country and Nordic events as members of the U.S. Ski Team. The athletes were found to possess high aerobic capacities, excellent balance and agility, and considerable strength and power. Moreover, they exhibited markedly little body fat (particularly the cross-country skiers). This is not to say that you cannot become a competent skier, and perhaps even a winning one, if you do not possess precisely these characteristics, but chances are you will not become an outstanding performer.

Weightlifting. "Champion weightlifters," according to Richard C. Nelson and Ray G. Burdett of the Biomechanics Laboratory at Penn

State University, "are highly mesomorphic, low in body fat and
. . . short of stature relative to their body weight." This much has
long been beyond dispute, since it is based on studies of weightlifters who have already shown themselves to be successful. Recently a team of investigators at Louisiana State University found
themselves wondering, however, whether a means might be found
for identifying gifted weightlifters in advance. Experimenting with
various tests on university students enrolled in a weight-training
course, they found that one such test showed a strikingly close
correlation with success as a weightlifter: the ability to jump ver-
tically. The reason, apparently, is that jumping requires power
(technically, force multiplied by velocity), just as weightlifting does.
Thus success in one activity indicates probable success in the other.
Conversely, if you are unable to jump higher than average, your
chance of making the Olympic weightlifting team is likely to be
slight.

Football. It hardly requires a scientific analysis to demonstrate
that the best football players tend to be both tall and heavy. In
one landmark study, conducted more than a decade ago by J. H.
Wilmore and W. L. Haskell, it was shown that professional offensive linemen and tight ends average six feet four inches in height
and weigh an average of 265 pounds, while even offensive backs,
most of whom are wispy by prevailing standards of the game,
average six feet tall and weigh more than 200 pounds.

On the other hand, it is apparent that not everyone who enjoys
such stature is suited to earn his living at football; some big people,
after all, are simply clumsy. Not long ago, therefore, researchers
at the University of Arkansas tried to find out if anatomical characteristics correlate reliably with success on the football field. Using as their subjects fifty-six players holding athletic scholarships,
the research team took numerous measurements and conducted
batteries of tests, ranging from determining height and weight to
assessing flexibility and strength. Two such indicators, it turned
out, proved to be the clearest signs of football ability. One was
good hip flexibility, the other a greater than average distance between the kneecaps while standing with the legs straight and the
feet together. From the midpoint of one kneecap to the midpoint
of the other averaged 6.18 inches in the superior football players.

These findings are neither so mystifying nor so unrelated as they
might at first appear. As long ago as the 1950's it was observed,

first, that people with widely spaced knees often toe in and, second, that toeing in requires that the hip joint be rotated. Since a modest degree of toeing in is known to contribute to running speed, a rough formula may be deduced: hip twisting = toeing in = speed = success at football.

Hockey. When researchers at three Canadian universities studied members of Canada's 1980 Olympic hockey team, they found their average height to be five feet eleven inches and their average weight slightly less than 180 pounds—unexceptional measurements by any standard. Furthermore, the players' aerobic capacity was only average and their strength, particularly when they were asked to flex their muscles quickly, was less than is commonly observed in other kinds of athletes. These hockey players, it seemed, excelled not in the tests they were given but, fittingly enough, in their ability to play hockey.

The researchers suggest that better training might benefit hockey players by improving aerobic fitness and increasing strength. On the other hand, a second, somewhat different conclusion seems equally plausible (even if not equally likely to prove popular among hockey players). This is that the athletes tested, having already been selected for their nation's Olympic team, were as fit as they needed to be and that hockey may thus be an ideal sport for people with only average physiological gifts.

Lacrosse. According to one student of the sport, lacrosse is unique because "it requires the physical and performance qualities (such as size, strength, power, speed, agility and endurance) of nearly all of the other sports combined." One would expect, therefore, that lacrosse players would excel in a variety of sports capacities, and that turns out to be exactly the case. Recently Dr. Larry G. Shaver of Vanderbilt University evaluated thirty intercollegiate lacrosse players. They proved to possess about half the body fat of the typical nonathlete (except for defensemen, including goalkeepers, who were somewhat less lean as befits their more placid roles). They were taller and heavier than comparable college-age men, and midfielders, the only players permitted to roam the entire playing field, had an aerobic fitness comparable to that of distance runners. (Aerobically, players at other positions yielded data much like that derived from football and basketball players.) As for strength, the lacrosse participants were as strong as basketball players, soccer players, gymnasts, swimmers and wrestlers. (They

DEMANDS MADE BY VARIOUS SPORTS ON STRENGTH, ENDURANCE, MOBILITY AND FLEXIBILITY OF DIFFERENT BODY AREAS

	SHOULDERS	BACK	TRUNK	ARMS	LEGS
AMERICAN FOOTBALL		● ▲	●	●	● ▲
BASEBALL	■			■	■
BASKETBALL					● ▲ ■
BOXING		● ▲	● ▲	● ▲ ■	● ▲ ■
CROSS-COUNTRY RUNNING		▲	▲		● ▲ ■
FENCING				■	● ■
FIELD HOCKEY		▲		■	● ▲ ■
GYMNASTICS	● ▲ ■	●	●	● ▲ ■	● ■
HANDBALL	■			● ■	● ▲ ■
HIGH JUMP		●	●		●
ICE HOCKEY		●	●	●	● ▲
JUDO		● ▲	● ▲	● ▲ ■	● ▲ ■
KARATE		● ▲	● ▲	● ▲ ■	● ▲ ■
LACROSSE	■			● ▲ ■	● ▲ ■
LONG JUMP		●	●		● ■
NORDIC SKIING	● ■	■	■	● ■	● ▲ ■
POLE VAULT	● ■	● ■	● ■	● ■	● ▲ ■
RACQUET BALL	● ■			● ■	● ▲ ■
ROWING	● ▲	● ▲	● ▲ ■	● ▲	▲
RUGBY				●	● ▲ ■
SOCCER					● ▲ ■
SPRINTING					● ■
SQUASH	● ■			● ■	● ▲ ■
SWIMMING	● ▲ ■	● ▲	● ▲	● ▲ ■	● ▲ ■
TENNIS	● ■			● ■	● ▲ ■
THROWING EVENTS	● ▲ ■	●		● ■	● ■
TUG-OF-WAR				■	● ▲ ■
VOLLEY BALL	■			● ▲ ■	● ▲
WATER POLO	■	▲		● ▲	▲
WATER SKIING	● ▲	▲	▲	● ▲	● ▲
WEIGHT LIFTING	● ▲	● ▲	● ▲	● ▲	● ▲
WRESTLING	● ▲ ■	● ▲ ■	● ▲ ■	● ▲ ■	● ▲ ■

● MUSCLE STRENGTH   ▲ MUSCLE ENDURANCE   ■ MOBILITY AND FLEXIBILITY

SOURCE: From The Diagram Group, *The Sports Fan's Ultimate Book of Sports Comparisons*. New York: St. Martin's Press, 1982.

were weaker than weightlifters, but then who isn't?) The moral seems to be that if you've always been known as an all-around athlete—fast, strong and tireless—lacrosse may be your game.

Volleyball. Like lacrosse, volleyball is a sport that calls for diverse skills. Not long ago researchers at Rice University, studying a group of top volleyball players, compared those who were chosen for the Pan-American team with those who were not. The selected players were heavier and taller, had longer arms and a greater aerobic capacity, and could jump higher and hop farther. Were top volleyball players and nonplayers to be compared, the discrepancies would almost certainly turn out to be even more pronounced. If you're tall, agile and have good endurance, volleyball may be a sport to consider.

Wrestling. When researchers studied a group of world-class wrestlers, all of them qualifiers for the 1979 U.S. Junior World Wrestling Team, they found that they differed significantly from less able wrestlers. Physically, they were taller and heavier and had lower heart rates during exercise. Psychologically, the top wrestlers showed less depression, fatigue, anger and confusion (but, perhaps because of competitive pressures, were more tense and anxious).

The investigators—John M. Silva III, Barry B. Schultz, Robert M. Haslam and Donald Murray—caution against concluding that champion wrestlers might one day be selected solely on the basis of tests like theirs. They do, however, write that "the present study did . . . reinforce the importance of aerobic fitness and low levels of precompetitive anger in maximizing wrestling performance." If you want to wrestle well, it seems, the secret is, first, to get into good shape and, second, to stay as sweet-tempered as possible. Although wrestling appears to be a combative activity, victory most often goes to the competitor who sees it not as warfare at all but simply as the game that it is.

Suppose you are a short, heavily muscled person who wants to compete in marathons. Or a tall, thin person who despite repeated urgings to play basketball is irresistibly drawn toward wrestling. Should you, knowing that your somatotype and physiological capacities are not ideal for the sport you enjoy most, abandon it and take up some other for which scientific research shows you to be better suited?

It can be argued that, yes, you should follow the sport for which science demonstrates you to be most appropriately fitted. It is, after all, in that sport that you have the greatest chance of excelling. But what if it is not excelling that primarily interests you but merely the pleasure of play? Few of us, after all, are charged with upholding our nation's Olympic honor; we are perfectly free to pursue whatever pastime we wish, with no thought that our patriotism, or even our common sense, might on that account be impugned.

That might seem to be justification enough for doing as we wish in our athletic pursuits. But there is still another reason, one that has relevance even at the highest levels of sport. An unfavorable background is no guarantee of failure, any more than a physique that looks as if it were handcrafted by the gods guarantees success. For example, Darrell Evans, one of the National League's most perennially reliable hitters, can barely see across a room without contact lenses. And Olympic figure skating champion Scott Hamilton had a childhood illness that arrested his growth (he stands only 5 feet 3 ½ inches).

Furthermore, sports that would seem, on the face of it, to require certain skills may not in fact require those skills at all. Two cases in point:

- Logic would suggest that depth perception should be crucial in basketball. So it seemed to Larry D. Isaacs, a researcher at Wright State University in Dayton, Ohio. Isaacs therefore tested a dozen basketball players for their ability to estimate depth. He then compared the results with the players' shooting performance, both free throws and field goals, during a twenty-three-game competitive season. His analysis, Isaacs reported in the journal *Perceptual and Motor Skills*, showed a relationship between depth perception and success at free throws, but none at all with respect to field goals.
- Spatial ability would seem to be important in squash, a sport that requires repeated rapid calculations of angles and trajectories. Yet when a researcher, Janet Graydon, compared international squash players with both nonplayers and players of low ability, she found no significant differences in spatial perception. "It may be," she concluded, "that any initial disadvantage that players low in spatial ability may suffer is soon overcome by other factors. It could also be argued that performance at squash racquets is so exceedingly complex that the contribution of a single factor such as spatial ability is likely to be minimal."

Not long ago at the University of California in San Francisco, several members of the Department of Medicine gathered for their weekly staff conference. The conversation turned to the composition of human muscle and its role in marathon running. It was observed that so-called slow-twitch fibers confer a distinct advantage in distance running. True enough, commented Dr. Richard Locksley, the chief medical resident and himself a 2:30 marathoner. Then he went on: "Training, however, is much more important than genetics in predicting success."

Dr. Locksley happened to be talking about marathon running, but he might just as well have been referring to any number of other sports. Jon Spaventa, an authority on sports psychology and a faculty member at the University of California at Santa Barbara, put it succinctly when he told the author, "Athletes are born and *then* made."

CHAPTER 10

Age and the Athlete

Getting older has made me a better quarterback.

—JIM HART, *St. Louis Cardinals*

ON AN AUTUMN DAY IN 1983, Carl Michael Yastrzemski, having labored for the Boston Red Sox for twenty-three years, laid down his bat for the last time and, to the familiar sounds of fans' cheers, finally retired as a baseball player. By any reckoning he had been an uncommonly gifted athlete—an eighteen-time all-star, a member of two World Series teams, an almost certain choice for the Hall of Fame, and a man whose quickness, agility and judgment had waned scarcely at all during his long years as Fenway Park's hero in residence. Unlike many athletes, both in and out of baseball, he had managed to pull every gram of his weight right up to the end, despite the fact that, at age forty-four, he was old enough to be the father of a good many of his teammates, not to mention his opponents.

There was a time, not too many years ago, when a career like Yastrzemski's would have been considered out of the ordinary, and for that matter out of the question. People in their forties simply didn't behave that way, for a twenty-year-old's mousetrap reflexes were not to be coaxed from ancient bone and muscle. One could, it was true, cite examples of aging athletes who had contrived to prolong their playing years beyond the normally allotted span:

Carl Yastrzemski

Clarence DeMar, still competing in foot races at age sixty-nine; Rumania's Lia Manoliu, an Olympic gold medal winner in the discus throw at age thirty-six and an Olympic competitor again four years later; the late Satchel Paige, still pitching at sixty; Bob Cousy, playing for the Boston Celtics until he was just short of forty-two years old; and Sam Snead, at seventy the only person to win a golf tournament in each of six decades. And there were others, to be sure. But they were considered remarkable not primarily as athletes but as curiosities who had somehow managed to wriggle free of the customarily imposed constraints. They were looked on as aberrations whose bodies were governed by principles other than those that chain most of us to more ordinary accomplishments.

Today our sense of astonishment at a Carl Yastrzemski is less acute than it might have been a decade or so ago. Though we still marvel, we have begun to accustom ourselves to the sight of athletes who continue at or near their peaks long after any reasonable person might expect them to do so: Jan Stenerud of the Minnesota Vikings, who at age forty began his seventeenth season as one of professional football's most reliable kickers; Al Oerter, in his mid-forties still a top discus thrower; Tom Seaver, a formidable pitcher though close to forty; Billie Jean King, who after some three decades on the courts still finds herself ranked among the top women in tennis; New Zealand's Jack Foster, who in his fifties ran a 2:20

marathon (good enough to satisfy, and more, all but the very fastest runners half his age); not to mention a sizable list of other athletes who are not just hanging on but going strong at forty and older, among them such baseball players as Joe Morgan, Jim Kaat, Pete Rose and Phil Niekro.

If aging athletes frequently jolt our sense of expected behavior, so, these days, do young ones. One of our country's most talented female gymnasts, Julianne McNamara, was national champion at age fourteen. Carling Bassett, the Canadian tennis pro, was upsetting top players at fifteen. Ron Francis of the Hartford Whalers was playing professional hockey as a teenager. And if as a swimmer you haven't made your mark by the time the orthodontist's first bill arrives, you would do well to look for some other line of work.

At both ends of the human age span, athletes today are extending our understanding of the extraordinary feats that can be attained through aptitude and training. Until only recently, leading performers in virtually all sports typically fell into a narrow ten years or so—roughly ages eighteen to twenty-eight. This range might on occasion be stretched by a Maureen Connolly, who won the national tennis championship at age sixteen, or by a Ken Rosewall, who held the men's title as a creaky antique of thirty-five. Such men and women were, it appeared, talented aberrations, and less gifted athletes were therefore able to take little cheer from their accomplishments.

Recent scientific research has rendered this impression no longer quite so accurate as it once seemed. Although we cannot, it is true, alter the year of our birth, any more than we can metamorphose a weightlifter's physique into that of a basketball player, we can discover ways to get the most out of the gifts and capacities that chance has seen fit to bestow upon us. Anyone watching a major marathon, such as Boston's or New York City's, will observe vast numbers of runners in their fifties, sixties and even seventies. Through training and dogged persistence practically all of them manage to stay the course and, often, to record thoroughly enviable times.

An older athlete's concerns are customarily twofold: to sustain youthful abilities as long as possible; and then, as reflexes slow and agility declines, to compensate through skill and tactical cunning. Many athletes can be cited who have done exactly that, but none has managed it more expertly or intelligently than Pancho Gonzales, who at age forty was still outsmarting and outmaneuvering tennis players half his age. In this quintessential young man's sport, in which quickness is paramount, Gonzales bestrode the court like an aging jungle cat, befuddling and confounding opponents with an unpredictably angled array of chips, chops, spins and slices. In order to retain as much speed afoot as possible, he purposely became thinner than he had ever been—gaunt to those who had known him in his prime—and he seemed not so much to *hit* a tennis ball as to will it to its destination, fashioning each stroke with feathery delicacy. Gonzales' extended heyday could not, of course, last forever, but while it did it was incomparable.

Performances like that of Gonzales have been effectively discouraged by deeply ingrained assumptions about which activities are proper and which improper for our aging citizenry. A decade ago the President's Council on Physical Fitness and Sports commissioned a survey of physical fitness practices. It found that, among Americans sixty and over, only 39 percent exercised regularly. Furthermore, of those who did, only 4 percent swam, only 3 percent bicycled, and only 1 percent jogged or engaged in weight training. (Most who exercised cited walking as their chief sport.)

Given the current enthusiasm for fitness, there can be no doubt that more older people are currently exercising than was the case when the survey was conducted. Nonetheless, participation falls far short of what it might be. C. Carson Conrad, former executive director of the President's Council, cites four misconceptions that inhibit older people from exercising more than they do:

1. They believe their need for exercise diminishes and finally disappears as they grow older.

2. They exaggerate the risks of exercise.

3. They overrate the benefits of light, sporadic exercise such as occasional walking.

4. They underrate their abilities and capacities.

A recent study of attitudes toward sports participation for men and women of various ages underscores the societal opposition older people must overcome. The investigators, Andrew C. Ostrow, Dianne C. Jones and David R. Spiker, asked a panel of undergraduates at West Virginia University how appropriate they felt various athletic activities were for people aged twenty, forty, sixty and eighty. While it was viewed as entirely appropriate for a twenty-year-old to participate in a marathon, play basketball, or ride a bicycle, such activities were considered markedly less suitable for an eighty-year-old, and even, for that matter, a sixty-year-old.

Not long ago a friend provided the author with a list entitled "How to Know When You're Getting Older." Although the list is plainly meant playfully, it betrays a cruel truth—that this is what too many of us expect of aging. Among the various indicators of aging were these:

• Everything hurts, and what doesn't hurt doesn't work.
• You feel like the morning after, but you didn't go anywhere the night before.
• All the names in your little black book end in "M.D."
• You join a health club but are too tired to go.
• You sit in a rocking chair but can't get it going.
• Your knees buckle but your belt won't.

Exactly how unfortunate such attitudes are is underscored by a study conducted by Drs. Daniel N. Kulund, David A. Rockwell and Clifford E. Brubaker at the University of Virginia. The three investigators studied fifty-six senior tennis players whose average age was seventy-four. Some had undergone surgical implantation of pacemakers to regulate their heartbeat and some had artificial heart valves. Even so, they continued to play three or four sets every other day or so. The researchers found that these aging athletes suffered from few injuries, had reaction times similar to those of college students (although physical response time was slower), and, in the words of a report on the study, displayed "high achievement motivation." Had they for some reason been prevented from playing tennis, they would have been deprived of a valuable aspect of their lives.

To argue that older men and women are capable not only of participating in athletics but of performing extremely well is hardly to insist, however, that the human body fails to change with age. In nearly every measure of performance that has a bearing on sports, age brings an inescapable decline. Reflecting on his final year in baseball at age forty-one, Babe Ruth wrote, "The harder I tried the worse I did. My old dogs just couldn't take it any longer. It was more and more of an effort to move over the outfield or run down to first base. I had tried hard to condition myself, but it was just torture." And the outfielder Stan Musial has said, "I didn't think of this game of baseball as work until I got to be about forty.

Those last couple of years it was much harder to get in shape and stay in shape. After a doubleheader I'd be stiff for two days."

The physical changes that the typical older person experiences are of several varieties:

- The maximum rate at which the heart is able to beat diminishes. This may, in fact, be the most significant difference between older and younger athletes, since a decline in heart rate is inevitably accompanied by a lessening of one's ability to process oxygen and, thus, to perform work.
- The heart pumps a smaller volume of blood with each beat. Less blood circulating through the body means, among other effects, a reduced oxygen supply for the working muscles.
- Aerobic power, the key factor in endurance, decreases.
- Anaerobic power, the key factor in brief, heavy work such as weightlifting or pole vaulting, similarly declines.
- Muscular strength diminishes. Maximum strength is reached at puberty in women and at about age seventeen in men and remains fairly stable until age forty-five or so. Thereafter, during the next twenty years, it declines by about 15 percent.
- Reaction time becomes increasingly sluggish.
- Protein synthesis does not occur as readily as it previously did. One result is slower conditioning effects.
- Recovery from injury and fatigue is not as rapid as it once was.
- Basal metabolism declines about 25 percent between youth and old age.
- Bones become less resilient. Furthermore, cartilage calcifies, decreasing skeletal elasticity.
- Thermoregulation becomes less precise and efficient.
- The typical man or woman becomes fatter.

This unwelcome catalogue of age's ravages and revenges might seem a compelling reason to retire to a rocking chair, were it not for one important fact that has emerged from recent research: through exercise most such changes can be postponed, in some instances for entire decades. "You reach your peak at about twenty-two years of age and go downhill after that," says the fitness expert Michael Quinn. "You can't stop this, but you can greatly slow it down."

After investigating the question for the *New York Times* the medical columnist Jane E. Brody wrote, "Whether you're twenty-eight, forty-eight or eighty-eight, accumulating evidence indicates that you can delay or reverse many of the deteriorating effects of age through exercise." This means that in all but extreme cases sports participation can not only continue but can be maintained at a higher intensity than was once thought possible. Not long ago in the journal *Primary Care* Dr. John Naughton, dean of the School of Medicine at the State University of New York at Buffalo, commented on a study by D. B. Dill in which people's health was examined over a twenty-five-year span. Wrote Naughton: "While the level of physical fitness decreased for the total group . . . the magnitude of decrease was related to each individual's life status. For the ex-athletes who remained physically active, healthy, and who did not gain body weight, the decrease over time was modest. For those who became sedentary and who gained weight, the rate of decrease in fitness was rather precipitous."

Where rapidity of aging is concerned, the differences between athletes and nonathletes are illustrated by numerous recent scientific investigations. Among them:

- A study at the University of Florida's College of Medicine showed that cardiovascular changes in track club members thirty-five to fifty-five years old were less pronounced than had previously been thought to be the case. In the words of an account published in the *Journal of Sports Medicine*, "Habitually taken physical activity delays cardiovascular aging."
- In the *Journal of the American Medical Association* Dr. Walter Bortz of the Palo Alto Medical Clinic drew a parallel between changes customarily associated with aging and those resulting from inactivity. Undesirable alterations in cardiac efficiency, blood chemistry, muscle mass, bone calcium, metabolism and other traditional measures of aging can all be delayed through exercise, he concluded.
- When Drs. Michael L. Pollock, Henry S. Miller, Jr., and Jack Wilmore investigated twenty-five champion runners from forty to seventy-five years old, they found that although performance, as anticipated, declines with age, it does so gradually and does not fall off sharply until athletes are about sixty years old.

One of the most persuasive fragments of evidence for the value of exercise, however, remains a study made public some years ago by Fred W. Kasch and Janet P. Wallace of San Diego State University. The two researchers followed sixteen men—eight university professors, a physician, a dentist, an engineer, two optometrists, an executive and two salesmen—for an entire decade in order to see what would happen to their physical condition during that time. At the start of the project the subjects ranged in age from thirty-two to fifty-six, and during the duration of the study all sixteen exercised regularly, running an average of fifteen miles each week.

From earlier investigations Kasch and Wallace knew what physiological changes normally occur as a person ages, and they were aware, too, that exercise would probably ameliorate at least some of these. On the other hand, they could hardly have anticipated the magnitude of their findings. For when they compared the sixteen men as they had been at the start of the study with what happened to them during the course of their ten years of exercise, they discovered two surprising things: First, the decline in such measures as oxygen-processing capacity and maximum heart rate had been markedly less than customarily occurs. Second, in some respects—among them breathing capacity—the men had actually improved, despite the fact that they were ten years older. Exercise, it seemed, had served to delay the aging process. Eventually, of course, we all must grow older, but it now appeared that, to some extent at any rate, we could choose our pace.

The implications for athletes of all kinds, from professional football and baseball players to recreational tennis players and golfers, are vast. For if, as seems clearly established by the Kasch-Wallace study, the aging process can to some degree be postponed, an athlete is able to view his playing career in a quite different way from what had previously been possible. Whether he plays for pay or solely for pleasure, he can look forward to a longer span of effective years than had at one time seemed possible. In return for the effort of athletics, it appears, a man or a woman receives a heightened capacity to invest still more effort.

As word of the Kasch-Wallace study spread, the traditional ages at which athletes had long been thought to peak—twenty-four years old in basketball, twenty-seven in hockey, twenty-eight in football and baseball, and so forth—no longer seemed quite so unshakably valid.

Furthermore, in the past several years it has become almost commonplace for elderly men and women to undertake activities that would once have been thought sufficient cause for an emergency psychiatric evaluation. Ruth Rothfarb, a retired shopkeeper, and Paul Spangler, a surgeon, were running in marathons at age eighty-two. Arthur Gutner, a gift-wrapping manufacturer, ran sixty kilometers (more than thirty-seven miles) to celebrate his sixtieth birthday. And a thousand or so downhill skiers from thirty states and several foreign countries hold membership in the 70-Plus Club (nearly sixty members are over eighty, and at last report one was ninety-seven).

One effect of the changing expectations of older athletes is the increasing incidence of comebacks, certainly one of the most difficult feats in sport. Al Oerter, who is in his late forties and won four gold medals in the Olympic games held from 1956 to 1968, qualified for the 1984 Olympic trials. It is beyond calculation how many former high school and college athletes, reminiscing as they have watched the World Series or the Olympics on television, have been inspired to come out of retirement for one final, brave effort.

Some such comebacks are strikingly successful, even after long layoffs. Dr. Ken Carman, to cite only one example, ran the mile in high school and competed in cross-country during college but stopped running when he entered medical school and did not run for some thirty years. He was inspired to take the sport up again when, entering a race on a whim, he was passed not just by an overweight woman but also by a Marine laden with full battle gear. Today he is the national 5,000-meter champion in the fifty-to-fifty-four age group and in one recent year won twenty-seven of the thirty-one races he entered.

In 1981 two members of the Memorial University of Newfoundland's Psychology Department, M. J. Stones and A. Kozma, aware that running performance characteristically declines with age, sought to devise a hypothesis that would account both for the phenomenon itself and for the fact that the steepness of the decline is not the same in all events. Studying world records for men forty to sixty-nine years old, the two scholars found that long-distance performance tends to fall off more sharply than sprinting ability. This seemed to suggest that the aerobic mechanism might for some reason age more rapidly than the anaerobic. If, therefore, an athlete were to specialize in events of short duration, he would presumably be able to retain more of his youthful speed.

As Stones and Kozma continued to explore the subject, however, they found themselves drawn to another hypothesis, one that, if ultimately proven valid, would shed considerable light on what older athletes are capable of doing. Citing a coaches' adage that "sprinters are born but distance runners are made," they pointed out that various events have dissimilar training requirements and, specifically, that the longer distances require heavier workouts than the sprints. Might it be possible, therefore, that older athletes simply fail to train hard enough?

As it happens, exactly such a possibility has been explored in considerable detail by Peter S. Riegel, a research engineer. Using complex mathematical analyses, Riegel found that the performances of the best athletes forty years old and over did not seem to be proportionately as distinguished as those of the most accomplished younger men and women. He suggests a reason: "With increasing responsibilities, few older men have the time to devote

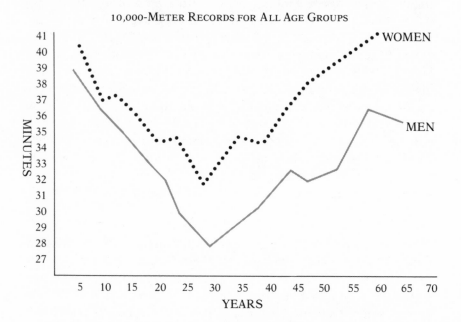

10,000-METER RECORDS FOR ALL AGE GROUPS

to covering the hundreds of kilometers typically run each week in training by elite distance competitors. It is quite unusual to find a world-class endurance athlete who also works hard at a nine-to-five job, as so many older runners do. It does not seem likely that an older man could possibly be trying as hard as a world-class competitor. They gain little glory, only the personal satisfaction that comes from a good performance. If substantial world recognition and acclaim were afforded to older athletes, their performance would surely become even more amazing."

This, then, may be the older athlete's ultimate secret—that by training harder he can gain an edge over competitors who are unprepared to make a similar investment. As solutions go, it is, as noted, not an easy one. It requires considerable effort, and no athlete need apologize for an unwillingness to make such an effort. It is, after all, one thing to train in hopes of someday hearing the applause of a crowded Olympic stadium, quite another to work out in the knowledge that at best only a few people will ever know of or appreciate your accomplishments.

Furthermore, at the top levels of sport, no matter what an athlete's age, even marginal improvements exact a high price. Peter Riegel calculates, for example, that if a world-class male runner hopes to achieve a 1 percent increase in speed, he must achieve a 13 percent increase in endurance—that is, he must improve enough to go 13 percent farther while maintaining his previous maximum pace. Plainly, this requires an effort of no inconsequential magnitude. For those who are willing to make such an effort, however, the rewards are abundant.

There can be no doubt that startlingly young men and women—in an increasing number of cases mere children—are capable, both physically and mentally, of becoming authentic athletes. An important question is: Should they?

We know that children, even quite young ones, are capable of deriving important physical and psychological benefits from sports participation. These benefits most reliably occur, however, when emphasis is on the pure fun of purposeful movement rather than narrowly focused on winning. Some coaches and parents—but, alas, by no means all of them—are wise enough to know this. Vic Braden, one of the nation's most respected tennis coaches, is ready to offer instruction to a child three or four years old, yet he insists that winning matches be no part of his student's goals. "If the coach is trying to develop champions," says Braden, "then he has to get out of the field because we don't need that approach. In tennis, his goals should be to introduce kids to a terrific hand-eye coordination game and let them have fun, get exercise, play in the sun. . . . The problem comes when the parents start shouting, 'You can do it, Johnny! . . . Oh, God, you missed it again.' "

In *Sports in America* James Michener relates the story of a father who was helping his son, a Little League participant, with batting practice. As Michener tells it, "The boy dug in, took a toehold, and laced one of his father's pitches against the outfield wall. On his next pitch he fired right at his son's head, knocking him flat. 'What was I supposed to do?' he asked a bystander. 'The little bastard hit my curve ball, didn't he?' "

Such parental attitudes are so common as to require no detailed documentation. Practically any Little League baseball diamond will yield examples, differing in their particulars, to be sure, but unhappily identical in effect. For either of two outcomes, equally undesirable, is likely when parents take an inordinate interest in their children's athletic performance. Through repeated failure a child may, on the one hand, become subtly persuaded that he is destined to do poorly not just in athletics but in much else as well. Or if he should by chance prove to have an early aptitude for sports, he may one day find that, though he hardly realized it at the time, he enjoyed his most glorious moments before he even left junior high school.

If this were not argument enough, there remain, in addition, other psychological reasons for not pressing ahead too hastily. Bill Mongovan, the high school track coach of Ceci Hopp, who became national junior 3,000-meter champion under his guidance, was certain his pupil was capable of running faster than she had thus far done. Nonetheless, he prudently declined to force the pace, reasoning that if her early workouts were not unreasonably arduous she would be more inclined to run hard later. Mongovan's theory turned out to be correct. In her freshman year at Stanford University she won the NCAA 3,000 meters, running significantly faster than she had a year earlier.

Let us suppose that we inhabited an entirely rational world in which no parent and no coach desired anything but what was best for young people, a world in which winning was seen to be of little consequence. (There is no reason to suppose that such a world will soon materialize, but imagine, your disbelief suitably suspended, that it had miraculously come about.) Freed of the need to dominate opponents, and seeking only those values that sport at its purest can bestow, how might children most profitably be exposed to athletic participation?

Above all, sports would not be introduced too early. Games are one thing—carefree, frolicsome activities, such as dodgeball and tag, that require no special training or conditioning. But true athletic contests, in which success depends upon skills and capacities that are acquired only through dedicated training, are best left for later. In a recent issue of a leading medical journal Dr. C. N. Stover, director of the Department of Orthopedics at the

Hunterdon Medical Center in Flemington, New Jersey, points out that becoming an adult takes longer than many people realize. "Since epiphyseal closure [full ossification of the bones] and other signs of maturation continue well into the twenties," he writes, "nearly all high school and college athletes are physically, physiologically, and, therefore, even psychologically immature."

Given the current enthusiasm for sports and the striking achievements of youthful participants, it is no doubt unreasonably utopian to expect large numbers of young people to refrain voluntarily from athletics until maturation is complete. The attraction of sports is too powerful and their rewards are too alluring for such restraint. Perhaps the most we should allow ourselves to hope for is a measure of moderation. For the most reliably informed opinion suggests that too early an exposure to hard workouts can have long-term adverse effects.

A report in a recent issue of the *Nike Research Newsletter*, for example, points out that "many sportsmedicine experts advise against regular long-distance running for preadolescents, saying that children's musculoskeletal systems are not developed enough to withstand the repeated poundings which occur during running." Similarly, Joe Paterno, Penn State's football coach and a fervent partisan of the game, questions the wisdom of participation in midget football. In his book *Winning Is Everything and Other American Myths*, Thomas Tutko, a frequently consulted sports psychologist, quotes Paterno as saying: "Kids of junior high school age are just not ready, physically or emotionally, for an organized football program. . . . Very often they become victims of injuries. It doesn't matter how much protection they have in the way of equipment. Their bones are soft and they are still growing. They don't know how to protect themselves and they can get hurt so easily in a scrimmage or a game. Frequently they sustain injuries that bother them for the rest of their lives."

Dangers lie in wait in other sports, too. Swimmers frequently suffer from shoulder tendinitis, the result of repetitive arm motions, as well as from breaststroker's knee, produced by the torque that repeatedly twists that joint. Baseball players are felled by Little League elbow, a combination of several disorders brought on by throwing a baseball too often. Gymnasts damage their epiphyses, the parts of the bones where growth occurs. Furthermore, pain—a warning sign no athlete prudently ignores, regardless of his or her age—is too frequently interpreted as a sign of weakness.

Says Tutko: "Some parents will even risk long-range physical damage by, for instance, allowing a cortisone shot in their twelve-year-old's ailing knee so that he can play in Saturday's 'important' game. One Houston pediatrician reported that parents have called him to ask if their son could play baseball with a broken nose." Is it any wonder that 31 percent of all sports injuries occur in children under fifteen years of age, the time of life when, because of maximum cartilage growth, we are most susceptible to injury?

It is too easy, however, to stack the deck unfairly by piling on examples of youthful injury and parental foolishness. For the fact is that not all young athletes hurt themselves, any more than that all older athletes do. Many play season after season in perfect comfort. Even so, there remain persuasive reasons for restraint in entering athletics too early or too strenuously.

In youth, for example, physical changes occur so quickly that children are likely to find themselves frustratingly awkward and, in many cases, puzzled and embarrassed by their sudden and unaccountable clumsiness. Robert K. Jensen, a researcher at Laurentian University in Ontario, recently studied twelve boys for a full year. He found that although their mean increase in height was only 4.7 percent and in weight only 15.8 percent, their rotational inertia—a measure of the force generated by movement—increased by as much as 92 percent. "It is necessary," wrote Colonel James L. Anderson of West Point in commenting on Jensen's investigation, "to understand the mechanical adjustments that children must make continually in order to keep performance levels on an upward slope. . . . Coaches who do not understand the relationships between growth patterns, strength development, and moments of inertia may think that the difficulties and frustrations experienced by young athletes are the result of poor attitude and practice rather than being a natural result of growing."

Even if young people were not subject to injury and awkwardness, there would remain yet another reason for restraint in pushing them into sport too early and in urging improvement on them before they are fully prepared for it. This is that such proddings may simply not be worth the effort. It has frequently been theorized that if children are introduced to athletics early in life, desirable physiological adaptations may take place that would not occur if training were delayed. Recent research suggests that this is perhaps not the case. At West Germany's Institute for Sports Medicine and Circulation Research not long ago, a researcher named R. Rost compared athletes who had started training as children with other athletes who waited until later on. Would the hearts of the two sets of subjects, he wondered, be different? Might not those who had trained in youth have developed more efficient cardiovascular systems? When Rost analyzed his data, he found no discernible differences. It appears that if you want to do well in athletics, there is no need to be in a hurry.

Dr. John Hiebert, a cardiologist at Stormont-Vail Medical Center in Topeka, Kansas, agrees with Rost's findings. "Prepubescent exercise," he told the author, "has little effect on ultimate development, so you might as well not push kids." The ideal time to start a training program, Hiebert said, is at age thirteen or fourteen. "This is when change can take place," he said. "A growth hormone is secreted with exercise, so people who start exercising at the onset of puberty may become larger and stronger than they otherwise would. Before that, nothing much of permanent value happens."

The validity of Rost's and Hiebert's views was borne out in 1981 when Dr. H. S. Sodhi of India's National Institute of Sports decided to investigate the ages at which some of his nation's top athletes, all of whom were participants in the Commonwealth and Asian Games, had started training. To be sure, some had begun when they were extremely young. Hockey players had started at a mean age of about twelve, while lightweight wrestlers had begun at ten. On the other hand, many athletes had not started until they were sixteen to eighteen years old, and some marathon runners and cyclists had delayed training until they were twenty or older. There is, it appears, no scientific justification for rushing into athletics.

CHAPTER 11

The Nutritional Advantage

There's an almost primitive belief that
there's something, somewhere, that you can eat
in order to perform better—that there's
just got to be some secret.

—PETER JOKL, M.D.

EVEN BEFORE sport had emerged as one of humankind's pervasive activities, athletes had begun to adopt special diets for
special purposes. A Spartan athlete of the seventh century B.C.,
Charmis by name, advocated dried figs as the ideal food. Often
combined with cheese, figs remained a popular dish until a two-
time Olympic winner, Dromeus of Stymphalus, came forward in
support of the view that what athletes needed, contrary to tradition, was meat in order to enhance strength and endurance.

The legendary strongman Milo, winner of no fewer than six
Olympic medals, was an irrepressibly faithful member of the Dromeus school, on one occasion consuming an entire ox and on another dining with relish on a four-year-old bullock. His daily diet,
if the historical record can be believed, was twenty pounds of meat,
a like amount of bread, and, lest all this prove burdensome to his
digestive apparatus, ten or so quarts of wine to ease it all down.
As M. I. Finley and H. W. Pleket explain in *The Olympic Games*,
Greek athletes relied on "common sense and empiricism and also
on faddism and mysticism."

So, in our day, do we. For more than half a century, Wheaties,
the "Breakfast of Champions," has been a training staple for hun-

dreds of thousands of Little Leaguers. By the groaning carload we ingest vitamin pills and mineral supplements, algae and bee pollen. We religiously eat meat or scrupulously avoid it altogether. We count our calories or are persuaded that calories don't count. On the day of competition some of us sit down to a hearty meal; others, ascetic as monks, prepare body and mind by fasting.

Even among leading amateur and professional athletes, strikingly little agreement exists on proper diet. Art Monk, wide receiver for the Washington Redskins, never eats breakfast and rarely sits down to lunch. (He makes up for his deprivations at night, however, often enjoying not just an enormous dinner but a bedtime bowl of ice cream as well.) Hubert Birkenmeier, goalkeeper for the New York Cosmos, is a believer in oatmeal and has his favorite variety specially imported from Germany. His teammate, Vladislav Bogicevic, adheres to no special diet but does limit himself to three bottles of beer per day. Champion archer Rick McKinney breakfasts on chocolate chip cookies and refers to "the basic four food groups"—a Big Mac, fries, a shake and a lemon tart. Jay Howells, of the New York Yankees' pitching staff, thinks the whole subject of diet has been blown out of proportion. "As long as you get the basics, you'll be all right," he insists. (Nonetheless, for safety's sake he takes a daily multiple-vitamin pill and several vitamin C tablets.)

What are we to make of such disparate views? If even those who earn their livings at sport are unable to agree on what they ought to eat, what hope is there for the rest of us? How can we arrive at a diet suited to our needs as lesser athletes?

Part of the problem is that top athletes not infrequently set dreadful examples. Hoping to discover a way to avoid, or at least to ease, the relentless rigors of high-level training, they often attach their hopes to fads. Says John Sumner of the Royal Melbourne Institute of Technology's Department of Food Science: "That athletes should seek to improve performance by methods outside training is understandable, considering their training grind of boring, time-consuming sessions for which the law of diminishing returns seems to have been specifically coined."

Not long ago the *Journal of Sports Medicine and Physical Fitness*, the official publication of the prestigious Fédération International de Médecine Sportive, printed a study based on interviews with varsity swimmers and basketball and ice hockey players at a Big Ten university. "The majority of the athletes," said the report, "skipped breakfast most of the time. Many never ate this meal. About one-quarter missed lunch fairly frequently." Analysis showed that the diets of many of the athletes provided too little vitamin A, vitamin C and calcium because the meals they ate were so deficient in green and yellow vegetables, fruits (especially citrus), eggs and milk. The diets of no fewer than 64 percent of the athletes were judged either "poor" or "fair."

This is particularly curious in the mid-1980's because so much is known about what constitutes an optimum diet for athletes of every kind. Here and there, some of this knowledge has, it is true, begun to penetrate the sports community. The New York Giants have for some time been benefiting from the services of a registered dietician, Merle Best, who among other training-table alterations has sought to limit the ingestion of fats and increase the use of complex carbohydrates—bread, cereal, pasta, beans and the like. Similarly, the Chicago White Sox recently sought the advice of Ann Grandjean, a University of Nebraska nutritionist. Other professional teams, including the Houston Oilers, the San Francisco 49ers and the Cleveland Browns, have also sought to alter players' diets in hopes of improving performance.

Despite such steps, much of athletic nutrition remains so encrusted with myth and superstition that we might as well still be living in the Dark Ages. At a recent ten-kilometer road race on Florida's West Coast, a group of bee-pollen enthusiasts displayed a banner urging fellow runners to adopt their dietary habit, even though no shred of scientific evidence thus far supports it. As long ago as 1980 the American Dietetic Association said it "does not recognize any unique ergogenic values of products such as wheat germ, wheat germ oil, vitamin E, ascorbic acid, lecithin, honey gelatin, phosphates, sunflower seeds, bee pollen, kelp or brewer's yeast." And the use of vitamin and mineral supplements is widespread despite persuasive evidence that most of us, vegetarians and nonvegetarians alike, derive all the nourishment we need or can make use of from an ordinary well-balanced diet.* About the best that can be said for such supplements is that the industry of which they are so lusty a part serves as a stimulant for the economy.

Other dietary misconceptions abound. Some athletes insist that

* Contrary to some reports, vegetarians are at no particular risk of undernutrition, particularly if they take pains to include protein in their diets. A growing body of evidence suggests, in fact, that vegetarians tend to be healthier than nonvegetarians, suffering less from high blood pressure, obesity, heart disease and cancer.

beer is the ideal fluid replacement. (It is not; water is.) They consume "pangamic acid," or vitamin B_{15}. (B_{15} is not a vitamin at all, since no need for its principal substances, dichloracetate and dimethylglycine hydrochloride, has been demonstrated.) They swallow salt tablets, exacerbating the very dehydration they seek to remedy, and ingest sugar, producing an insulin response that reduces available energy. When Dr. David L. Costill, director of the Human Performance Laboratory at Ball State University, surveyed 360 college athletes, he reported that their diets were not only largely ineffective but in many cases accomplished exactly the opposite of what they were trying to achieve.

Costill is not alone in his assessment of athletes' diets. In the *American Journal of Sports Medicine* not long ago, Dr. Nathan J. Smith of the University of Washington Medical School wrote, "No population group is more vulnerable to food faddism, cultism, misinformation, and the promotions of the nutrition charlatan than seriously committed athletes. They are bombarded with threatening information by a host of nutrition quacks, faddists, cultists, charlatans and hucksters of all kinds. . . . In recent years, athletes have been involved in abusive intakes of vitamin A, vitamin C, protein mixtures, electrolyte drinks and powders, supplements of multiple nutrient compounds, etc., etc., all of which are potentially dangerous, needlessly expensive, and completely useless in upgrading performance."

The essentials of eating sensibly, for both athletes and nonathletes, are easily summarized:

1. If body weight is neither too low nor too high, maintenance requires fifteen kilocalories (usually referred to simply as "calories") per pound, plus whatever additional calories exercise consumes. Thus a 150-pound jogger who runs three miles per day would need 2,250 calories (150 × 15) as well as an additional 300 calories to compensate for his daily workout, or a total of 2,550 calories per day. If a person wants to lose weight, he must either eat less or exercise more (a combination, however, has been demonstrated to be most effective). The chart on the following page, listing the calories expended in various sports, will enable the reader to make calculations to suit his or her own needs.

2. A balanced diet, according to recent nutritional research, consists of the following percentages of calories from protein, carbohydrate and fat sources:

Protein	10–20%
Carbohydrate	55–60%
Fat	25–30%

The listed percentage of fat reflects a recommended reduction based on studies suggesting a relationship between fat consumption (in particular saturated fats, such as those found in meats and dairy products) and such medical problems as atherosclerosis and coronary heart disease.

CALORIES EXPENDED FOR 30 MINUTES
OF ENTHUSIASTIC PHYSICAL ACTIVITY*

Baseball (except pitcher)	140
Basketball	210
Bicycling—5.5 mph	150
13 mph	320
Bowling (non-stop)	200
Dancing—moderate	125
vigorous	170
Golf	120
Football/Soccer	250
Martial Arts	150
Racquetball/Squash	270
Rowing—2.5 mph	150
3.5 mph	330
12 mph	750
Running—5.5 mph	325
7 mph	425
Skating—ice skating (10 mph)	200
roller skating (9 mph)	235
Skiing—cross-country	350
downhill	290
water	220
Swimming—backstroke—20 yd./min	115
crawl—20 yd./min	145
Tennis—singles	225
doubles	180
Volleyball/Badminton	155
Walking—downstairs	200
upstairs	525
2 mph	105
4 mph	185

* Based on calorie expenditures of a 150-lb. person

One exception to the recommended percentages occurs in the case of athletes engaged in contact sports, such as football and hockey, whose bodies frequently suffer injury through bumping, battering and bruising and who must therefore continually synthesize new tissue. This process requires extra protein. Otherwise exercise, no matter how intense or prolonged, appears not to increase the need for protein.

An athlete's life would be simple if he or she could just follow a tidy list of foods recommended daily in order to be properly nourished no matter what the competitive occasion. Unfortunately, he cannot quite do this, for nutritional requirements vary from sport to sport. We shall now turn, therefore, to some supplementary principles that govern the food and drink that athletes of various kinds should consume in order to achieve peak efficiency.

Be at the right weight for your sport. Gary Fencik of the Chicago Bears has an enviable problem. A few years ago, having reported to training camp at 190 pounds, he became aware that he was being pushed around by opposing players more than he liked. Deliberately, therefore, he set out to gain weight and was gratified to notice that an additional seven or eight pounds allowed him better to stand his ground in professional football's frequent collisions. "When I was lighter," he observes, "I was always getting beaten up."

Most athletes, however, have a quite different problem. Because they are in excellent health and enjoy good appetites, they tend to become heavier than they ought to be. Rosie Casals, a tennis player in her late thirties, recently lost some twenty pounds, feeling she would be able to move more quickly on the court if she weighed less. Her theory proved correct. "I don't feel I've lost an edge because of age," she told the author. "I've compensated for it by being lighter."

For every sport there exists an ideal weight range. Football players and weightlifters are typically the heaviest. Gymnasts and distance runners need to be as light as possible. Baseball, lacrosse and soccer players are somewhere in the middle. Particularly gifted athletes who are unusually large or small occasionally perform well—the Atlanta Falcons' Reggie Smith stands 5 feet 4 inches tall and weighs a mere 159 pounds—but such deviations are exceptional. (You can try in vain to think of a top marathon runner who is so much as five pounds overweight.) Thus when Bob Horner, the Atlanta Braves' third baseman, signed a contract for the 1983 season, it provided for a $100,000 bonus if his weight did not exceed 215 pounds. (He had played at 237 the previous season.)

Research shows that dieting alone is an inefficient way to lose

RELATIVE BODY FAT VALUES FOR MALES AND FEMALES
IN VARIOUS SPORTS

SPORT	MALES PERCENT FAT	FEMALES PERCENT FAT
Baseball/Softball	12–14	16–26
Basketball	7–10	16–27
Football	8–18	—
Gymnastics	4–6	9–15
Ice Hockey	13–15	—
Jockeys	12–15	—
Skiing	7–14	18–20
Soccer	9–12	—
Speed Skating	10–12	—
Swimming	5–10	14–26
Track and Field		
Sprinters	6–9	8–20
Middle-Distance Runners	6–12	8–16
Distance Runners	4–8	6–12
Discus	14–18	16–24
Shot Put	14–18	20–30
Jumpers and Hurdlers	6–9	8–16
Tennis	14–16	18–22
Volleyball	8–14	16–26
Weightlifting	8–16	—
Wrestling	4–12	—

* The values represent the range of means reported in various published and unpublished studies. Table reprinted with permission from Ross Laboratories.

weight. When we reduce our intake of nutrients, our bodies consume glycogen in their search for energy. Since each pound of glycogen is inevitably associated with 2.7 pounds of water, much of our initial weight loss is nothing more than fluid. When the body eventually switches over to consuming fat instead of glycogen, weight loss slows markedly.

At this point, people who are singlemindedly determined to lose weight sometimes redouble their efforts, virtually starving themselves in order to achieve their goal. On one memorable occasion, according to a report in *Sports Illustrated*, the world-class power-lifter John Gamble, seeking to lose weight in preparation for a meet, shed nineteen pounds in a day and a half by means of steam baths, lack of sleep, starvation and—so he reported—worry.

Such measures, according to recent research, should play no part in a sensible athlete's regimen. Not long ago Michael E. Houston, Donald A. Marrin and Howard J. Green of the University of Waterloo in Ontario studied Olympic wrestlers as they systematically lost nearly 7 percent of their body weight over a four-day period.

During this time, the researchers found, the wrestlers' glycogen stores—their prime source of energy—diminished by an average of 54 percent. Even after they had regained half their lost weight, glycogen levels were found to be only marginally higher. The study's chief conclusion is a useful cautionary lesson for any athlete contemplating rapid weight loss: "Muscle glycogen concentrations are markedly reduced during acute weight loss. . . . Therefore many wrestlers may compete with greatly reduced muscle carbohydrate stores." The observation applies equally, of course, to athletes in other sports.

Nor are so-called diet aids a solution. In *The Runner* magazine not long ago, Dr. Gabe Mirkin, a respected sportsmedicine authority, debunked such current weight-loss fads as spirulina, starch blockers and glucomannan.* None, he reported, is effective, either in scientific theory or in actual practice.

Where, then, is an athlete to turn if he needs to lose weight? Logically enough, to more exercise, combined, if need be, with a somewhat reduced intake of food. If, for example, an overweight baseball or football player were to add forty minutes or so of jogging to his off-season workouts he would lose ten pounds in two months without ever feeling hungry. (If, in addition, he were to eat less he would lose weight even more rapidly.)

Exercise confers side benefits as well. Among other effects, it serves as an appetite suppressant, easing feelings of hunger for several hours after a workout. It also prompts the release of beta-endorphin, a natural tranquilizer that reduces tensions of the sort that prompt many people to overeat. Finally, it speeds up the metabolism, causing men and women who exercise to consume calories at a beneficially accelerated rate for several hours after a workout.

In their search for the lowest possible weight, athletes occasionally find themselves subject to such eating disorders as anorexia nervosa and bulimia. (This is an entirely different matter from the kind of deliberate crash diet mentioned above.) Cathy Rigby McCoy, an Olympic gymnast in 1968 and 1972 and more recently a commentator for ABC Sports, became involved with bulimia—overeating followed by self-induced vomiting—while training for the

---

* Spirulina is an algae that is said to reduce hunger. Starch blockers are substances that supposedly prevent the transformation of starch to sugar. Glucomannan, derived from a tuber grown in Japan, is said to absorb many times its weight in water and thus bring a feeling of satiety.

1968 games. "I wanted to be a top gymnast," she said. "Nobody can tell you that you're thin enough."

Consider dividing intake among several meals rather than the usual three. This practice is particularly useful for endurance athletes such as cyclists and marathon runners—those who train heavily and who therefore need more than the customary quantities of food and drink. When K. A. Kirsch and H. von Ameln of the Free University of Berlin recently examined the eating habits of cyclists and distance runners they found that the athletes tended to consume from four to seven distinct meals each day. Only in this way could they obtain their necessary caloric requirement and fully replace the fluids they were expending during workouts.

Drink enough water. As mentioned in Chapter 3, athletes should replace lost fluids as promptly as possible. Water is the primary ingredient of our cells and blood as well as of such products as sweat and urine. In the absence of the proper amount of water, cellular activity—tissue replenishment, the production of energy and the like—slows, blood volume diminishes, and urine is inadequate to rid the body of waste.

Countless scientific studies document the harmful effects of a failure to drink enough water. A recent report in the *South African Medical Journal*, for example, showed that when rugby players lose an average of 2¼ quarts of fluid during a match their rising internal temperature brings a measurable decline in athletic ability. The researchers explained, "At rectal temperatures above 39 degrees C. [102.2 degrees F.] . . . endurance is usually curtailed even in highly trained and heat-acclimatized men. The demand for dissipation of heat decreases the intensity of exercise that can be sustained for long periods because the circulating blood volume is inadequate to supply oxygen to the muscles and simultaneously transport heat to the body surface."

Studies show, incidentally, that plain water is just as effective as commercially marketed fluids.

For sustained events, try carbohydrate loading. This dietary regimen, sometimes called glycogen loading or supercompensation, has been looked upon as an important aid in endurance sports ever since its discovery two decades ago by Scandinavian researchers. Its physiological principles are easily described. The muscles normally contain a fixed amount of glycogen, the intracellular form of glucose. So long as glucose, a sugar, is available in sufficient quantities, high-intensity work is able to continue. When glucose is finally exhausted, however, work must inevitably cease because the muscles' fuel is gone. (This is what happens when, eighteen or twenty miles into a marathon, runners encounter the dreaded "wall.")

The pioneer Scandinavians tried to find a way to increase the customary levels of glycogen and thereby enable work to continue longer than usual. What they finally arrived at was the familiar week-long carbohydrate-loading program: an exhausting workout followed by approximately three days of a low-carbohydrate diet (meat, eggs, cheese and the like) and finally another three days or so of a high-carbohydrate diet consisting of such foods as pasta, vegetables and fruits. Apparently the muscles, physically exhausted and purposely starved of their normal fuel, become more absorptive than usual. When finally exposed to carbohydrates, therefore, they soak up an exceptionally large amount.

There is no doubt that carbohydrate loading is effective. The *Journal of Human Nutrition* reports that an athlete may be able to work at high intensity for 50 percent longer after following a supercompensation diet. Research shows, furthermore, that those who practice carbohydrate loading typically complete a marathon anywhere from six to eleven and a half minutes faster than non-loaders. (In one test, cyclists were able to continue for 37 percent longer after three days on a high-carbohydrate diet.) For these reasons carbohydrate loading has become common in all sustained sports, including cross-country skiing.

Recent research has shown, however, that the process has several disadvantages:

1. Its initial depletion phase is uncomfortable, leaving an athlete tired and hungry. Fortunately, Dr. David Costill's research over the past several years suggests that carbohydrate loading works fairly well if this phase is ignored and an athlete simply starts with the high-carbohydrate diet, particularly if he allows for plenty of rest in the days preceding competition.

2. Athletes who follow carbohydrate loading usually gain three or four pounds because glycogen, as we have seen, is associated with nearly three times its weight in water. Furthermore, since the water lodges primarily in the muscles most directly involved in an athlete's particular sport, he experiences a sensation of pressure and fullness exactly where it is most bothersome.

3. Carbohydrate loading is not noticeably effective in events lasting less than an hour and a half since muscle glycogen is not significantly depleted in this time unless exercise is of extremely high intensity.

4. No one has yet determined whether repeated carbohydrate loading is harmful, nor is it known whether the process can be engaged in on successive occasions with equal effect. Warns *Medical Times*: "Glycogen loading should be limited to preparing for a few important competitions each season. It is not, in any sense, to be thought of as a recommended training diet plan."

Despite these drawbacks it is likely that athletes, searching for advantages wherever they are to be found, will continue to practice carbohydrate loading in preparation for competition. Present research, as well as the experience of thousands of athletes who have used the technique, suggests that it is effective and has few if any undesirable side effects.

After competition, eat carbohydrates. While the uses of precompetition carbohydrate loading have long been known, the value of a related practice—post-exercise adherence to a high-carbohydrate diet—has only recently been established. Explored by Dr. Costill and several associates at Ball State University's Human Performance Laboratory, the procedure consists of consuming more than the usual amount of carbohydrates following a hard workout in order to replenish muscle glycogen quickly.

In the study that demonstrated the effectiveness of this diet, volunteers first took a hard eight-mile run and then subjected themselves to five sprints of a minute's duration each, becoming thoroughly tired in the process. They then went on a diet of carbohydrates, fats and proteins in a 70:20:10 ratio. Although muscle glycogen levels had been greatly reduced by the intense exercise, they were largely restored within twenty-four hours. Concluded the researchers: "It appears that muscle glycogen can be normalized between daily strenuous running activity."

Although Costill and his colleagues experimented only on runners, there is no reason to suppose that their findings would not hold equally true for athletes in other sports.

If you are a woman, have your iron levels monitored from time to time. Among other physiological functions, iron in the hemoglobin molecule helps carry oxygen to the various parts of the body, including the muscles, and is thus of particular importance to athletes. Need for dietary iron is one respect in which men and women have been shown to differ. While men, even those who regularly engage in strenuous exercise, almost always derive whatever iron they need from an ordinary diet, women are likely to require more than they naturally consume.*

Dr. Gabe Mirkin has calculated that some 20 to 25 percent of American women are deficient in iron. Thus women athletes will do well to ask their doctors to check their iron levels whenever they have a physical examination.

A study conducted not long ago by Sharon A. Plowman and Patricia C. McSwegin undertook to find out whether iron supplements could serve as a corrective. After administering such supplements (combined with vitamin C to enhance absorption) to high school and college cross-country runners, 36.4 percent of whom were iron-deficient, they reported a marked increase in iron storage.

Most iron deficiencies can be satisfactorily treated through diet alone. At least two readily available breakfast cereals, Most and Total, provide 100 percent of the U.S. recommended daily allowance. Dr. George Sheehan, a resourceful student of women's athletics, recently made a practical suggestion: Cook in iron pots. The use of iron cookware, he reports, greatly increases the iron in foods. For example, the iron content of spaghetti sauce that has been simmered in an iron pot for three hours has been shown to rise from three to eighty-eight milligrams.

Use vitamin supplements sparingly. Among the most common (and, unfortunately, least helpful) dietary aids are vitamins. Even many athletes who are aware of the dubious reputation of such supplements superstitiously use them "just in case." A well-known tennis player who takes several vitamin tablets every day assured the author, "Whatever the body can't use, it will get rid of." (This is not entirely true. So-called megadoses can prove chemically toxic.)

No evidence exists for the efficacy of vitamin supplements. According to Nancy Clark, a sports nutritionist and author of *The Athlete's Kitchen*, "Supplements offer no benefits for either the average person or the athlete. . . . Money spent on vitamin supplements can be better spent on more fruit and vegetables."

---

* The difference in requirements, about 15 milligrams a day, cannot always be met even by a diet rich in such iron sources as liver, eggs, fish, fowl and dried fruits.

In large doses, furthermore, supplements can produce undesirable effects. Vitamin C can destroy vitamin B_{12}. Vitamin E is suspected to be a cause of headaches, nausea, dizziness, fatigue and blurred vision. Vitamin A can have an adverse effect on the nerves, vitamin D a similar effect on the kidneys.

For most athletes, extra vitamins, whether in doses small or large, should play no part in a training program.

Nor is there any reason to spend the extra money invariably charged for so-called health foods. Not long ago researchers at New York City's Department of Consumer Affairs compared prices at twenty-three health food stores with those charged by conventional outlets. Health foods, they reported, often cost twice as much and, moreover, "are in no way demonstrably superior."

What, then, do all these dietary principles—as well as scores of others to be found in the literature on the subject—add up to? If scrupulously followed, can they create a winning athlete? Sad to say, there is no evidence that they can. What they *may* be able to do is eliminate a possible adverse factor that might otherwise prevent an athlete from performing at his or her best. For anyone serious about athletics, that is reward enough.

CHAPTER 12

Staying Well

Most injuries go away by themselves.
That's why I'm always telling colleagues,
"You'd better hurry up and operate because if you don't
he's going to get better."

—PETER JOKL, M.D.

F EW TOPICS are of greater or more sustained interest to men and women involved in sport, from top professionals to those whose efforts are largely recreational, than their athletic health. For avoiding injury or, should it occur, treating it promptly and effectively is essential both to improvement and to enjoyable participation. In this chapter, therefore, we examine some important principles of athletic medicine, mostly of recent origin, particularly those that promise to let athletes devote more time to their sport and fewer days per year to mending after assorted misadventures.

This chapter undertakes to describe those medical findings that are likely to be of practical value to athletes. Among its chief themes are the two subjects that most commonly concern the serious athlete, whether he plays for money, for fun or for both: the prevention of injury and treatment when injury occurs.

Where health is concerned, sport is a balancing act of formidable intricacy. Although we must be in excellent health to achieve maximum performance, it is precisely when we most assiduously seek to attain this state that we place ourselves at greatest risk. Danger—often of a considerable magnitude—is inescapable in many if not most athletic undertakings. In our search for excellence we are tempted to train more than we profitably are able. As a consequence we tear muscles and tendons, sprain joints, incur stress fractures, and not infrequently become so tired that we find ourselves wondering whether the prize (if indeed there is to be one) is worth the effort.

Nor are our contests themselves ideal settings in which to pursue radiant well-being. On the football, soccer and rugby fields we allow our bodies to be ignominiously battered, bruised and trampled upon. In hockey and lacrosse we place ourselves in uneasy proximity to implements that might more suitably serve as weapons of combat. If we are endurance athletes—marathon runners, cross-country skiers or mountaineers—we assault not only our muscles, bones and mind but the very chemistry of our cells.

This is not to suggest that it is improper that athletes should behave as they do. On the contrary, a measure of risk is inherent in sport, and ought to be. Writing in the *New York Times* not long ago, a former member of the Kansas City Chiefs, Michael Oriard, convincingly articulated the allure of danger in football. "It's that meeting of violence and artistry," he wrote, "the tension between the two, that so appeals. It's that instant when ball, receiver and defender converge, when artistry is threatened by violence and the outcome is in doubt, that epitomizes the game's attraction. . . . Injuries are not aberrations in football, or even a regrettable by-product. They are essential to the game."

James Michener, an even-handed student of the subject and certainly no proponent of pointless mayhem, acknowledges the value of vigorous competition. "We live in a competitive world whose rules are harsher than we might prefer," he writes in *Sports in America*. "But competition is inescapable, and much superior to a bland existence with no challenge."

It is, paradoxically, the search for superior competitive performances that often makes further competition impossible. Early in 1982 Eamonn Coghlan, the world's fastest indoor miler, began a routine training run. He was looking forward to the Millrose Games a month later. He was, after all, not only a four-time winner of the meet's prestigious Wanamaker Mile but, at the San Diego Sports Arena two years earlier, had set an indoor record of 3 minutes 50.6 seconds. By the end of the day, however, Coghlan's plans lay in ruins. He had developed a stress fracture and could not race for an entire year.

The more intense the competition, the greater the likelihood of

injury. Studies show that some 10 percent of sports participants
under twelve years of age suffer mishaps. That figure rises to 30
percent among high school athletes and to 70 percent among those
in college. Injuries among professional athletes, because they play
so intensely and are rarely afforded time for proper recovery, no
doubt approach 100 percent.*

Time lost through mishaps might matter little if it merely afforded an opportunity for rest. At one time or another, after all,
most men and women who are serious about sport train too hard,
tearing themselves down instead of building themselves up. At such
times they would unquestionably benefit from a few days' respite.
Here, however, we encounter a second athletic balancing act—the
perilously thin line between beneficial rest and unwelcome deconditioning.

A layoff of three or four days invariably benefits an athlete, allowing him to return to action stronger, fresher and more eager to
compete. A longer rest, however, permits the onset of deconditioning. Muscular strength and efficiency decline, skills deteriorate,
and the cardiovascular system loses its ability to function at maximum capacity. The difference between a champion and an also-
ran may be nothing more than the number of days lost to injury.

The running career of Mary Decker is a well-known case in point.
An astonishingly gifted runner at 1,500 and 3,000 meters, she has
repeatedly been beset by lower-leg problems that have required
several surgical operations. When she is able to avoid layoffs and
train consistently, she is all but unconquerable, customarily taking
an early lead and breaking the tape in lofty isolation from all rivals.
When injury curtails her workouts, however, she is as frustratingly
handicapped as anyone in similar circumstances would be.

Or consider the seemingly indestructible Steve Garvey of the
San Diego Padres, who in the spring of 1983, at age thirty-four,

* Chief among athletic pursuits in which injury is all but inevitable is professional
boxing. From a medical point of view boxing is, however, so bizarre a sport that
it is accorded little attention in these pages. Dr. Ernst Jokl of the University of
Kentucky has performed a signal service by analyzing the various skull traumas
that produce the common boxer's condition known as punch-drunkenness. These
injuries consist of deformations, compressions, decompressions, bruises, hemor-
rhages and concussions. Dr. Jokl points out that it is the rare professional boxer
whose central nervous system is undamaged. Recently Dr. George D. Lundberg,
editor of the *Journal of the American Medical Association*, commented, "Some have
argued that boxing has a redeeming social value in that it allows a few disadvan-
taged or minority individuals an opportunity to rise to spectacular wealth and
fame. This does occur, but at what price?"

tied the National League record for consecutive games played (1,117, dating back to 1975). Said Billy Williams, the co-record holder: "Only he and I know what you have to go through—playing hurt, staying lucky."

Such consistency is not, however, attainable by every athlete. Most athletes sooner or later break down in one way or another, developing pulled muscles, stress fractures, chronic fatigue or other signs of excessive training over too long a period. Even those who manage to escape physical injury would be likely, after several years of continuous workouts (or even, in many instances, several weeks), simply to lose interest and ask themselves what purpose can possibly be served by such unremitting effort. Among the warning signs are the following:

• Soreness that fails to disappear between workouts.
• Frequent headaches and colds.
• Insomnia.
• Inability to concentrate.
• Irritability.
• Excessive weight loss.

Until only recently the principal preoccupation of sportsmedicine specialists was not such premonitory complaints but the more obvious varieties of ailment—pulled muscles and the like. In the last few years, however, a parallel and increasingly fruitful concern has begun to manifest itself. This is the prevention of injury. For if injury can be avoided, fewer playing days—and, even more important, fewer *training* days—need be lost than with even the most swift and efficient rehabilitative measures.

If proof were needed, one need only study a single career—that of Mike Bell, a defensive end for the Kansas City Chiefs. In his first four seasons Bell sat out no fewer than twenty-three games, victim of a strained knee, a torn biceps, and pulled groin and hamstring muscles. A weightlifter and devoted believer in conditioning, Bell was puzzled by the frequency of his injuries. "I was beginning to think maybe it was my fate," he said. "I'd look around and see guys who hadn't worked out nearly as hard as I did go the entire season without getting hurt. I couldn't figure it out."

Eventually Bell, who at 245 pounds appears to be a man who would evoke a respectful attitude even among the careening behemoths of professional football, paid a visit to the Olympic Training Center in Colorado Springs. There he was told he ought to supplement his weightlifting regimen with stretching, running and flexing. Almost immediately, his susceptibility to injury lessened.

Injury prevention has three primary components. Among them are adequate conditioning and full acquisition of the skills necessary in a given sport.* Studies have repeatedly shown that most athletic injuries occur early in a playing season. When, for example, Dr. Harlan C. Hunter examined the injury records of 4,393 football players enrolled in St. Louis high schools, he found that half the mishaps they suffered occurred during the season's third to fifth weeks. Thereafter injuries, which afflicted 51 percent of participants, became less frequent. Dr. Hunter attributes the skewing of the injury records to the fact that most athletes do not become fully fit, and therefore fully resistant to injury, until well into the season.

Even in noncontact sports, conditioning is essential if injuries are to be avoided. There are, in fact, no athletic activities in which muscles are not occasionally pulled and tendons torn—and unrecoverable training time thereby forfeited. The sportsmedicine authority Dr. Fred L. Allman, Jr., has outlined the chief components of conditioning as follows:

• Acquiring endurance.
• Developing strength.
• Maximizing flexibility.
• Improving coordination.
• Reducing reaction time.
• Achieving the proper weight.
• Achieving a winning attitude.

These, the reader will notice, are much the same principles that have been outlined in earlier chapters of this book. They are effective in preventing injury not just because a flexible, well-conditioned athlete is more durable than his less fully conditioned fellows but also because his speed and skills allow him to escape hazardous situations. (A batter who is able to move his head quickly out of the way of an errant fastball not only enjoys a clear athletic advantage over a more sluggish teammate but enjoys a less anxiety-ridden life as well.) The primary principle of injury avoidance, therefore, is to get oneself into the best possible condition.

This includes, in addition to the conditioning goals enumerated

* A third component, use of proper protective equipment, is discussed in Chapter 13.

in Dr. Allman's valuable list, sleeping enough. Although in the heat of competition few athletes feel drowsy, no matter how little they have slept, research demonstrates that efficiency falls off whenever sleep deprivation occurs. Not long ago Bruce J. Martin of Indiana University conducted an experiment in which men and women were deprived of sleep for thirty-six hours. Their performances on a treadmill were then tested and compared with their capability when fully rested. Loss of sleep, it turned out, reduced work time by an average of 11 percent. Although few athletes have occasion to forfeit an entire night's sleep before competition, lesser degrees of deprivation no doubt have their effect as well.

Working oneself into playing condition is not only a matter of preparing the muscles and developing the necessary skills. It also consists of adapting to environmental conditions. Chief among the conditions that put an athlete under stress are heat, cold and high altitudes. Any of the three can not only intefere with performance but can also, in extreme cases, endanger life. Fortunately, simple and reliable methods exist for coping with all three.

Heat. Of the principal environmental hazards, this is the one most commonly encountered. Assessing its impact is not always easy for an inexperienced observer, however, since its severity depends not just on air temperature but also on humidity, solar radiation, clothing, the amount of work being performed, and the athlete's degree of adaptation. On a sunny September day, when lightly dressed soccer players are enjoying an entirely comfortable workout, a football team, encumbered by helmets, padding, and the varied paraphernalia of their sport, may be experiencing considerable distress.

High-temperature problems range from heat cramps, a comparatively mild ailment, to heatstroke, which frequently causes death. Chief among the preliminary symptoms of heat distress are cramps in the arms, legs and abdomen; such cramps are readily treated by resting for a day or two and by using extra salt.

If cramps are permitted to go untreated, the next major stage—heat exhaustion—may occur. In addition to cramps, symptoms include headache, dizziness, nausea and diarrhea. Cool salt water and rest constitute the recommended treatment. It is also important to limit hot-weather workouts for several days, or even several weeks if temperatures are extreme, since the body is more susceptible to episodes of heat exhaustion once it has suffered an initial attack.

TRAINING IN THE HEAT

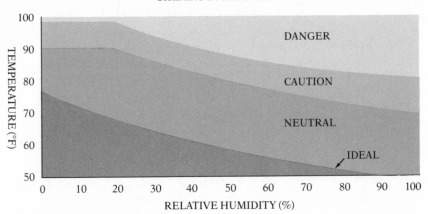

SOURCE: E.C. Frederick, Ph.D.

Heatstroke is characterized by a high temperature (often over 106° F.), dry skin, rapid pulse, irrationality and unconsciousness. On-the-spot emergency treatment consists primarily of cooling the skin. Prompt medical aid is essential.

All heat injuries are preventable. The chief way to avoid them is to limit workouts whenever the weather is severe and to be alert for warning signs. It is also important to allow enough time for acclimatization. The process requires a week or two and consists of such changes as a near-normal body temperature even when the surrounding air is extremely warm, a lowered pulse, and a more precisely adjusted rate of sweating. One's adjustment to hot weather begins with the first workout (research shows that simply spending time in the heat without working out does little good) and proceeds rapidly provided enough water is ingested. Once attained, such acclimatization lasts about two weeks, then gradually disappears unless it is renewed through continued hot-weather workouts.

Cold. If proper clothing is worn, cold usually presents no particular problem. Even the condition known as "burned lungs" is largely mythical, at least under conditions prevailing in most of the United States. By the time air has been warmed by the mouth, nose and throat it is unlikely to damage the body's remoter airways.

Athletes who customarily work out in cold weather—distance runners, skiers, paddle tennis players and the like—soon discover, in fact, that overdressing is more hazardous than underdressing.

Wind Chill Index

				ACTUAL THERMOMETER READING (°F)								
	50	40	30	20	10	0	−10	−20	−30	−40	−50	−60
WIND SPEED IN MPH	EQUIVALENT TEMPERATURE (°F)											
CALM	50	40	30	20	10	0	−10	−20	−30	−40	−50	−60
5	48	37	27	16	6	−5	−15	−26	−36	−47	−57	−68
10	40	28	16	4	−9	−21	−33	−46	−58	−70	−83	−95
15	36	22	9	−5	−18	−36	−45	−58	−72	−85	−99	−112
20	32	18	4	−10	−25	−39	−53	−67	−82	−96	−110	−124
25	30	16	0	−15	−29	−44	−59	−74	−88	−104	−118	−133
30	28	13	−2	−18	−33	−48	−63	−79	−94	−109	−125	−140
35	27	11	−4	−20	−35	−49	−67	−82	−98	−113	−129	−145
40*	26	10	−6	−21	−37	−53	−69	−85	−100	−116	−132	−148

LITTLE DANGER	INCREASING	GREAT DANGER
(FOR PROPERLY CLOTHED PERSON)	DANGER	
	DANGER FROM FREEZING OF EXPOSED FLESH	

*WIND SPEEDS GREATER THAN 40 MPH HAVE LITTLE ADDITIONAL EFFECT.

SOURCE: From Brian J. Sharkey, *Physiology of Fitness*. Champaign, Ill.: Human Kinetics Publishers, 1979.

Wearing too much clothing can cause excessive sweating as well as impede movement.

So long as one is comfortable, it can safely be assumed that dress is adequate, particularly if care is taken to protect the nose, ears and other parts of the body that are particularly subject to frostbite.

High altitude. The 1968 Mexico City Olympics, conducted at 7,350 feet, stimulated the curiosity of researchers interested in the precise effects of altitude on athletic performance. Their interest had several causes. First, at high altitudes air resistance is diminished. Second, gravitational force is less than at sea level. Finally, less oxygen is available.

The first two conditions enhance performance. Bob Beamon's still-unmatched long jump of 29 feet 2 ½ inches—almost two feet farther than the then existing world record—was no doubt partly attributable to lessened air resistance and gravity. On the other hand, a reduction in available oxygen can only serve to limit performance, particularly in endurance events such as the 10,000-meter run and the steeplechase.

This is why athletes planning to compete at high altitudes often prepare themselves by training well above sea level. This is why, too, they occasionally suffer from the hazards indigenous to such locales. The chief such hazard is so-called mountain sickness, characterized by headache, nausea, sleepiness and, in advanced cases, nausea, vomiting and pulmonary problems. Mountain sickness usually begins to develop after two or three hours at altitudes above 7,000 feet, although some people are afflicted at only 5,000 feet (less than the altitude of Denver). If pulmonary edema—commonly signaled by coughing and labored breathing—develops, medical treatment and removal to a lower attitude are necessary. Otherwise, symptoms usually disappear without treatment in a few days.

The severity of mountain sickness can be markedly alleviated by spending a day or two at an intermediate altitude before going to one's ultimate training altitude.

What, ideally, should this altitude be? Since oxygen use by the body necessarily decreases some 3 percent for every 1,000 feet, physical efficiency falls off as altitude increases. Recent research suggests that there is little point in training above 12,500 feet, and some authorities consider 7,500 feet the useful maximum.

An increasingly common atmospheric hazard these days is air pollution. Dr. Lawrence Folinsbee of the Institute for Environmental Stress at the University of California's Santa Barbara campus described for the author a study in which seven cyclists worked out for an hour during a typical Southern California smog alert. All but one experienced adverse respiratory symptoms, and performance ability decreased by an average of 10 percent. Dr. Folinsbee pointed out, however, that athletes who regularly train in smog suffer from progressively fewer symptoms as time goes by. It has not yet been determined, however, whether long-term exercise in such conditions has undesirable residual effects.

Despite the varied measures athletes take to avoid injury, mishaps inevitably occur. When these happen, treatment of one kind or another, if only a day's rest or the application of a Band-Aid, may be needed. Medical attention is not always necessary, however. The reason is that, as Dr. Peter Jokl puckishly puts it, "Most injuries go away by themselves. That's why I'm always telling colleagues, 'You'd better hurry up and operate because if you don't he's going to get better.'"

Because so many injuries heal perfectly well without attention, sportsmedicine enjoys its share of folk remedies and superstitions. When John Montefusco developed a blister on his thumb during his 1983 season as a New York Yankees pitcher, he treated it with pickle brine that Billy Martin, then the team's manager, obtained from the Stage Delicatessen. (Montefusco stopped following Martin's prescription after five days, explaining, "I couldn't sleep because it stunk.")

Unfortunately, not all sports injuries are so easily alleviated. Some require bona fide medical treatment, either by a physician or by the athlete himself. When professional aid must be sought, particularly if the practitioner is a sports specialist, relief these days is likely to be far quicker and more successful than it would have been even a few years ago. The chief reason is that medical knowledge has expanded vastly, bringing an array of new techniques and equipment that are revolutionizing sportsmedicine. Muscle problems are alleviated with ultrasound treatments, foot injuries are diagnosed with the $10,000 Electrodynogram force sensor and computer, and knees are repaired by surgeons who use the versatile arthroscope to tiptoe their way through procedures

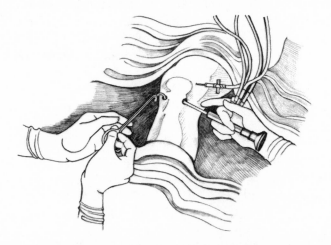

that not infrequently permit the resumption of sports activity almost before the anesthetic has worn off. Joan Benoit's arthroscopic knee surgery only seventeen days before she won the 1984 Olympic marathon trials is a prominent case in point. And when Ken Morrow of the New York Islanders underwent arthroscopic removal of cartilage from his knee in 1983, he was on the Nassau Coliseum ice less than three days after surgery. A decade ago he would have been out of action for as long as two months, all the while undergoing intense physiotherapy.

Sports injuries are broadly classifiable into two categories: those that are traumatically induced and those that result from overuse. Strains, sprains, bruises, fractures and the like are in the first category, while blisters, runner's knee and Achilles tendinitis fall into the second. It is not within the scope of this book to describe the entire range of injuries to which athletes are subject. Nonetheless, it may be useful to examine briefly their main types and some of the treatments that athletes are likely to find useful.

Blisters. Although blisters are usually considered minor problems, even a small one can have a significant effect on performance. Prevention is therefore the most desirable rule; properly fitted equipment, particularly shoes and socks, is essential.

A blister's warning signs, appearing well before the familiar raised skin and fluid are present, consist of redness and tenderness. Once these have appeared, stop play if possible and apply adhesive tape or moleskin. Allow it to remain on the skin for two or three days, or until the redness and discomfort are entirely gone.

If an actual blister is present, puncture the skin close to its edge with a sterilized needle and squeeze the fluid out. Allow the top layer of the skin to remain as protection for the more tender skin underneath, and clean the blister with antiseptic and cover with a sterile dressing. If improperly treated, an infected blister can lead to septicemia (blood poisoning).

Bruises. In collision sports such as football, bruises of the body's soft tissues are common. Except in extreme cases (those, for example, in which considerable internal bleeding has occurred), ice-pack applications every two or three hours, combined with rest, are usually sufficient treatment. Severe bruises may require a doctor's attention.

A second type of bruise is the bone bruise, which is most likely to affect the foot. Common in basketball players, gymnasts and distance runners, it typically starts with a trauma such as landing too hard or stepping on a stone. Ice treatments, administered promptly and continued for about 48 hours, will limit internal bleeding and speed recovery.

Chondromalacia patellae. Often called runner's knee, this is the most common injury to which runners are subject. Caused by excessive wear between the kneecap and the femur, or thigh bone, it involves the wearing away of cartilage and, as a consequence, the development of swelling, stiffness, pain and occasionally a grinding sensation whenever the leg is flexed. (This comes from bone rubbing on bone rather than on cartilage.) Reducing mileage, applying ice and exercising to strengthen the quadriceps—the muscles at the front of the upper leg—usually bring relief.

Cramps. Cramps are spasms that most often affect the calf muscle, but they are occasionally encountered in virtually all the voluntary muscles. Cramps can almost always be prevented by drinking enough water, eating a balanced diet (to ensure a full complement of electrolytes and minerals) and avoiding excessive fatigue. A cramp can be eased by slowly stretching the affected muscle. Resting for a day or two usually prevents the cramp's return; if exercise is resumed immediately it may recur.

Inflammations. No doubt the most common inflammation, because of the millions of men and women who currently participate in running, is Achilles tendinitis. (The suffix *itis* means "inflammation.") Caused by straining or excessive stretching of the calf, it affects the sheath within which the tendon at its lower end moves. The early stages of Achilles tendinitis can often be relieved by ice massage, aspirin both before and after workouts, and gentle (not vigorous) stretching. In one study, conducted at the University of Toronto by R. Peter Welsh and Judy Clodman, such exercises were found to reduce symptoms in most athletes.

Since Achilles tendinitis is often brought on by excessive stretching of a tendon that is too short, anything that will limit this effect is recommended—running on flat surfaces rather than uphill, confining workouts to hard surfaces rather than soft, wearing shoes with adequately elevated heels, and so forth.

Other inflammations, such as tennis elbow and the various similar problems that occur in the muscles and joints as a result of excessive exertion, are effectively treated with rest, massage, stretching, warm baths and two aspirin tablets taken four times daily. If it is feasible, however, the most effective treatment by far is alteration of the action that produced the inflammation in the first place. An important study of tennis elbow, described a few years ago in *The Physician and Sportsmedicine,* showed that changing one's stroke brings relief more reliably than any other measure, including rest, exercise, cortisone treatments, and use of an elbow brace.*

When inflammation is the result of trauma rather than overuse, elevate, wrap and ice the injury for several hours to limit internal bleeding. Heat should not be used for two or three days, since the accompanying increased circulation may cause a resumption of bleeding. Thereafter, however, moderate heat—it should not be any warmer than bath temperature—will facilitate the reabsorption of blood.

Overuse injuries (miscellaneous). Occasionally an injury cannot be precisely identified, at least by a layman, but is clearly the result of working out in one's sport. Typically, such injuries start slowly, manifesting themselves with only moderate and perhaps intermittent discomfort, but become increasingly severe as training continues over the next several days. Among such injuries are swimmer's shoulder, baseball elbow, and the various leg, hip and foot pains common to runners.

Much research into the most effective treatments for such injuries has been conducted in recent years. The most widely accepted are rest (partial or total), ice massage, heat treatments, anti-inflammatory medicines and ultrasound.

Shin splints. Characterized by pain in the lower leg, shin splints are most commonly an irritation of both the tendons and the periosteum, or bone covering. Running surfaces, either those that are too hard (e.g., cement) or too soft (e.g., sand), are among the likely causes, as are running on the toes and wearing inadequately padded shoes. Discomfort, which can range from mild to quite severe, is invariably relieved by ice massage, aspirin and exercises that increase calf strength and flexibility. The podiatrist Mark E. Wolpa, author of *The Sports Medicine Guide*, says he usually obtains good results with hydrotherapy and ultrasound treatments, both of which increase the blood supply. (See also Stress Fractures, below.)

Sprains. A sprain, or injury to the ligaments that stabilize a joint,

---

* Tennis elbow, one of the most common action-induced inflammations, is by no means confined to tennis players but can afflict anyone who moves his arms in a repetitive fashion over a long period of time. Orchestra conductors, among others, are notoriously subject to this malady. In early 1984, to cite only one example, Zubin Mehta of the New York Philharmonic was obliged to take several weeks' leave from his conducting duties in order to undergo surgery for "tennis" elbow.

is caused by a sudden torque or pressure that falls short of producing a dislocation or fracture. Most commonly seen in the ankle
and knee, sprains usually heal in six to eight weeks. If a sprain is
serious enough to prevent weight-bearing, a doctor should be consulted. Otherwise, ice packs, elevation of the leg, and taping are
normally sufficient treatment. Pain and swelling usually lessen
within forty-eight hours, and the leg should feel fairly normal within
two weeks. Because the joint will not have returned to full strength
for six weeks or more, however, caution is imperative.

Strains. Commonly called a muscle pull, a strain can affect either
muscle alone or the meeting sites of muscle and tendon. Stretching
exercises, which relieve tension on muscle-tendon systems, are the
recommended preventative. Once a strain occurs, however, treatment should consist of icing, taping and rest. A physician need be
consulted only if serious injury, such as an Achilles tendon rupture,
is suspected.

Stress fractures. Occasionally a stress fracture, or incomplete bone
break, is mistaken for shin splints (see above). Stress fractures are
characterized by tenderness, usually at a single spot in the foot or
leg, and take four to six weeks to heal. Normal training should be
discontinued or at the very least curtailed during this period; swimming is a good substitute for more jarring activities.

Where sports performance is concerned, both age and sex are important influences. In the case of injuries, however, this is not
necessarily the case. As men and women grow older, it is true, their
bodies are inherently more subject to damage. But because they
ordinarily train and compete less strenuously, their injuries are
not significantly more frequent or severe than those of younger
athletes. (They may, however, be somewhat different.)

Furthermore, older athletes are more inclined to take a long view
of their sports careers and, should they suffer injury, allow themselves whatever rest is necessary. (California's Walt Stack, still a
regular runner at age seventy-seven, has devised an appropriate
motto: "Start slowly and taper off.") A younger athlete, by contrast,
frequently seems to feel that today's match, meet or race is the
most important in the history of sport. If a child feels that by failing
to win he will badly disappoint the adults who are most important
to him, he is likely to try harder than is sensible, keep injuries

secret, and in general become so singleminded about athletics that little else matters.

Nor, contrary to what has long been thought, are well-trained women any more subject to injury than men. Medical records at the U.S. Military Academy show that incoming women cadets experience more injuries than do men, presumably because they have had less involvement with high school sports and because few of them have enjoyed the benefits of knowledgeable coaching. Once they are in good condition, however, their injury rate diminishes sharply and eventually declines to roughly that of male cadets. All the evidence suggests that, with perhaps a single exception, women are every bit as durable as men.

The exception is that women appear to be somewhat more subject to leg injuries. Mark Wolpa, the podiatrist and author who was quoted earlier in this chapter, theorizes that the chief cause is women's wider pelvises. "This gives them a different gait, with more of an inward tilt," he says. "Also, a lot of women insist on wearing stylish high-heeled shoes that put the leg in an abnormal position. Those shoes are murder for anyone trying to be an athlete."

CHAPTER 13

The Gadgetry
of Sport

If you told an athlete to wear a strand of garlic
around his neck and that it would make him run
faster, he would wear it and he would run faster.

—Dr. Charles Greene

IN THE BEGINNING, vaulting poles were fashioned of whatever
happened to be at hand—spruce and fir among the softwoods,
ash, oak and hickory among the hardwoods. Because these clumsy,
unyielding implements were better suited to serve as battering
rams than pole vaulters' implements, improvement was necessarily slow; in the nearly half a century after 1853, when competitive
vaulting first appeared as part of Scotland's Caledonian Games,
the record advanced, it is true, but its progress was scarcely stratospheric.

Not long after the 1900 Olympics most vaulters eagerly switched
to bamboo, preferring its lightness and flexibility, and by 1927 the
record stood at a lofty fourteen feet. In 1948, with the introduction
of fiberglass, it soared again; currently it is just over nineteen feet.

The evolution of pole-vaulting equipment, including changes in
the vaulting box and landing pit, constitutes a persuasive illustra-
tion of the central role sports gear has played, and continues to
play, in the development of athletics. For no matter how skillful
vaulters themselves might have become, had they not had the use
of bamboo and later fiberglass they would almost certainly not be
soaring to their present vertiginous altitudes. The chief reason is

that fiberglass is not simply *better* than ash or spruce or bamboo; it is an entirely *different* order of substance. Unlike wood, it makes possible the construction of an unprecedentedly appropriate instrument, one that facilitates an efficient transfer of kinetic to potential energy and back again as the athlete's momentum is stored in the bent pole and then swiftly liberated.

The example of pole vaulting is not unique. In other sports as well, improvements in equipment have brought numerous benefits. Using graphite racquets, tennis players produce harder, more precisely struck shots than with the once-dominant wooden racquet. Bicyclists, reaping the rewards of lighter, stronger alloys and more aerodynamic design, pedal faster and do so with less fatigue.* Using angled paddles, canoe racers move through the water more swiftly. Runners, benefiting from advances in shoe technology, cover their miles in less time while expending less energy. With scientifically matched clubs, golfers play more consistently. (If their consciences will let them use the illegal Polara ball, with its scientifically designed configuration of dimples, they can even reduce their hooks and slices by as much as 75 percent.)

That recent innovations in athletic equipment have demonstrably enhanced our games has led, perhaps unavoidably, to a pervasive fallacy. This is the optimistic conviction that in the end it is chiefly the gear we use, and not the practice we undertake or the skill we thereby acquire, that determines our ability as athletes. The result is that across the entire spectrum of sport, from the most popular activities to the most obscure, we currently witness a burgeoning array of gadgets, gimcracks and devices of such astonishing variety that the "fitness market" (equipment, clothing, food, vitamins, and so forth) has become a $35-billion-per-year industry.† Among randomly selected samples of the wares currently offered:

* In winning the gold medal in the 1984 Olympic 4,000-meter individual pursuit race Steve Hegg used one of the most significant advancements in recent sports equipment. Hegg pedaled to victory on an 11-pound bicycle designed by the Huffy Corporation. The bicycle, costing $40,000, had in place of a traditional rear wheel a carbon fiber-laminated Kevlar honeycomb disc, material commonly used for bulletproof vests. According to Huffy technician Michael Melton, the solid disc has 30 percent less drag than a spoked wheel and can reduce a top cyclist's time by about one second per kilometer.

† The reader interested in comparative expenditures may find significance in the fact that this is more than one-third what the nation currently devotes to public education.

- Contrivances that permit us to hang upside down in order to counteract, in the words of one promoter, the "ill effects of gravity on the upright human posture." Said to relax muscles and enhance alertness by improving the brain's blood supply, such devices have at least one unwanted side effect: recent studies show that they can produce dangerous, albeit short-lived, hypertension.
- A baseball bat with a double bend at the handle end. According to the manufacturer, the curvature puts the arms into proper alignment and lets the bat reach the ball more quickly.

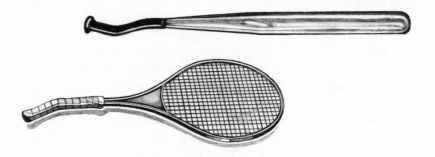

- Calculators and computers that keep golf scores, analyze one's swing and even remember wagers.
- Taped music that is said to promote scientific synchronization of one's internal rhythms with the rhythms of one's sport.
- Electronic treadmills that calculate speed and distance as you run. Although some models cost as much as $6,000, they offer the welcome side benefit that you need never again exercise in the rain. (To point out that you can buy sixty or more rainsuits for the same price would be churlish.)

If the range of available equipment is not exactly infinite, it sometimes seems very nearly so. Heavyhands increase the intensity of workouts. Exercise clothing is not only more cheerful to behold than the ghost-gray sweatsuit of bygone days but is more artfully suited to weather conditions. Specially designed swimsuits increase drag during training by the use of pockets that flare out like airport wind socks. Sports watches offer striking versatility, including alarms, all manner of arcane timing functions and even devices for monitoring an athlete's heartbeat. Finally, Nautilus apparatus, with its mesmerizing appeal, has lured thousands of men and women who might otherwise avoid exercise altogether.

Equipment and efforts at its improvement have always been part of sport. Greek long jumpers carried weights—*halteres*—to add impetus to their efforts, and certainly the Romans were interested in the technology of the racing chariot. In our own century, no American needs to be reminded of the sustained attention that has been lavished on such artifacts of civilization as the bicycle, the tennis racquet, and the running shoe.

What is new today is that, for the first time, the full panoply of contemporary scientific knowledge is being applied to athletic concerns. Not long ago *Mechanical Engineering* magazine published a report on the ways in which engineering principles are being used in the design of sports equipment. One important result, observed the magazine, is that the heyday of the solitary inventor, the eccentric folk hero awaiting inspiration in a cluttered basement workshop, is gone forever. " 'Eureka'-type inventions will be rarer in the future," said the magazine's report, "as technology invades the realm of sport. Engineers and computers will design, manufacture and test equipment. They will analyze the movement of athletes and correct the stride, stroke and swing. Coaches will become engineers and engineers coaches and play diagrams will become equations."

At the Nike Research and Development Center in Exeter, New Hampshire, for example, computers have long been used in designing athletic shoes. Data provided by Nike's research and development staff are supplied to an instrument that not only analyzes the characteristics of a proposed product but also provides a finished drawing of its appearance. Once a design is approved, molds are automatically made in a computerized milling shop. "It does away with the engineer designing on the back of a napkin," observes Dr. John Ochs of Lehigh University, a mechanical engineer and computer specialist.

Elsewhere, the range of scientific intervention in sport is also considerable. In preparation for 1984's Olympic Games, both summer and winter, U.S. athletes were subjected to unprecedented scrutiny and analysis in hopes that performance might thus be enhanced. Members of the women's volleyball team were assessed biomechanically and their strengths and weaknesses pinpointed by computer. The arousal and tension levels of shooters and archers were electronically monitored and their anxiety reduced through biofeedback.

An important recent achievement that would almost surely not have occurred without scientific analysis was the development of the *Gossamer Albatross*, the first aircraft to traverse the English Channel under human power alone. Creation of the *Gossamer Albatross* was possible only because of a close application to scientific principles governing airfoils, wing loadings and the efficient transfer of human energy.

The fruits of scientific application are becoming visible in more conventional sports as well. For baseball players, the Japanese manufacturer Mizuno has designed digital catcher-pitcher communication systems, gloves with built-in polyurethane sunglasses lenses, and radio receivers that fit inside a cap or helmet in order to eliminate missed signals. In golf, clubs designed to control both the moment of inertia and oscillation time are said to improve the quality of play. And tennis players, if they wish, can choose from a growing array of racquets fitted with improbably angled heads and handles that are claimed to be more effective than conventional models. (Not everyone agrees, however, that such racquets constitute an improvement. "The racquet doesn't make the player, the player makes the racquet," says Vitas Gerulaitis, Sr., a respected teaching pro.)

Recent innovations in athletic equipment fall into four principal categories: clothing, safety equipment, training aids and playing surfaces.

Clothing. If a Rip Van Winkle, having slumbered through the past several years, were to reappear and survey the athletic apparel currently available, his eye would no doubt be attracted first by the dazzling range of its style and color. Athletic clothing has become so attractive that it is routinely worn to supermarkets, offices, airports, even churches. Behind the surface glitter, however, lies something more significant: a steadfast concern with function. Polypropylene, an artificial fabric of woven nylon, offers insulating properties unmatched by most natural materials. (Wool remains an important exception.) Gore-Tex lets molecules of perspiration escape but keeps raindrops out.

Nowhere are the results of contemporary technology more usefully visible, however, than in the design of athletic shoes. At the

Nike Sport Research Laboratory, researchers have learned how to lessen impact by the use of various designs and cushioning materials, how to limit undesirable movements of the feet, and how to minimize the physiological damage often associated with prolonged exercise. In pursuing their various projects, Nike investigators have undercut a number of myths. Recently, for example, a research team discovered that the energy demands of running are not nearly as dependent on the weight of one's shoes as had generally been assumed. Rather, the chief influence is cushioning; the more resilient the sole the less work a runner needs to do, even if a shoe is relatively heavy.*

Such research, by Nike as well as by other investigators, is producing footwear that is far more exactingly suited to the needs of athletes than anything previously available. Not too many years ago runners were advised to work out on soft surfaces whenever possible, in order to keep the shock of impact to a minimum. With today's shoes, this is no longer necessary. The cushioning properties of the best-made footwear make it the equivalent of the most yielding surfaces.

Safety equipment. Risk is inherent in sports, even those in which the dangers appear to a novice to be slight. In the village church

EFFECT OF FACE MASKS AND DENTAL GUARDS ON INJURIES

YEAR	PROTECTION	PLAYERS	FACIAL AND DENTAL INJURIES	INCIDENCE/100
1954	No face masks or dental guards	15,714	356	2.26
1955	Face masks introduced	15,714	288	1.83
1959	Face masks mandatory; few dental guards	22,969	275	1.20
1963	Face masks and dental guards mandatory	30,357	143	0.47
1966	Face masks and dental guards mandatory	34,298	115	0.33

SOURCE: Gordon Stoddard, "Protective Equipment." In *Sports Medicine*, edited by A. J. Ryan and F. L. Allman, Jr. New York: Academic Press, 1974.

* A definitive book on athletic shoes, embodying much of the recent research on the subject, appeared in 1984 under the editorship of Nike's research director, E. C. Frederick. Titled *Sport Shoes and Playing Surfaces: Biomechanical Properties*, it is published by Human Kinetics Publishers, Box 5076, Champaign, IL 61820.

in Elford, England, stands an ancient memorial effigy. Fashioned in about 1460, it depicts a curly-haired boy. He holds in one hand a tennis ball, the apparent cause of his death, while the other points to a spot behind his ear. An inscription reads *Ubi dolor, ibi digitus.* ("Where my finger points, there was my injury.")

If a fifteenth-century child could be killed by a tennis ball, how much more likely is injury in sports like football, baseball and basketball. This is why so much attention has been given in recent years to the fashioning of protective gear. Using complex analyses that show exactly what undesirable forces affect the body and to what degree, safety specialists have pinpointed deficiencies in equipment and in some cases have made, or at least recommended, important improvements.

At the Department of Mechanical Engineering of the University of California at Berkeley, for example, researchers recently tested baseball headgear by firing balls at it with a compressed-air cannon. (Speeds ranged from 50 to 120 miles per hour, approximating the velocities encountered in professional baseball games.) After analyzing their data the investigators, Werner Goldsmith and J. Michael Kabo, concluded that currently used headgear is far less effective than it should be in dissipating impact. They suggested that more effective gear could be designed if the shell were more flexible and therefore offered more "give." Perhaps one day their findings will result in greater safety for baseball players.

Similarly, analysis of skiing injuries has led to safety bindings that lessen the frequency of mishap by releasing skis before forces become severe. In one study, injuries declined by 65 percent over a fifteen-year period. A newly developed computerized binding promises to bring even more impressive results.

In other sports as well, safety has improved because of the use of scientifically designed equipment. Football face guards have evolved continually since their introduction in the 1950's, and facial injuries have declined nearly sevenfold in the intervening years. Basketball shoes have reduced the frequency of ankle injuries. Hockey helmets have minimized injuries caused by sticks and pucks. Finally, runners in large numbers have turned to the use of orthotics—supports that change the manner in which the foot strikes the ground and absorbs shock. In a recent Nike study, excessive flexing of the subtalar joint was found to be associated with common injuries of the hip, knee, Achilles tendon and foot; use of orthotics in concert with stable shoes, analysis showed, minimizes such flexing and therefore presumably lowers the incidence of injury. And runners who work out at night are less subject to automobile mishaps because of the growing variety of reflective gear that has become available.

Not all protective equipment is the product of research laboratories. Recently the Miami Dolphins' Woody Bennett began marketing a foam-padded girdle that he helped design. Called the Bennett 34 after his jersey number, it is said to give protection from many of the insults to which football players are subject. Having worn the girdle during the 1983 season, Bennett said, "I haven't had a bruise all year."

Training aids. On several occasions in these pages we have had occasion to observe that athletes are undiscourageable in their hope that they will someday find a substitute for the rigors of conventional training. A vitamin supplement, a device, a diet— wouldn't life's pleasures be wonderfully enhanced if one of these could somehow replace the endless hours of workouts?

An entire industry has, in fact, been built on just this fond hope. A magazine advertisement, for example, promises "3,000 sit-ups without moving an inch . . . 10 miles of jogging lying flat on your back." The secret, we are told, is "Europe's miracle body shaper," described as an "amazing NO-WORK exerciser." In a similarly optimistic vein, a brochure lists the multitudinous benefits of commercially prepared plankton, "nature's most potent supplement," which is said to contain numerous vitamins and minerals as well as such energy sources as glycogen and rhamnose, "an unusual sugar that is absorbed by the blood and quickly made available to the muscles."

All manner of equipment is also available to augment the benefits and ease the discomforts of training—motorized treadmills, rowing machines, miniature trampolines, and even video games that can be played while pedaling a stationary bicycle. Not long ago, when *Runner's World* undertook to compile a directory of such aids, it found nearly 130 specifically intended for participants in the single sport with which the magazine concerns itself. The abundance is no less spectacular in other sports.

The usefulness of such devices varies. If they elevate the heart rate and increase the breathing frequency, they are probably worthwhile as conditioning adjuncts. If, on the other hand, they require little effort, chances are they don't do much good. A person using a popular variety of miniature trampoline, for example, spends so much time resting between bounces that the exercise obtained is slight. And some devices, promising as they may sound in theory, simply don't seem to confer any measurable benefits.

An example is the so-called MORA, or mandibular orthopedic repositioning appliance. Based on the principle that problems in the jaw's temporomandibular joint can lessen muscular strength and endurance in other parts of the body, the MORA seeks to correct the jaw's functioning and thus allow an athlete to achieve maximum strength. In a study conducted at the University of Pennsylvania, however, a group of basketball players showed no change in strength after being fitted with the appliances. Dr. Charles Greene of the University of Illinois Medical Center suggests that MORA proponents promise more than they can deliver to athletes. "If you told an athlete to wear a strand of garlic around his neck and that it would make him run faster, he would wear it and he would run faster. Every scientific study so far says [the MORA] is nothing more than a placebo."

Furthermore, a device that provides excellent exercise in one respect may not appreciably improve conditioning for one's sport. The reason, as described in Chapter 5, is the apparently unalterable principle of specificity—that we improve only at what we practice. A man or woman who works out vigorously on a stationary bicycle, for example, will develop endurance for cycling but will not improve noticeably at tennis or squash.

Two instruments whose ultimate usefulness to athletes seems beyond doubt, however, are video recorders and computers. Thus far neither has been widely used, but the success of initial experiments suggests that they will one day become standard fixtures in sport.

Video recorders allow a coach or athlete to analyze technique at the playing site, thereby providing immediate criticism or reinforcement. Recently two researchers, Laura Kessler Cooper and Anne L. Rothstein, used videotape replay as an instructional aid for tennis players as they practiced ground strokes and serves. Results varied with the precise methods used but were generally encouraging.

To date the computer industry has been characterized by such a confusion of competing hardware and programs that devices for sport remain far short of their potential. Although a number of exercise and diet programs are available, not many have been sufficiently inventive to use the full range of a computer's capacities. Says John Hawkins, executive vice president of the software firm Micro Education Corporation of America: "As computers become more broadly used by the general population, programs will be written to meet the precise needs of the people who have access to them. So far, that hasn't happened in very many instances."

For a glimpse of what computers might one day do for athletes, one need look no further than a weightlifting system designed by the biomechanist Dr. Gideon Ariel. Called ArielTek, it consists of a program linked to a machine that provides a variety of exercises—sit-ups, squats, the bench press and others. When an athlete using ArielTech exerts himself, variable air resistance ensures that he continually exerts maximum effort, no matter what his muscle angle or state of fatigue. At $18,000, ArielTek may be too costly for the average weekend athlete. Still, it and other computers appear to represent the shape of sport's future.*

Playing surfaces. Athletes have long known that the surface on which a game is played exerts a significant influence. As long ago as 1925 Bill Tilden lamented that tennis was played on such a variety of surfaces that no one could become fully accustomed to any one of them. The same problem, of course, exists today. Not long ago Ivan Lendl said, "The widely held opinion that I can't play on grass is not true. . . . But for me the problem is that I'm a hard-court specialist. I also get on all right on clay. And with the exception of the two weeks of Wimbledon we're playing on these surfaces all year around. That's why it's extremely difficult and very time- and energy-consuming to adapt to grass."

Surfaces play an important role in other sports as well. Studies show that artificial turf is hotter than grass surfaces, making summer workouts more difficult and, in extreme conditions, more dangerous. Furthermore, artificial turf exposes athletes to a greater risk of injury (although the mishaps that occur, according to one study, are not usually as serious as those sustained on grass). Finally, artificial turf can affect the quality of play. Analysis shows that the Kansas City Royals, to cite one prominent instance, are more likely to win games played on artificial turf than on grass.

---

* Not all athletes would agree. Martina Navratilova, who at one time used a computer to analyze the playing styles of rivals, revealed not long ago that she has abandoned the practice. People, she explained, can do the job more effectively than computers.

From 1980 to 1982 the team compiled a winning percentage of .571 on artificial turf and .531 on grass. Since the Royals' batting average is only slightly different on the two surfaces—a mere .002 point, with artificial turf favored—no one is quite sure of the reason for the magnitude of the difference.

Probably the most closely studied playing surface in sports today is Harvard University's so-called tuned track, which according to mathematical projections that appeared in a 1978 *Scientific American* article was expected to produce a new era of record-breaking. Analysis shows, however, that the improvement in running times made possible by the scientifically designed track during two recent competitive seasons was only slightly more than 1.5 percent, or three seconds in a four-minute mile. This slight an improvement might be fully explained by nothing more than the track's banked turns, since most of the events with which Harvard performances were compared were held on flat surfaces. It has also been suggested that the tuned track may offer a placebo effect. That is, athletes simply *expect* to run faster on it and therefore do.

In the end the chief lesson of Harvard's tuned track may turn out to be one hardly intended by its designers—that athletic excellence, even in an era of scientific marvels, comes primarily from the athletes themselves rather than from the equipment they use.

CHAPTER 14
Outer Limits

> The participatory and spectator sports in
> the Western world now offer more objects
> for men's spiritual concerns than all
> the formal religions combined.
>
> —RICHARD D. MANDELL

I N THIS FINAL CHAPTER we turn our attention away from sport's history and current manifestations, the topics that have chiefly preoccupied us in these pages, to its future and the shape it is likely one day to take. For if sport, like most other aspects of our lives, constitutes not discrete, unrelated moments but a continuing drama, then the past is indeed not just history but prologue, and by looking in the right places we may be able, if we can decide what to look for, to discern the pattern of accomplishments yet to come. For sports records, it is true, may for a time have seemed inviolable— could anyone possibly run a mile in less than four minutes or pole vault higher than twelve feet?—but in the end the marvelous has always occurred and someone has managed to accomplish what the collective wisdom had decreed no one could possibly do.

There is no reason to suppose such improvement will cease. On the contrary, the opposite is true: There is every reason to argue, first, that in the years ahead records will be broken in unprecedented numbers and, second, that the great run of athletes, those whose gifts ensure that they will never be asked to play for pay or even for much applause, will benefit from the progress at the top.

Several influences, some of them already alluded to, suggest that

WORLD RECORDS FOR THE MARATHON

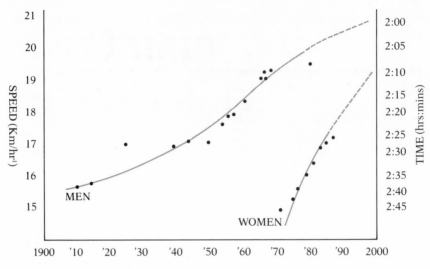

SOURCE: E.C. Frederick, Ph.D.

such a pattern can be confidently predicted. Despite its multitude of undeniably frenetic pressures, our society affords more leisure than ever before, and increasing portions of that leisure are devoted to sports. In 1983 a survey showed that almost half of all Americans participate in one sport or another nearly every day, and when respondents were asked whether they engage in sport at least once a week, the figure reached 71 percent.

This widespread interest in sports, particularly among the young, increases the likelihood that talented athletes will come to light rather than be lost through neglect. Examples of precisely this process of discovery abound. At age seventeen the Edmonton Oilers' Wayne Gretzky was the youngest athlete in North America to be playing a major-league sport. At age nineteen Tom Petranoff, who had not even seen a javelin thrown until two days earlier, threw 198 feet 10 inches and won his first collegiate meet. (Fulfilling his early promise, he has since set a world record.) And at the same age Severiano Ballesteros, the gifted Spanish golfer, led the British Open for the first three rounds. (He, too, has done spectacularly well, going on to win the British Open, the Masters and over $1.5 million in prize money.)

The financial lure of professional sports has been an essential element in the general improvement of athletics. While only the rare athlete will ever be offered the multimillion-dollar contract of a Rich Gossage or a Steve Young, the fact that such rewards exist has a mesmerizing attraction for countless young athletes.

Finally, sport offers prestige. Money aside, top sports participants are respected and even lionized. The same survey cited above found that 75 percent of Americans believe athletes are desirable role models for children, and 59 percent believe they are not infrequently the very best examples children can have. In a society in which being well known and widely admired are regarded as being of considerable importance, this function of sport should not be ignored.

Sports, in short, are seen not as trivial pastimes, mere optional diversions, but as fundamental aspects of our society. In *Sport: A Cultural History*, Richard D. Mandell writes: "Sport in our newspapers occupies more space and is the object of more passionate reader concern than domestic and international politics combined. The ways or extent in which sport occupies the symbolic inner life of modern man must remain a subject of conjecture. However, proportional representation in the printed and electronic media and the extent to which our sports are socially sanctioned conversational subjects all suggest that the participatory and spectator sports in the Western world now offer more objects for men's spiritual concerns than all the formal religions combined."

When interest in any human enterprise is passionate, extraordinary accomplishments almost always follow. It was religious passion that built the cathedrals of the Middle Ages, the Renaissance passion for knowledge that so spectacularly expanded the scientific boundaries of our world, and the passion for space exploration in our own time that has made the solar system our front yard. There is no reason to suppose that the current passion for sport will, in its realm, ultimately accomplish any less.

Aside from the mere numbers of sports participants today, several other phenomena point to a period of remarkable athletic achievement.

Foremost, perhaps, are advances in the psychology of sport, a development discussed at length in Chapter 4. A comparatively new field of inquiry, sports psychology has been explored with any thoroughness only during the past two decades. Despite impressive accomplishments, therefore, its greatest achievements almost certainly lie ahead. Not only its practitioners but many athletes themselves feel that psychology may, in fact, soon become the single most important source of improvement in sports. As Roger Bannister declared not long ago, "It is psychological factors beyond the ken of physiology which set this razor's edge between defeat and victory and which determine how closely an athlete comes to the absolute limits of performance."

Some of the research currently being undertaken in sports psychology appears to hold considerable promise. The psychologist William P. Morgan, for example, has experimented with telling volunteers that he is increasing their workload as they pedal stationary bicycles. Actually, however, he keeps the workload exactly as it has been all along. Remarkably, the volunteers' oxygen use—the chief measure of how hard the body senses its various systems to be working—increases.

If oxygen use can be artificially increased through suggestion, might it not also be lessened? This is exactly what has happened in related experiments in which volunteers experience a reduced oxygen demand when they practice the kinds of relaxation techniques outlined by Herbert Benson in his book *The Relaxation Response.*

Despite these and other discoveries, sports psychology is still so much in its infancy that no one, including most of its practitioners, is entirely certain what its purposes ought to be. Is the sports psychologist's proper goal to produce victory or well-integrated human beings? Should his loyalty be to a team or to its individual players? It is perhaps tempting to argue that a sports psychologist, like a coach or trainer, should primarily serve the cause of winning, yet what if such an effort conflicts with an individual's values?

Because of questions like these, sports psychology is currently the subject of considerable debate. "It is now critical," says a recent article in the *Journal of Sport Psychology,* "that we develop congenial relationships between physical education and psychology. The birth of a new field requires the cooperation and support of both parents." Once it has been determined what forms such cooperation and support ought to take, there is little doubt that sports psychology will go on to accomplish far more than anyone has yet imagined.

A second development that has already contributed much to the improvement of sports is the vast quantity of medical and physiological research that is currently taking place. In preparation for the 1984 Olympics, investigators working under the aegis of the

United States Olympic Committee looked into such questions as the manner in which the time of day influences athletic performance, recent equipment technology and its usefulness to athletes, and the effect of anabolic steroids on the various physiological systems.* Working independently, other researchers have been seeking to determine exactly what attributes—body fat, strength, speed and so forth—contribute to success in various sports, how potentially superior athletes can be identified early, and how men and women can reach top condition at the precise moment of competition.

As a result of such inquiries, many present-day athletes are training quite differently from those of earlier times. Martina Navratilova, for example, attributes the current extraordinary level of her game partly to a program of "tennis kinetics." Taught by Rick Elstein, a trainer and teaching pro, tennis kinetics emphasizes proper movement on the court rather than merely hitting the ball well. "My footwork and overall movement have gotten much better," says Miss Navratilova. "People pay so much attention to hitting the ball, when movement is really the key. Learning to hit a tennis ball without learning proper movement is like a hockey player learning to shoot a puck without learning how to skate."

The study of movement has, in fact, been at the forefront of sports research for quite some time. Biomechanics, the science of human motion, is commonly traced to the writings of Aristotle, in particular his *De Motu Animalium* ("The Movements of Animals") and *De Incessu Animalium* ("The Parts of Animals"). It was not until the 1870's, however, that the photographer Eadweard Muybridge devised a means of making sequential images that for the first time permitted motion to be scientifically analyzed rather than merely theorized about. Thereafter, progress came swiftly. Using cadavers, pioneering researchers determined the centers of gravity of the

---

* The application of drugs to sport is, of course, vastly controversial. Anabolic steroids, the most widely used illegal substances, are synthetic male hormones that stimulate muscle growth but can also damage the liver, cause heart attacks and prostate enlargement, and very likely produce cancer. The biochemist Van Rensselaer Potter explains, "There's no free lunch. Steroids shouldn't be used. The right way is to put the athlete into a stress situation in which he produces hormones by himself." Says Dr. Gabe Mirkin, author of *The Sportsmedicine Book*: "It still amazes me that any athlete would be tempted to take them." Athletes argue, on the other hand, that in sports that depend heavily upon strength—weightlifting, the shotput, wrestling and the like—there is no way to attain international caliber *without* using steroids. So long as even a few athletes resort to these drugs, the problem will almost certainly be with us.

body's various parts. Others analyzed the movements intrinsic to the several sports, while still others studied their physiological implications.

The result is a formidable library of material on exactly how the human body functions—and should function—during virtually every type of sports activity. By consulting the appropriate authorities, almost any athlete can find methods for improving his manner of movement. To cite only one example, several years ago researchers at Penn State University's Biomechanics Laboratory compared the styles of elite and less gifted runners as they worked out on a treadmill. The elite runners, it turned out, had an average stride length of 1.56 meters and took 191 steps per minute, while the others averaged 1.64 meters and took only 182 steps per minute. It may be, therefore, that if an average runner were deliberately to shorten and quicken his stride, he would be more successful. Similar instances from other sports abound.

Nor, in their concern with facilitating the emergence of excellence for a given season's efforts, do investigators ignore the shape of things to come. In the *Canadian Journal of Applied Sports Science* not long ago, E. W. Banister and T. W. Calvert of Simon Fraser University in British Columbia pointed out that it is not enough for a gifted young athlete to train with an eye to breaking the records that currently exist. Rather, he must school himself to break tomorrow's records, which will inevitably be more severe than today's. The athlete's problem is thus much like that of a skeet shooter—he must aim not where the target is but where it will be, or at least, with any luck, may be.

A third influence that promises to bring an improvement in sport is the continuing development of equipment technology, including the use of videotape (for on-the-spot motion analyses) and computers (for devising precisely individualized training programs, developing strategy, analyzing diet and performing a growing range of other functions). As noted in the preceding chapter, we are currently in the midst of a sometimes bewildering explosion of new equipment, not a little of which is of doubtful usefulness. Much of what has become available, however, has provided a distinct service by improving the efficiency with which sports can be played.

Finally, athletes today train harder than those of any other time. Top athletes have always realized the importance of training. As long ago as 1925 Bill Tilden wrote, "I am a great believer in practice, but above all in intensive practice. My idea of intensive practice is to pick out one stroke and hammer away at that shot until it is completely mastered." A half-century ago not many athletes had yet adopted Tilden's view of training; today many have. Greg Meyer, currently one of the world's most gifted marathon runners, told the author recently, "I train hard and consistently. I'm running well because I've been training very consistently for about three years now."

Nowhere is the movement toward intense training more impressively visible than among women athletes. No longer fettered by widespread prejudice, and inspired by the examples of the growing number of accomplished women athletes, women today are compiling a list of achievements that would once have seemed not

Joan Benoit

only unlikely but out of the question. In 1979, in the *International Journal of Sport Psychology*, an article on "Female Sport Today" expressed an opinion common to that period: "Sport is a human behavior to be shared equally by both males and females; that realization is long overdue throughout the world." Only a few years later, the realization referred to is so prevalent as to be entirely unremarkable. Women, like men, may fail to excel through lack of ability or perseverance, but it is rare today that they need do so through an absence of opportunity.

The trend toward increasingly intense efforts has also influenced older athletes, those who in an earlier time would have been content to be mere shuffling dabblers. Any spectator watching tennis players like Ken Rosewall and Fred Stolle, who have lived approximately a half-century apiece, has good cause for wondering whether he might be in the presence of competitors half their age. And it is doubtful that in an earlier era an athlete like Marion Irvine, a nun in her mid-fifties, would have qualified for the Olympic marathon trials. With a time of 2 hours 51 minutes 1 second, she is the oldest person ever to meet the trials standards in a running event of any distance.

For all these reasons—science, technology, the inexorable march of research, and above all the rising expectations of athletes themselves—sports performance will beyond question continue to exceed its apparent limits. Knowledgeable authorities have, for example, only recently predicted the attainment of a 110-mile-per-hour fastball in baseball, a seventy-five-yard field goal in football, a sub-3:40 mile in track, a 2:06 men's marathon, a 45-second 100-meter men's freestyle in swimming, as well as the equaling of Bob Beamon's "mutation" long jump of 29 feet 2½ inches. These achievements, improbable as some of them may seem, are foreseeable merely by extrapolating from the present rates of improvement. Mathematically, therefore, it will be more remarkable if they should *not* occur than if they do.

There is also, however, an additional source of improvement in sports, and by its nature it is beyond the reach of science or any other influence we may seek to apply. This is nothing less than physical genius, the appearance of which is utterly and wondrously beyond prediction. Ineffable and marvelous, it is genius that, more than anything else, is responsible for revealing the athletic prodigies of which men and women are finally capable. We cannot know in advance upon whom such genius will bestow itself. We can only be certain that sooner or later it will surely do so, and that when it does we will witness achievements about which we have not yet thought to dream.

Selected References

CHAPTER 1: The Science Explosion

Brancazio, Peter J. *SportScience*. New York: Simon and Schuster, 1984.

Brundage, Avery. *The Speeches of Avery Brundage*. Lausanne: Comité International Olympique, 1968.

Cruikshank, John. *Albert Camus and the Literature of Revolt*. London: Oxford University Press, 1959.

Finley, M.I., and H.W. Pleket. *The Olympic Games: The First Thousand Years*. New York: Viking, 1976.

Guttman, Allen. *The Games Must Go On: Avery Brundage and the Olympic Movement*. New York: Columbia University Press, 1984.

———. *From Ritual to Record: The Nature of Modern Sports*. New York: Columbia University Press, 1978.

Hanlon, R.J. "Misinformation Burdens Runners." (Letter.) *New York Times*, March 20, 1983.

Hill, A.V. "The Scientific Study of Athletics." *Scientific American*, April 1926.

Jokl, Ernst. "Record Physiology." *Medicine and Sport*, Vol. 9, 1976.

———. "Running and Swimming World Records." *Olympic Review*, September–October 1976.

Kazantzakis, Nikos. *Report to Greco*. New York: Simon and Schuster, 1965.

Miller Brewing Company. *The Miller Lite Report on American Attitudes Toward Sports*. Milwaukee, Wis.: Miller Brewing Co., 1983.

Nelson, Richard C. "Biomechanical Research Applied to Sports in the

United States." Paper presented at the International Symposium on Biomechanics of Sport, Cologne, West Germany, December 1980.

Rasmussen, Stanley A. "Exercise Physiology at the Cellular Level." *Journal of Sports Medicine and Physical Fitness*, June 1972.

Umminger, Walter. *Supermen, Heroes, and Gods*. New York: McGraw-Hill, 1963.

CHAPTER 2: The Invention of Excellence

Bodnar, Leslie M. "Historical Role of Women in Sports." *American Journal of Sports Medicine*, Vol. 8, No. 1, 1980.

Durant, John, and Otto Bettman. *Pictorial History of American Sports*. Cranbury, N.J.: A.S. Barnes, 1965.

Fishler, Stan, and Shirley Fishler. *The Best, Worst and Most Unusual in Sports*. New York: Thomas Y. Crowell, 1977.

Gardiner, E. Norman. *Athletics of the Ancient World*. Chicago: Ares Publishers, 1978.

Glubok, Shirley, and Alfred Tamarin. *Olympic Games in Ancient Greece*. New York: Harper & Row, 1976.

Gontang, Austin. "The Mind of the Runner." *San Diego Running News*, May 1982.

Guttman, Allen. *From Ritual to Record: The Nature of Modern Sports*. New York: Columbia University Press, 1978.

Jokl, Ernst. "Future Athletic Records." *Running & Fitness*, March–April 1984.

———. "Running, Psychology and Culture." *Annals of the New York Academy of Sciences*, October 31, 1977.

Konner, Melvin. *The Tangled Wing: Biological Constraints on the Human Spirit*. New York: Holt, Rinehart and Winston, 1982.

Manchester, Herbert. *Four Centuries of Sport in America*. New York: Benjamin Blom, 1968.

Mandell, Richard D. *Sport: A Cultural History*. New York: Columbia University Press, 1984.

———. "The Invention of the Sports Record." *Stadion*, Vol. 2, No. 2, 1976.

Murrell, John. *Athletics, Sports and Games*. London: George Allen & Unwin, 1975.

Nye, Russel Blaine. *The Cultural Life of the New Nation*. New York: Harper & Brothers, 1960..

Pollock, John Crothers. "America's Love of Sports: How Strong the Feeling?" *New York Times*, March 20, 1983.

Reed, J.D. "America Shapes Up." *Time*, November 2, 1981.

Ryan, Allan J. "The Limits of Human Performance." In *Sports Medicine*, edited by Allan J. Ryan and Fred L. Allman, Jr. New York: Academic Press, 1974.

Schöbel, Heinz. *The Ancient Olympic Games*. London: Studio Visa Limited, 1966.

Strutt, Joseph. *The Sports and Pastimes of the People of England*. Detroit: Singing Tree Press, 1968.

Willoughby, David P. *The Super Athletes*. New York: A.S. Barnes, 1970.

CHAPTER 3: The Path to Peak Performance

Beattie, Bob. "A Look at America's Success in Skiing." *New York Times*, March 27, 1983.

Bentivegna, Angelo, James E. Kelley, and Alexander Kalenak. "Diet, Fitness and Athletic Performance." *The Physician and Sportsmedicine*, October 1979.

Blair, Steven N., et al. "Comparison of Nutrient Intake in Middle-Aged Men and Women Runners and Controls." *Medicine and Science in Sports and Exercise*, Vol. 13, No. 5, 1981.

Daniels, J.T., R.A. Yarbrough, and C. Foster. "Changes in VO_2 Max and Running Performance with Training." *European Journal of Applied Physiology*, Vol. 39, 1978.

Frederick, E.C. "Our Best Hour." *Running*, March–April, 1983.

Frisancho, A. Roberto. "Functional Adaptation to High Altitude Hypoxia." *Science*, January 1975.

Gleim, Gilbert W., Philip A. Witman, and James A. Nicholas. "Indirect Assessment of Cardiovascular 'Demands' Using Telemetry on Professional Football Players." *American Journal of Sports Medicine*, May–June 1981.

Gunby, Phil. "Increasing Numbers of Physical Changes Found in Nation's Runners." *Journal of the American Medical Association*, February 13, 1981.

Hickson, R.C. "Skeletal Muscle Cytochrome *c* and Myoglobin, Endurance and Frequency of Training." *Journal of Applied Physiology*, Vol. 51, No. 3, 1981.

———. "Time Course of the Adaptive Responses of Aerobic Power and Heart Rate to Training." *Medicine and Science in Sports and Exercise*, Vol. 13, No. 1, 1981.

———, and Maureen A. Rosenkoetter. "Reduced Training Frequencies and Maintenance of Increased Aerobic Power." *Medicine and Science in Sports and Exercise*, Vol. 13, No. 1, 1981.

———, et al. "Reduced Training Duration Effects on Aerobic Power, Endurance and Cardiac Growth." *Journal of Applied Physiology*, Vol. 53, No. 1, 1982.

Houston, M. E., and H.J. Green. "Skeletal Muscle and Physiologic Characteristics of a World Champion Masters Distance Runner: A Case Study." *International Journal of Sports Medicine*, Vol. 2, 1981.

Houston, M.E., et al. "The Effect of Rapid Weight Loss on Physiologic Functions in Wrestlers." *The Physician and Sportsmedicine*, November 1981.

Jacobs, Jody. "Beautiful People True Believers in Survival of Fittest." *Minneapolis Star and Tribune*, September 8, 1983.

Lavoie, Jean-Marc, Albert W. Taylor, and Richard R. Montpetit. "Physiological Effects of Training in Elite Swimmers as Measured by a Free Swimming Test." *Journal of Sports Medicine*, Vol. 21, 1981.

Luce, John M. "Respiratory Adaptation and Maladaptation to Altitude." *The Physician and Sportsmedicine*, June 1979.

Macková, Eva V., et al. "Enzyme Activity Patterns of Energy Metabolism in Skiers of Different Performance Levels (M. Quadriceps Femoris)." *European Journal of Applied Physiology*, Vol. 48, 1982.

Monahan, Gene. *The Winter Months*. New York: New York Yankees, undated.

Mumford, Michael, and Ravi Prakash. "Electrocardiographic and Echocardiographic Characteristics of Long-Distance Runners." *American Journal of Sports Medicine*, Vol. 9, No. 1, 1981.

Muyhre, L.G., G.H. Hartung, and D.M. Tucker. "Plasma Volume and Blood Metabolites in Middle-Aged Runners During a Warm-Weather Marathon." *European Journal of Applied Physiology*, Vol. 48, 1982.

Namath, Joe Willie, with Dick Schaap. *I Can't Wait Until Tomorrow . . . 'Cause I Get Better-Looking Every Day*. New York: Random House, 1969.

Newcombe, Jack. *The Best of the Athletic Boys*. New York: Doubleday, 1975.

Nimmo, M.A., and D.H. Snow. "Time Course of Ultrastructural Changes in Skeletal Muscle After Two Types of Exercise." *Journal of Applied Physiology*, Vol. 52, No. 4, 1982.

O'Neil, T.K. "The Art of Peaking." *The Runner*, September 1983.

Osler, Tom. *The Conditioning of Distance Runners*. Los Altos, Calif.: Tafnews Press, 1977.

Quigley, Brian M. " 'Biorhythms' and Australian Track and Field Records." *Journal of Sports Medicine and Physical Fitness*, March 1981.

Rasmussen, Stanley A. "Exercise Physiology at the Cellular Level." *Journal of Sports Medicine and Physical Fitness*, June 1972.

Robinson, Earl P., and J. Mark Kjeldgaard. "Improvement in Ventilatory Muscle Function with Running." *Journal of Applied Physiology*, Vol. 52, No. 6, 1982.

Rodgers, Bill, and Joe Concannon. *Marathoning*. New York: Simon and Schuster, 1980.

Rost, R. "The Athlete's Heart." *European Heart Journal*, Vol. 3, 1982.

Ryan, E. Dean, and Jeff Simons. "Cognitive Demand, Imagery and Frequency of Mental Rehearsal as Factors Influencing Acquisition of Motor Skills." *Journal of Sport Psychology*, Vol. 3, 1981.

Shinnick, Phil. "The Russians Are Coming." *Runner's World*, May 1983.

Siebers, Lynn S., and Robert G. McMurray. "Effects of Swimming and Walking on Exercise Recovery and Subsequent Swim Performance." *Research Quarterly for Exercise and Sport*, Vol. 52, No. 1, 1981.

Siegel, Arthur J., Lawrence M. Silverman, and Robert E. Lopez. "Creatine Kinase Elevations in Marathon Runners: Relationship to Training and Competition." *Yale Journal of Biology and Medicine*, Vol. 53, 1980.

Smith, St. John Francis. "The Influence of Interpolated Work on Experimentally Produced Muscle Soreness." Master's thesis, Graduate Division, University of California, 1949.

Staron, Robert S., Fredrick C. Hagerman, and Robert S. Hikida. "The

Effects of Detraining on an Elite Power Lifter." *Journal of the Neurological Sciences*, Vol. 51, 1981.

Subotnick, Steven I. "Variations in Angles of Gait in Running." *The Physician and Sportsmedicine*, April 1979.

Temple, Cliff. "Take a Break." *The Runner*, March 1983.

Vondra, K. "Effect of Sleep Deprivation on Activity of Selected Metabolic Enzymes in Skeletal Muscle." *European Journal of Applied Physiology*, Vol. 47, 1981.

Wieling, Wouter, et al. "Echocardiographic Dimensions and Maximal Oxygen Uptake in Oarsmen During Training." *British Heart Journal*, Vol. 46, 1981.

Wiktorsson-Möller, Margareta, et al. "Effects of Warming Up, Massage, and Stretching on Range of Motion and Muscle Strength in the Lower Extremity." *American Journal of Sports Medicine*, Vol. 11, No. 4, 1983.

Yates, Alayne, Kevin Leehey, and Catherine Shisslak. "Running—An Analogue of Anorexia?" *New England Journal of Medicine*, February 3, 1983.

Ziegler, Susan G., James Klinzing, and Kirk Williamson. "The Effects of Two Stress Management Training Programs on Cardiorespiratory Efficiency." *Journal of Sport Psychology*, Vol. 4, 1982.

CHAPTER 4: Mind Over Muscle

Anderson, James L., and Martin Cohen. *The Competitive Edge*. New York: William Morrow, 1981.

Åstrand, Per-Olof, and Kaare Rodahl. *Textbook of Work Physiology*. New York: McGraw-Hill, 1977.

Bell, Keith F. *Winning Isn't Normal*. Austin, Tex.: Keel Publications, 1982.

Bennett, James G., and James E. Pravitz. *The Miracle of Sports Psychology*. Englewood Cliffs, N.J.: Prentice-Hall, 1982.

Berkow, Ira. "Can Mind Games Win Games?" *New York Times*, January 17, 1983.

———. "The Many Moods of John McEnroe." *New York Times*, January 22, 1983.

Brown, Elizabeth Y., James R. Morrow, Jr., and Stephen M. Livingston. "Self-Concept Changes in Women as a Result of Training." *Journal of Sport Psychology*, Vol. 4, 1982.

Cady, Steve. "Yastrzemski Seeks the Perfect Swing in His Final Innings." *New York Times*, September 26, 1983.

Carron, Albert V. "Cohesiveness in Sport Groups: Interpretations and Considerations." *Journal of Sport Psychology*, Vol. 4, 1982.

Cohen, D.A., and M.L. Young. "Self-Concept and Injuries Among Female High School Basketball Players." *Journal of Sports Medicine and Physical Fitness*, Vol. 21, 1981.

Dickey, Glenn. "The Giants Analyze Their Slump." *San Francisco Chronicle*, April 21, 1983.

Dishman, Rod K. "Contemporary Sport Psychology." *Exercise and Sport Sciences Reviews*, Vol. 10, 1982.

Doherty, J. Kenneth. *Modern Track and Field*. Englewood Cliffs, N.J.: Prentice-Hall, 1963.

Dorsey, Barbara, Patricia Lawson, and Vera Pezer. "The Relationship Between Women's Basketball Performance and Will to Win." *Canadian Journal of Applied Sports Science*, Vol. 5, No. 2, 1980.

Epstein, Martha L. "The Relationship of Mental Imagery and Mental Rehearsal to Performance of a Motor Task." *Journal of Sport Psychology*, Vol. 2, 1980.

Ferstle, Jim. "Accentuating the Positive." *Running*, January–February 1983.

Fisher, A. Craig, and Elizabeth F. Zwart. "Psychological Analysis of Athletes' Anxiety Responses." *Journal of Sport Psychology*, Vol. 4, 1982.

Frederick, E.C. "Why the 'High'?" *Running*, January–February, 1982.

Gould, Daniel, Maureen Weiss, and Robert Weinberg. "Psychological Characteristics of Successful and Nonsuccessful Big Ten Wrestlers." *Journal of Sport Psychology*, Vol. 3, 1981.

Greenspan, Emily. "Conditioning Athletes' Minds." *New York Times Magazine*, August 28, 1983.

Gruber, Joseph J., and Gary R. Gray. "Responses to Forces Influencing Cohesion as a Function of Player Status and Level of Male Varsity Basketball Competition." *Research Quarterly for Exercise and Sport*, Vol. 53, 1982.

Hale, Bruce D. "The Effects of Internal and External Imagery on Muscular and Ocular Concomitants." *Journal of Sport Psychology*, Vol. 4, 1982.

Heyman, Steven R. "Comparisons of Successful and Unsuccessful Competitors: A Reconsideration of Methodological Questions and Data." *Journal of Sport Psychology*, Vol. 4, 1982.

Highlen, Pamela S., and Bonnie B. Bennett. "Psychological Characteristics of Successful and Nonsuccessful Elite Wrestlers: An Exploratory Study." *Journal of Sport Psychology*, Vol. 1, 1979.

Hogg, John M. "Anxiety and the Competitive Swimmer." *Canadian Journal of Applied Sport Sciences*, Vol. 5, No. 3, 1980.

Huizinga, Johan. *Homo Ludens: A Study of the Play Element in Culture*. Boston: Beacon Press, 1955.

Ito, M. "The Differential Effects of Hypnosis and Motivational Suggestions on Muscular Strength." *Japanese Journal of Physical Education*, Vol. 24, 1979.

Jares, Joe. "We Have a Neurotic in the Backfield, Doctor." *Sports Illustrated*, January 18, 1971.

Journal of Sport Psychology, editors of. "Biofeedback Reduces Tension and Leads to Enhanced Performance." *Journal of Sport Psychology*, Vol. 1, 1979.

———. "Developing Athletic Skills Through Biofeedback." *Journal of Sport Psychology*, Vol. 3, 1981.

———. "Injury Rates and Psychological Health." *Journal of Sport Psychology*, Vol. 3, 1981.

———. "Pain: Mind Over Matter." *Journal of Sport Psychology*, Vol. 1, 1979.

Kauss, David R. *Peak Performance: Mental Game Plans for Maximizing Your Athletic Potential*. Englewood Cliffs, N.J.: Prentice-Hall, 1980.

Kiesling, Stephen. "Connoisseurs of Pain." *American Health*, November–December 1983.

King, Billie Jean. *Billie Jean*. New York: Harper & Row, 1974.

Klavora, Peter, and Juri V. Daniel. *Coach, Athlete and the Sport Psychologist*. Champaign, Ill.: Human Kinetics Publishers, 1979.

Loehr, James E. *Athletic Excellence: Mental Toughness Training for Sports*. Denver: Forum Publishing Co., 1982.

McCutcheon, Lynn. "The Psychology of the Ultra Woman." *Ultrarunning*, January–February 1982.

McLaughlin, Loretta. "Study Says Compulsive Runners, Dieters Share Woes." *Boston Globe*, February 3, 1983.

Mifflin, Lawrie. "Goalie's Postgame Anguish." *New York Times*, March 10, 1983.

———. "Greg Louganis Is Raising His Art to New Levels." *New York Times*, July 11, 1983.

Molotsky, Irvin. "Mixing of Sexes Urged in Sports." *New York Times*, November 5, 1983.

Monagan, David. "The Failure of Coed Sports." *Psychology Today*, March 1983.

Morgan, William P. "The Mind of the Marathoner." *Psychology Today*, April 1978.

———. "Test of Champions." *Psychology Today*, July 1980.

Nelson, Jonathan. "From Inactivity to Marathons: Motivations and Self-Perceptions of Middle-Aged Distance Runners." Unpublished paper.

Nideffer, Robert M. *The Inner Athlete: Mind Plus Muscle for Winning*. New York: T.Y. Crowell, 1976.

Noel, Richard C. "The Effect of Visuo-Motor Behavior Rehearsal on Tennis Performance." *Journal of Sport Psychology*, Vol. 2, 1980.

Powell, Frank M., and James P. Verner. "Anxiety and Performance Relationships in First-Time Parachutists." *Journal of Sport Psychology*, Vol. 4, 1982.

Rosenblum, Stephen. "Psychologic Factors in Competitive Failures in Athletes." *American Journal of Sports Medicine*, May–June 1979.

Rushall, Brent S., and D.C. Fry. "Behaviour Variables in Superior Swimmers." *Canadian Journal of Applied Sports Science*, Vol. 5, No. 3, 1980.

Russell, Bill. *Go Up for Glory*. New York: Coward-McCann, 1966.

Ryan, Allan J., and Fred L. Allman. *Sports Medicine*. New York: Academic Press, 1974.

Ryan, E. Dean, and Jeff Simons. "Efficacy of Mental Imagery in Enhancing Mental Rehearsal of Motor Skills." *Journal of Sport Psychology*, Vol. 4, 1982.

Sauer, George, Jr. "Playing for the N.F.L. Title: Anxiety Amid the Glory." *New York Times*, January 23, 1983.

Saxon, Lee. "Hypnotic Projection in Sport." *Australian Family Physician*, March 1981.

Silva, John M., III. "Behavioral and Situational Factors Affecting Concentration and Skill Performance." *Journal of Sport Psychology*, Vol. 1, 1979.

Silva, John M., III. "An Evaluation of Fear of Success in Female and Male Athletes and Nonathletes." *Journal of Sport Psychology*, Vol. 4, 1982.

Sime, Wesley E. "A New Look at Association/Dissociation in Long Distance Runners." *Running Psychologists*, Winter 1982.

Straub, William F. "Sensation Seeking Among High-and Low-Risk Male Athletes." *Journal of Sport Psychology*, Vol. 4, 1982.

Suinn, Richard M. *Psychology in Sports*. Minneapolis: Burgess Publishing Co., 1980.

Tuite, James. "Ranger Goalie Plays Mind Games First." *New York Times*, January 22, 1983.

Tutko, Thomas, and William Bruns. *Winning Is Everything and Other American Myths*. New York: Macmillan, 1976.

Tutko, Thomas, and Umberto Tosi. *Sports Psyching: Playing Your Best Game All of the Time*. Los Angeles: J.P. Tarcher, 1976.

Valliant, Paul M., Fay A.B. Bennie, and Jonathan J. Valliant. "Do Marathoners Differ from Joggers in Personality Profile: A Sports Psychology Approach." *Journal of Sports Medicine*, Vol. 21, 1981.

Van Schoyck, Stephen R., and Anthony F. Grasha. "Attentional Style Variations and Athletic Ability: The Advantages of a Sports-Specific Test." *Journal of Sport Psychology*, Vol. 3, 1981.

Varca, Philip E. "An Analysis of Home and Away Game Performance of Male College Basketball Teams." *Journal of Sport Psychology*, Vol. 2, 1980.

Weinberg, Robert S., and Marvin Genuchi. "Relationship Between Competitive Trait Anxiety, State Anxiety and Golf Performance: A Field Study." *Journal of Sport Psychology*, Vol. 2, 1980.

Weinberg, Robert S., and Allen Jackson. "Mental Preparation Strategies, Cognitions, and Strength Performance." *Journal of Sport Psychology*, Vol. 2, 1980.

Weinberg, Robert S., Daniel Gould, and Allen Jackson. "Relationship Between the Duration of the Psych-Up Interval and Strength Performance." *Journal of Sport Psychology*, Vol. 3, 1981.

———. "Expectations and Performance: An Empirical Test of Bandura's Self-Efficacy Theory." *Journal of Sport Psychology*, Vol. 1, 1979.

Widmeyer, W.N., and J.S. Birch. "The Relationship Between Aggression and Performance Outcome in Ice Hockey." *Canadian Journal of Applied Sport Science*, Vol. 4, 1979.

Wilson, V.E., N.C. Morley, and E.I. Bird. "Mood Profiles of Marathon Runners, Joggers and Non-Exercisers." *Perceptual and Motor Skills*, Vol. 50, 1980.

Zgoda, Jerry. "They Use the Shrinks on the Links." *Boston Globe*, September 5, 1983.

CHAPTER 5: Becoming Strong

Anderson, Tim, and Jay T. Kearney. "Effects of Three Resistance Training Programs on Muscular Strength and Absolute and Relative Endurance." *Research Quarterly for Exercise and Sport*, Vol. 53, 1982.

Clarkson, Priscilla M., Walter Kroll, and Anthony M. Melchionda. "Iso-kinetic Strength, Endurance and Fiber Type Composition in Elite American Paddlers." *European Journal of Applied Physiology*, Vol. 48, 1982.

Darden, Ellington. *Superfitness Handbook*. Philadelphia: George F. Sticky Co., 1980.

———. "Winning with Strength." *Athletic Purchasing and Facilities*, January 1979.

Gardiner, E. Norman. *Athletics of the Ancient World*. Chicago: Ares Publishers, 1978.

Getchell, Bud. *Being Fit: A Personal Guide*. New York: Wiley, 1982.

———. *Physical Fitness: A Way of Life*. New York: Wiley, 1976.

Gettman, Larry R., Paul Ward, and R.D. Hagan. "A Comparison of Combined Running and Weight Training With Circuit Weight Training." *Medicine and Science in Sports and Exercise*, Vol. 14, No. 3, 1982.

Glubok, Shirley, and Alfred Tamarin. *Olympic Games in Ancient Greece*. New York: Harper & Row, 1976.

Gollnick, P.D. "Relationship of Strength and Endurance with Skeletal Muscle Structure and Metabolic Potential." *International Journal of Sports Medicine*, Vol. 3, 1982.

Gonyea, William J. "Role of Exercise in Inducing Increases in Skeletal Muscle Fiber Number." *Journal of Applied Physiology*, Vol. 48, No. 3, 1980.

———, and Flemming Bonde-Petersen. "Alterations in Muscle Contractile Properties and Fiber Composition After Weight-Lifting Exercise in Cats." *Experimental Neurology*, Vol. 59, 1978.

———, George Diepstra, and Jere H. Mitchell. "Cardiovascular Response to Static Exercise During Selective Autonomic Blockade in the Conscious Cat." *Circulation Research*, October 1980.

———, Kathryn H. Muntz, and Jere H. Mitchell. "Cardiac Hypertrophy in Response to an Isometric Training Program in the Cat." *Circulation Research*, November 1981.

———, and D. Sale. "Physiology of Weight-Lifting Exercise." *Archives of Physical Medicine and Rehabilitation*, May 1982.

———, et al. "Cardiovascular Response to Static Exercise in the Conscious Cat." *Circulation Research*, Supplement I, June 1981.

Green, W.K., et al. "Effect of Viewing Selected Colors on the Performance of Gross and Fine Motor Tasks." *Perceptual and Motor Skills*, Vol. 54, 1982.

Haymes, Emily M., and Arthur L. Dickinson. "Characteristics of Elite Male and Female Ski Racers." *Medicine and Science in Sports and Exercise*, Vol. 12, No. 3, 1980.

Jensen, Clayne R., and A. Garth Fisher. *The Scientific Basis of Athletic Conditioning*. Philadelphia: Lea & Febiger, 1979.

Kroll, Walter, et al. "Isometric Knee Extension and Plantar Flexion Muscle Fatigue and Fiber Type Composition in Female Distance Runners." *Research Quarterly for Exercise and Sport*, Vol. 52, No. 2, 1981.

Larsson, Lars. "Physical Training Effects on Muscle Morphology in Sedentary Males at Different Ages." *Medicine and Science in Sports and Exercise*, Vol. 14, No. 3, 1982.

Mirkin, Gabe, and Marshall Hoffman. *The Sportsmedicine Book*. Boston: Little, Brown, 1978.

Monahan, Gene. *The Winter Months*. New York: New York Yankees, undated.

Nideffer, Robert M. *The Inner Athlete: Mind Plus Muscle for Winning*. New York: T.Y. Crowell, 1976.

Parker, Michael G. "Characteristics of Skeletal Muscle During Rehabilitation: Quadriceps Femoris." *Athletic Training*, Summer 1981.

Riley, Daniel P., ed. *Strength Training by the Experts*. West Point, N.Y.: Leisure Press, 1977.

Ryan, Allan J., and Fred L. Alman, Jr. *Sports Medicine*. New York: Academic Press, 1974.

Sanders, Michael T. "Comparison of Two Methods of Training on the Development of Muscular Strength and Endurance." *Journal of Orthopedic and Sports Physical Therapy*, Spring 1980.

Schmidtbleicher, D., and G. Haralambie. "Changes in Contractile Properties of Muscle After Strength Training in Man." *European Journal of Applied Physiology*, June 1981.

Schöbel, Heinz. *The Ancient Olympic Games*. London: Studio Vista Limited, 1966.

Sharkey, Brian J. *Physiology of Fitness*. Champaign, Ill.: Human Kinetics Publishers, 1979.

Silva, John M., III, et al. "A Psychophysiological Assessment of Elite Wrestlers." *Research Quarterly for Exercise and Sport*, Vol. 52, 1981.

Smith, Michael J., and Paul Melton. "Isokinetic Versus Isotonic Variable-Resistance Training." *American Journal of Sports Medicine*, July–August 1981.

Weinberg, Robert S., Daniel Gould, and Allen Jackson. "Mental Preparation Strategies, Cognitions and Strength Performance." *Journal of Sport Psychology*, Vol. 2, 1980.

―――. "Relationship Between the Duration of the Psych-up Interval and Strength Performance." *Journal of Sport Psychology*, Vol. 3, 1981.

Willoughby, David P. *The Super Athletes*. New York: A.S. Barnes, 1970.

Wind, Herbert Warren. *The Realm of Sport*. New York: Simon and Schuster, 1966.

CHAPTER 6: The Forever Factor

Anderson, Tim, and Jay T. Kearney. "Effects of Three Resistance Training Programs on Muscular Strength and Absolute and Relative Endurance." *Research Quarterly for Exercise and Sport*, Vol. 53, No. 1, 1982.

Andzel, Walter D., and Charles Busuttil. "Metabolic and Physiological Responses of College Females to Prior Exercise, Varied Rest Intervals and a Strenuous Endurance Task." *Journal of Sports Medicine*, Vol. 22, 1982.

Buskirk, Elsworth R., et al. "Muscle Fuel for Competition." *The Physician and Sportsmedicine*, January 1979.

Conley, Douglas L., and Gary S. Krahenbuhl. "Running Economy and Distance Running Performance of Highly Trained Athletes." *Medicine and Science in Sports and Exercise*, Vol. 12, No. 5, 1980.

Costill, David L., W.J. Fink, and M.L. Pollock, "Muscle Fiber Composition and Enzyme Activities of Elite Distance Runners." *Medicine and Science in Sports*, Vol. 8, No. 2, 1978.

Docherty, D. "A Comparison of Heart Rate Responses in Racquet Games." *British Journal of Sports Medicine*, June 1982.

Dolgener, Forrest. "Oxygen Cost of Walking and Running in Untrained, Sprint Trained and Endurance Trained Females." *Journal of Sports Medicine*, Vol. 22, 1982.

Dressendorfer, Rudolph H. "Endurance Training of Recreationally Active Men." *The Physician and Sportsmedicine*, November 1978.

Elliott, B.C., and A.D. Roberts. "A Biomechanical Evaluation of the Role of Fatigue in Middle-Distance Running." *Canadian Journal of Applied Sport Sciences*, Vol. 5, No. 4, 1980.

Farrell, Peter A., et al. "Plasma Lactate Accumulation and Distance Running Performance." *Medicine and Science in Sports*, Vol. 11, No. 4, 1979.

Farrell, Peter A., Jack Wilmore, and Edward F. Coyle. "Exercise Heart Rate as a Predictor of Running Performance." *Research Quarterly for Exercise and Sport*, Vol. 51, No. 2, 1980.

Fred, Herbert L. "The 100-Mile Run: Preparation, Performance and Recovery." *American Journal of Sports Medicine*, Vol. 9, No. 4, 1981.

Gettman, Larry R., Paul Ward, and R.D. Hagan. "A Comparison of Combined Running and Weight Training with Circuit Weight Training." *Medicine and Science in Sports and Exercise*, Vol. 14, No. 3, 1982.

Gleim, Gilbert W., Philip A. Witman, and James A. Nicholas. "Indirect Assessment of Cardiovascular 'Demands' Using Telemetry on Professional Football Players." *American Journal of Sports Medicine*, May–June 1981.

Gollnick, P.D. "Relationship of Strength and Endurance with Skeletal Muscle Structure and Metabolic Potential." *International Journal of Sports Medicine*, Vol. 3, 1982.

Hagan, R.D., M.G. Smith, and L.R. Gettman. "Marathon Performance in Relation to Maximal Aerobic Power and Training Indices." *Medicine and Science in Sports and Exercise*, Vol. 13, No. 3, 1981.

Holloszy, John O. "Muscle Metabolism During Exercise." *Archives of Physical Medicine and Rehabilitation*, May 1982.

Jensen, Clayne R., and A. Garth Fisher. *The Scientific Basis of Athletic Conditioning*. Philadelphia: Lea & Febiger, 1979.

Kanehisa, Hiroaki, and Mitsumasa Miyashita. "An Attempt at the Classification of Adolescents Into Sprint or Endurance Types." *Journal of Sports Medicine*, Vol. 20, 1980.

Keul, J., et al. "The Athlete's Heart—Haemodynamics and Structure." *International Journal of Sports Medicine*, Vol. 3, 1982.

Komi, P., et al. "Muscle Metabolism, Lactate Breaking Point and Biomechanical Features of Endurance Running." *International Journal of Sports Medicine*, Vol. 2, 1981.

Lathan, S. Robert, and John D. Cantwell. "A Run for the Record: Studies on a Trans-American Ultramarathoner." *Journal of the American Medical Association*, January 23–30, 1981.

Lesmes, George R., Noel D. Nequin, and Douglas S. Garfield. "Physiological Profiles of Two Champion Ultramarathoners." *The Physician and Sportsmedicine*, May 1983.

Loke, Jacob, Donald A. Mahler, and James A. Virgulto. "Respiratory Muscle Fatigue After Marathon Running." *Journal of Applied Physiology*, Vol. 52, No. 4, 1982.

Martin, Bruce J. "Effect of Sleep Deprivation on Tolerance of Prolonged Exercise." *European Journal of Applied Physiology*, Vol. 47, 1981.

———, and H.-I. Chen. "Ventilatory Endurance in Athletes: A Family Study." *International Journal of Sports Medicine*, Vol. 3, 1982.

———, and Joel M. Stager. "Ventilatory Endurance in Athletes and Nonathletes." *Medicine and Science in Sports and Exercise*, Vol. 13, No. 1, 1981.

Mirkin, Gabe, and Marshall Hoffman. *The Sportsmedicine Book*. Boston: Little, Brown, 1978.

Montgomery, David L., Virginia Malcolm, and Ellen McDonnell. "Comparison of Intensity of Play in Squash and Running." *The Physician and Sportsmedicine*, April 1981.

Nagle, F., et al. "Lactic Acid Accumulation During Running at Submaximal Aerobic Demands." *Medicine and Science in Sports*, Vol. 2, No. 4, 1970.

Niemela, K., I. Palatsi, and J. Takkunen. "The Oxygen Uptake–Work Output Relationship of Runners During Graded Cycling Exercise: Sprinters vs. Endurance Runners." *British Journal of Sports Medicine*, December 1980.

Nike Research Newsletter, editors of. "The Effect of Shoe Weight on the Aerobic Demands of Running." *Nike Research Newsletter*, Fall 1982.

Pohl, A.P., M.W. O'Halloran, and P.R. Pannall. "Biochemical and Physiologic Changes in Football Players." *Medical Journal of Australia*, May 2, 1981.

Pollock, Michael L., Andrew S. Jackson, and Russell R. Pate. "Discriminant Analysis of Physiological Differences Between Good and Elite Distance Runners." *Research Quarterly for Exercise and Sport*, Vol. 51, No. 3, 1980.

Riegel, Peter S. "Athletic Records and Human Endurance." *American Scientist*, May–June 1981.

Runyan, William S., and Jacqueline Puhl. "Relationships Between Selected Blood Indices and Competitive Performance in College Women Cross-Country Runners." *Journal of Sports Medicine*, Vol. 20, 1980.

Ryan, Allan J., and Fred L. Allman, Jr. *Sports Medicine*. New York: Academic Press, 1974.

Sanders, Michael T. "Comparison of Two Methods of Training on the Development of Muscular Strength and Endurance." *Journal of Orthopedic and Sports Physical Therapy*, Spring 1980.

Sjödin, B., and I. Jacobs. "Onset of Blood Lactate Accumulation and Marathon Running Performance." *International Journal of Sports Medicine*, Vol. 2, 1981.

Stipe, Peter, ed. "The Effect of Shoe Weight on the Aerobic Demands of Running." *Nike Research Newsletter*, Fall 1982.

Tanaka, K., and Y. Matsuura. "A Multivariate Analysis of the Role of Certain Anthropometric and Physiological Attributes in Distance Running." *Annals of Human Biology*, Vol. 9, No. 5, 1982.

Waitz, Grete. "Getting Ready to Race." *The Runner*, February 1983.

Wells, Christine, Joel R. Stern, and Lillian H. Hecht. "Hematological Changes Following a Marathon Race in Male and Female Runners." *European Journal of Applied Physiology*, Vol. 48, 1982.

Western Journal of Medicine, editors of. "Fuel Utilization in Marathons: Implications for Performance." *Western Journal of Medicine*, December 1980.

Wilmore, Jack H., et al. "Physiological Alterations Consequent to 20-Week Conditioning Programs of Bicycling, Tennis and Jogging." *Medicine and Science in Sports and Exercise*, Vol. 12, No. 1, 1980.

CHAPTER 7: **Searching for Speed**

Angier, Natalie. "How Fast? How High? How Far?" *Running* (England), March 1983.

Barnes, William S. "Selected Physiologic Characteristics of Elite Male Sprint Athletes." *Journal of Sports Medicine and Physical Fitness*, March 1981.

Bowerman, William J., and Gwilym S. Brown. "The Secrets of Speed." *Sports Illustrated*, August 2, 1971.

Bramble, Dennis M., and David R. Carrier. "Running and Breathing in Mammals." *Science*, January 21, 1983.

Christina, Robert W. "Minimum Visual Feedback Processing Time for Amendment of an Incorrect Movement." *Perceptual and Motor Skills*, Vol. 31, 1970.

———, et al. "Simple Reaction Time as a Function of Response Complexity: Memory Drum Theory Revisited." *Journal of Motor Behavior*, Vol. 14, No. 4, 1982.

———, and Noreen L. Goggin. "Reaction Time Analysis of Programmed Control of Short, Rapid Aiming Movements." *Research Quarterly*, Vol. 50, No. 3, 1979.

Costill, David L. *A Scientific Approach to Distance Running*. Los Altos, Calif.: *Track & Field News*, 1979.

Doherty, J. Kenneth. *Modern Track and Field*. Englewood Cliffs, N.J.: Prentice-Hall, 1963.

———. *Track and Field Omnibook*. Los Altos, Calif.: Tafnews Press, 1980.

Frederick, E.C. "Hot Times." *Running*, January–February 1983.

Galloway, Jeff. "Peaking for Top Performance." *Running Advice*, Vol. 1, No. 5, 1982.

———. "Speed Pays Off." *The Runner*, September 1983.

Gregor, R.J., et al. "Skeletal Muscle Properties and Performance in Elite

Female Track Athletes." *European Journal of Applied Physiology*, Vol. 47, 1981.

Hagerman, F.C., G.R. Hagerman, and T.C. Mickelson. "Physiologic Profiles of Elite Rowers." *The Physician and Sportsmedicine*, July 1979.

Hayes, Aden. *Getting There First: A Guide to Better Racing*. Canton, N.Y.: Achilles Sports International, 1981.

Kanehisa, Hiroaki, and Mitsumasa Miyashita, "An Attempt at the Classification of Adolescents into Sprint or Endurance Types." *Journal of Sports Medicine*, Vol. 20, 1980.

Manchester, Herbert. *Four Centuries of Sport in America*. New York: Benjamin Blom, 1968.

Mirkin, Gabe, and Marshall Hoffman. *The Sportsmedicine Book*. Boston: Little, Brown, 1978.

Olsen, Eric. "How to Sprint." *The Runner*, October 1983.

Ryan, Allan J. *The Physician and Sportsmedicine Guide to Running*. New York: McGraw-Hill, 1980.

Subotnick, Steven I. "Variations in Angles of Gait in Running." *The Physician and Sportsmedicine*, April 1979.

Thomas, Jerry R., Jere D. Gallagher, and Gracie J. Purvis. "Reaction Time and Anticipation Time: Effects of Development." *Research Quarterly for Exercise and Sport*, Vol. 52, No. 3, 1981.

Whitt, Frank Roland, and David Gordon Wilson. *Bicycling Science*. Cambridge, Mass.: MIT Press, 1982.

Wolman, B.B., ed. "Skilled Motor Performance: Anticipatory Timing." In *International Encyclopedia of Psychiatry, Psychology, Psychoanalysis and Neurology*. New York: Van Nostrand Reinhold, 1977.

CHAPTER 8: **Gracefulness Under Pressure**

Beaulieu, John E. "Developing a Stretching Program." *The Physician and Sportsmedicine*, November 1981.

Bhanot, J.L., and L.S. Sidhu. "Comparative Study of Reaction Time in Indian Sportsmen Specializing in Hockey, Volleyball, Weight Lifting and Gymnastics." *Journal of Sports Medicine*, March 1980.

Brancazio, Peter J. *SportScience: Physical Laws and Optimum Performance*. New York: Simon and Schuster, 1984.

Cornelius, William L. "Two Effective Flexibility Methods." *Athletic Training*, Spring 1981.

Doherty, J. Kenneth. *Track and Field Omnibook*. Los Altos, Calif.: Tafnews, 1980.

Durant, John, and Otto Bettman. *Pictorial History of American Sports*. Cranbury, N.J.: A.S. Barnes, 1965.

Dyson, Geoffrey H.G. *The Mechanics of Athletics*. New York: Holmes and Meier, 1977.

Frederick, E.C. "Extrinsic Biomechanical Aids." In *Ergogenic Aids in Sport*, M. Williams, ed. Champaign, Ill.: Human Kinetics Publishers, 1983.

———. "Stretching Things a Bit." *Running*, May–June 1982.

Gardner, Howard. *Frames of Mind: The Theory of Multiple Intelligences.* New York: Basic Books, 1983.

Hay, James G. *The Biomechanics of Sports Techniques.* Englewood Cliffs, N.J.: Prentice-Hall, 1978.

Jokl, Ernst. *Collected Works.* Privately printed; undated.

Konner, Melvin. *The Tangled Wing: Biological Constraints on the Human Spirit.* New York: Holt, Rinehart and Winston, 1982.

Marshall, John L., et al. "Joint Looseness: Function of the Person and the Joint." *Medicine and Science in Sports and Exercise,* Vol. 12, 1980.

Nelson, Richard C. "Biomechanics: Past and Present." In *Biomechanics Symposium Proceedings.* Bloomington, Ind.: Indiana University, 1980.

———. "Introduction to Sport Biomechanics." In *Biomechanics of Motion,* A. Morecki, ed. New York: Springer-Verlag, 1980.

Nideffer, Robert M. *The Inner Athlete: Mind Plus Muscle for Winning.* New York: T.Y. Crowell, 1976.

Schultz, Paul. "Flexibility: Day of the Static Stretch." *The Physician and Sportsmedicine,* November 1979.

Thomas, Jerry R., Jere D. Gallagher, and Gracie J. Purvis. "Reaction Time and Anticipation Time: Effects of Development." *Research Quarterly for Exercise and Sport,* Vol. 52, No. 3, 1981.

Wipfler, R.W. "Mental Approach to Batting." *Athletic Journal,* January 1981.

Yannis, Alex. "Cosmos Fans See Rarity by Romero." *New York Times,* May 3, 1983.

CHAPTER 9: **Natural Gifts**

Anderson, James L., and Martin Cohen. *The Competitive Edge.* New York: William Morrow, 1981.

Arnold James A., et al. "Anatomical and Physiologic Characteristics to Predict Football Ability." *American Journal of Sports Medicine,* March–April, 1980.

Boileau, R.A., et al. "Physiological Characteristics of Elite Middle and Long Distance Runners." *Canadian Journal of Applied Sport Sciences,* Vol. 7, No. 3, 1982.

Burke, Edmund J., Edward Winslow, and William V. Strube. "Measures of Body Composition and Performance in Major College Football Players." *Sports Medicine,* Vol. 20, 1980.

Clarkson, Priscilla M., Walter Kroll, and Anthony M. Melchionda. "Isokinetic Strength, Endurance and Fiber Type Composition in Elite American Paddlers." *European Journal of Applied Physiology,* Vol. 48, 1982.

Conley, Douglas L. "Percentage of Maximal Heart Rate and Distance Running Performance of Highly Trained Athletes." *Sports Medicine,* Vol. 21, 1981.

Darden, Ellington. *Superfitness Handbook.* Philadelphia: George F. Sticky, 1980.

Dunn, Kathleen. "Twin Studies and Sports: Estimating the Future?" *The Physician and Sportsmedicine,* May 1981.

Graydon, Janet. "Spatial Ability in Highly Skilled Women Squash Players." *Perceptual and Motor Skills*, Vol. 50, 1980.

Guttman, Allen. *From Ritual to Record: The Nature of Modern Sport*. New York: Columbia University Press, 1978.

Haymes, Emily M., and Arthur L. Dickinson. "Characteristics of Elite Male and Female Ski Racers." *Medicine and Science in Sports and Exercise*, Vol. 12, No. 3, 1980.

Isaacs, Larry D. "Relationship Between Depth Perception and Basketball-Shooting Performance Over a Competitive Season." *Perceptual and Motor Skills*, Vol. 53, 1981.

Kane, Martin. "Black Is Best." *Sports Illustrated*, January 18, 1971.

King, Billie Jean. *Billie Jean*. New York: Harper & Row, 1974.

Michener, James A. *Sports in America*. New York: Random House, 1976.

Morris, Alfred F. "A Scientific Explanation for Eric Heiden's Unique Olympic Performance." *Journal of Sports Medicine*, Vol. 21, 1981.

Shaver, Larry G. "Body Composition, Endurance Capacity and Strength of College Lacrosse Players." *Journal of Sports Medicine*, Vol. 20, 1980.

Silva, John M., III, et al. "A Psychophysiological Assessment of Elite Wrestlers." *Research Quarterly for Exercise and Sport*, Vol. 52, No. 3, 1981.

Sjøgaard, Gisela, et al. "Subgrouping of Fast-Twitch Fibers in Skeletal Muscles of Man: Critical Appraisal." *Histochemistry*, Vol. 58, 1978.

Slaughter, M.H., and T.G. Lohman. "An Objective Method for Measurement of Musculo-Skeletal Size to Characterize Body Physique with Application to the Athletic Population." *Medicine and Science in Sports and Exercise*, Vol. 12, No. 3, 1980.

Smith, D.J., et al. "Physiological Profiles of the Canadian Olympic Hockey Team (1980)." *Canadian Journal of Applied Sport Sciences*, Vol. 7, No. 2, 1982.

Spence, D.W., et al. "Descriptive Profiles of Highly Skilled Women Volleyball Players." *Medicine and Science in Sports and Exercise*, Vol. 12, No. 4, 1980.

Stine, C. Douglas, Michael R. Arterburn, and Norman S. Stern. "Vision and Sports: A Review of the Literature." *Journal of the American Optometric Association*, August 1982.

Stone, Michael H., et al. "Relationship Between Anaerobic Power and Olympic Weightlifting Performance." *Journal of Sports Medicine*, Vol. 20, 1980.

Syuzo, Kumagai, et al. "Relationships of the Anaerobic Threshold with the 5 km, 10 km and 10 Mile Races." *European Journal of Applied Physiology*, Vol. 49, 1982.

Tanaka, K., and Y. Matsuura. "A Multivariate Analysis of the Role of Certain Anthropometric and Physiological Attributes in Distance Running." *Annals of Human Biology*, Vol. 9, No. 5, 1982.

Tedford, W.H., Jr., W.R. Hill, and L. Hensley. "Human Eye Color and Reaction Time." *Perceptual and Motor Skills*, Vol. 47, 1978.

Vodak, Paul A., et al. "Physiological Profile of Middle-Aged Male and Female Tennis Players." *Medicine and Science in Sports and Exercise*, Vol. 12, No. 3, 1980.

Western Journal of Medicine, editors of. "Fuel Utilization in Marathons: Implications for Performance." *Western Journal of Medicine*, December 1980.

Withers, R.T., and R.G.D. Roberts. "Physiological Profiles of Representative Women Softball, Hockey and Netball Players." *Ergonomics*, Vol. 24, No. 8, 1981.

CHAPTER 10: Age and the Athlete

American Academy of Pediatrics position paper. "Competitive Sports for Children of Elementary School Age." *Pediatrics*, June 1981.

Barnes, L. "Preadolescent Training—How Young Is Too Young?" *The Physician and Sportsmedicine*, October 1979.

Brody, Jane E. "Exercising to Turn Back the Years." *New York Times*, June 6, 1979.

———. "Exercise for Young Children: Are Stars Born or Must They Be Carefully Made?" *New York Times*, March 2, 1983.

Clarke, H. Harrison, ed. "Exercise and Aging." *Physical Fitness Research Digest*, April 1977.

Davies, C.T.M. "Thermoregulation During Exercise in Relation to Sex and Age." *European Journal of Applied Physiology*, October 1979.

Gardiner, E. Norman. *Athletics of the Ancient World*. Chicago: Ares Publishers, 1978.

Gutin, Bernard, Lenore R. Zohman, and Jeffrey L. Young. "Case Report: An 80-Year-old Marathoner." *Journal of Cardiac Rehabilitation*, Vol. 1, No. 5, 1981.

Heath, G.W., et al. "A Physiological Comparison of Young and Older Endurance Athletes." *Journal of Applied Physiology*, Vol. 51, No. 3, 1981.

Houston, M.E., and H.J. Green. "Skeletal Muscle and Physiologic Characteristics of a World Champion Masters Distance Runner: A Case Study." *International Journal of Sports Medicine*, Vol. 2, 1981.

Jokl, Ernst, et al. "Sports Medicine." In *Jokl: Collected Works*. Privately printed, undated.

Kasch, Fred W., and Janet P. Wallace. "Physiological Variables During Ten Years of Endurance Exercise." *Medicine and Science in Sports*, Vol. 8, No. 1, 1976.

Kramer, Jack, and Frank Deford. *The Game: My Forty Years in Tennis*. New York: Putnam, 1979.

Kulund, Daniel N., David A. Rockwell, and Clifford E. Brubaker. "The Long-Term Effects of Playing Tennis." *The Physician and Sportsmedicine*, April 1979.

Larsson, Lars. "Physical Training Effects on Muscle Morphology in Sedentary Males at Different Ages." *Medicine and Science in Sports and Exercise*, Vol. 14, No. 3, 1982.

Maud, P.J., et al. "Fifty Years of Training and Competition in the Marathon: Wally Hayward, Age 70—A Physiological Profile." *South African Medical Journal*, Vol. 59, 1981.

Michener, James A. *Sports in America*. New York: Random House, 1976.

Naughton, John. "Physical Activity and Aging." *Primary Care*, March 1982.

Nelson, Janet. "Outdoors: Fun for the Older Skier." *New York Times*, February 14, 1983.

Ostrow, Andrew C., Dianne C. Jones, and David R. Spiker. "Age Role Expectations and Sex Role Expectations for Selected Sport Activities." *Research Quarterly for Exercise and Sport*, Vol. 52, No. 2, 1981.

Pollock, Michael L., Henry S. Miller, and Jack Wilmore. "Physiological Characteristics of Champion American Track Athletes 40 to 75 Years of Age." *Journal of Gerontology*, Vol. 29, No. 6, 1974.

Riegel, Peter S. "Athletic Records and Human Endurance." *American Scientist*, May–June 1981.

Rost, R. "The Athlete's Heart." *European Heart Journal*, Vol. 3, Supplement A, 1982.

Schöbel, Heinz. *The Ancient Olympic Games*. London: Studio Vista Limited, 1966.

Sherwood, David E., and Dennis J. Selder. "Cardiorespiratory Health, Reaction Time and Aging." *Medicine and Science in Sports and Exercise*, Summer 1979.

Sodhi, H.S. "A Study of Age and Participation in Different Physical Activities." *Journal of Sports Medicine*, Vol. 21, 1981.

Stones, M.J., and A. Kozma. "Adult Age Trends in Athletic Performances." *Experimental Aging Research*, Vol. 7, No. 3, 1981.

———. "Adult Age Trends in Record Running Performances." *Experimental Aging Research*, Vol. 6, No. 5, 1980.

Stover, C.N. "Physician Conditioning of the Immature Athlete." *Orthopedic Clinics of North America*, July 1982.

Tutko, Thomas, and William Bruns. *Winning Is Everything and Other American Myths*. New York: Macmillan, 1976.

Willoughby, David P. *The Super Athletes*. New York: A. S. Barnes, 1970.

Wright, Thomas W., Christian W. Zaunder, and Robert Cade. "Cardiac Output in Male Middle-Aged Runners." *Journal of Sports Medicine*, Vol. 22, 1982.

CHAPTER 11: **The Nutritional Advantage**

Allman, Fred L., Jr., and Edward W. Watt. "The Role of Exercise in Disease Prevention." In *Sports Medicine*, edited by Allan J. Ryan and Fred L. Allman, Jr. New York: Academic Press, 1974.

American Dietetic Association, statement by. "Nutrition and Physical Fitness." *Journal of the American Dietetic Association*, May 1980.

Barry, A., et al. "A Nutritional Study of Irish Athletes." *British Journal of Sports Medicine*, Vol. 15, 1981.

Bentivegna, Angelo, James E. Kelley, and Alexander Kalenak. "Diet, Fitness and Athletic Performance." *The Physician and Sportsmedicine*, October 1979.

Blair, Steven N., et al. "Comparison of Nutrient Intake in Middle-Aged Men and Women Runners and Controls." *Medicine and Science in Sports and Exercise*, Vol. 13, No. 5, 1981.

Bloom, Mark. "Power Eating." *American Health*, November–December 1983.

Brody, Jane E. "New Research on the Vegetarian Diet." *New York Times*, October 12, 1983.

———. "To Lose Weight, More Exercise Is the Key." *New York Times*, August 3, 1983.

Buskirk, Elsworth R. "Muscle Fuel for Competition." *The Physician and Sportsmedicine*, January 1979.

———. "Nutrition for the Athlete." In *Sports Medicine*, edited by Allan J. Ryan and Fred L. Allman, Jr. New York: Academic Press, 1974.

Caldarone, G., et al. "Nutrition of Athletes: The Role of Confectionary (and Ice Cream) in the Diet of Young Girls in Training." *Journal of Sports Medicine*, Vol 22, 1982.

Clark, Nancy, with Amby Burfoot. "The Truth About Caffeine." *Runner's World*, February 1983.

Cohen, I., et al. "The Effect of Water Deficit on Body Temperature During Rugby." *South African Medical Journal*, Vol. 60, 1981.

Costill, David L., et al. "The Role of Dietary Carbohydrates in Muscle Glycogen Resynthesis After Strenuous Running." *American Journal of Clinical Nutrition*, September 1981.

Dale, Edwin, and Dana L. Goldberg. "Implications of Nutrition in Athletes' Menstrual Cycle Irregularities." *Canadian Journal of Applied Sport Sciences*, Vol. 7, No. 2, 1982.

Derderian, Tom. "The Inside Story." *Running*, March–April 1983.

Durnin, J.V.G.A. "Muscle in Sports Medicine—Nutrition and Muscular Performance." *International Journal of Sports Medicine*, Vol. 3, 1982.

Farrell, Peter A., et al. "A Comparison of Plasma Cholesterol, Triglycerides, and High Density Lipoprotein-Cholesterol in Speed Skaters, Weightlifters and Non-Athletes." *European Journal of Applied Physiology*, Vol. 48, 1982.

Felig, Philip, et al. "Hypoglycemia During Prolonged Exercise in Normal Men." *New England Journal of Medicine*, April 15, 1982.

Finley, M.I., and H.W. Pleket. *The Olympic Games: The First Thousand Years*. New York: Viking Press, 1976.

Hanley, Daniel F. "Basic Diet Guidance for Athletes." *Journal of the Florida Medical Association*, April 1980.

Herbert, Victor D. "Megavitamin Therapy." *New York State Journal of Medicine*, February 1979.

Houston, Michael E. "Diet, Training and Sleep: A Survey Study of Elite Canadian Swimmers." *Canadian Journal of Applied Sport Sciences*, Vol. 5, No. 3, 1980.

———, et al. "The Effect of Rapid Weight Loss on Physiologic Functions in Wrestlers." *The Physician and Sportsmedicine*, November 1981.

Hursh, Laurence M. "Food and Water Restriction in the Wrestler." *Journal of the American Medical Association*, March 2, 1979.

Ivy, J.L., et al. "Influence of Caffeine and Carbohydrate Feedings on Endurance Performance." *Medicine and Science in Sports and Exercise*, Spring 1979.

Jensen, Clayne R., and A. Garth Fisher. *Scientific Basis of Athletic Conditioning.* Philadelphia: Lea and Febiger, 1979.

Jones, N.L., et al. "Fat Metabolism in Heavy Exercise." *Clinical Science,* Vol. 59, 1980.

Journal of Human Nutrition, editors of. "Diet and Athletic Performance." *JHN,* August 1980.

Kirsch, K.A., and H. Von Ameln. "Feeding Patterns of Endurance Athletes." *European Journal of Applied Physiology,* October 1981.

Koivisto, Veikko A., Sirkka-Liisa Karonen, and Esko A. Nikkilä. "Carbohydrate Ingestion Before Exercise: Comparison of Glucose, Fructose and Sweet Placebo." *Journal of Applied Physiology,* October 1981.

Kramer, Jack, and Frank Deford. *The Game: My Forty Years in Tennis.* New York: G.P. Putnam, 1979.

McCutcheon, Lynn, and Alex Ayres. "Are Runners *Really* Like Anorexics?" *Running Times,* June 1983.

Maughan, R.J., and D.C. Poole. "The Effects of a Glycogen-Loading Regimen on the Capacity to Perform Anaerobic Exercise." *European Journal of Applied Physiology,* Vol. 46, 1981.

Milkereit, Joanne. "Nutrition Training for Runners." *Running & Fitness,* July–August 1983.

Plowman, Sharon A., and Patricia C. McSwegin. "The Effects of Iron Supplementation on Female Cross Country Runners." *Journal of Sports Medicine,* Vol. 21, 1981.

Ryan, Allan J. "The Limits of Human Performance." In *Sports Medicine,* edited by Allan J. Ryan and Fred L. Allman, Jr. New York: Academic Press, 1974.

Schöbel, Heinz. *The Ancient Olympic Games.* London: Studio Vista Limited, 1966.

Sherman, W.M., et al. "Effect of Exercise-Diet Manipulation on Muscle Glycogen and Its Subsequent Utilization During Performance." *International Journal of Sports Medicine,* Vol. 2, 1981.

Smith, Nathan J. "Nutrition and the Athlete." *American Journal of Sports Medicine,* Vol. 10, No. 4, 1982.

———. "Nutrition and Athletic Performance." *Medical Times,* August 1981.

Sumner, John. "Nutrition and Athletic Performance." *Food and Nutrition,* Vol. 37, No. 3, 1980.

Western Journal of Medicine, editors of. "Fuel Utilization in Marathons: Implications for Performance." *Western Journal of Medicine,* December 1980.

CHAPTER 12: Staying Well

Alles, Wesley F. "National Athletic Injury-Illness Reporting System Three-Year Findings of High School and College Football Injuries." *Journal of Orthopedic and Sports Physical Therapy,* Fall 1979.

Allman, William F. "The Knee." *Science 83,* November 1983.

Anderson, Bob. *Stretching.* Bolinas, Calif.: Shelter Publications, 1980.

Baum, Erika, Kurt Brück, and Peter Schwennicke. "Adaptive Modifications in the Thermoregulatory System of Long-Distance Runners." *Journal of Applied Physiology*, March 1976.

Bernhang, Arthur M. "The Many Causes of Tennis Elbow." *New York State Journal of Medicine*, August 1979.

Boyle, Robert H., and Wilmer Ames. "Too Many Punches, Too Little Concern." (On boxing injuries.) *Sports Illustrated*, April 11, 1983.

Cavanagh, Peter R. "Advances in Diagnosing the Runner's Injuries." *Runner's World*, August 1980.

————. *The Running Shoe Book*. Mountain View, Calif.: Anderson World, 1980.

Chambers, Richard B. "Orthopedic Injuries in Athletes (Ages 6–17): Comparison of Injuries Occurring in Six Sports." *American Journal of Sports Medicine*, May–June 1979.

Clement, D.B., et al. "A Survey of Overuse Running Injuries." *The Physician and Sportsmedicine*, May 1981.

————, and J.E. Taunton. "A Guide to the Prevention of Running Injuries." *Australian Family Physician*, March 1981.

Coddington, R., and J. Troxell. "The Effect of Emotional Factors on Football Injury Rates—a Pilot Study." *Journal of Human Stress*, Vol. 6, 1980.

Cooter, G.R. "Amphetamines and Sport Performance." *Journal of Physical Education and Recreation*, October 1980.

Costrini, Anthony M. "Cardiovascular and Metabolic Manifestations of Heat Stroke and Severe Heat Exhaustion." *American Journal of Medicine*, February 1979.

Davies, C.T.M. "Thermoregulation During Exercise in Relation to Sex and Age." *European Journal of Applied Physiology*, October 1979.

Dressendorfer, R.H., et al. "Cold Tolerance of Long-Distance Runners and Swimmers in Hawaii." *International Journal of Biometeorology*, Vol. 21, No. 1, 1977.

————, Charles E. Wade, and Ezra A. Amsterdam. "Development of Pseudoanemia in Marathon Runners During a 20-Day Road Race." *Journal of the American Medical Association*, September 11, 1981.

Faria, Irvin E., and Bruce J. Drummond. "Circadian Changes in Resting Heart Rate and Body Temperature, Maximal Oxygen Consumption and Perceived Exertion." *Ergonomics*, Vol. 25, No. 5, 1982.

Frederick, E.C. *The Running Body*. Mountain View, Calif.: World Publications, 1973.

————. "Running in the Heat." *Running*, Spring 1978.

Gleim, Gilbert W., Philip A. Witman, and James A. Nicholas. "Indirect Assessment of Cardiovascular 'Demands' Using Telemetry on Professional Football Players." *American Journal of Sports Medicine*, May–June 1981.

Glickman, Harold B. "Stress Fractures." *Running and Fitness*, January–February 1983.

Grisogono, Vivian. "The Knee." *Running* (England), March 1983.

Gruchow, H. William, and Douglas Pelletier. "An Epidemiologic Study of

Tennis Elbow: Incidence, Recurrence and Effectiveness of Prevention Strategies." *American Journal of Sports Medicine*, July–August 1979.

Hanson, Peter G. "Heat Injury in Runners." *The Physician and Sportsmedicine*, June 1979.

Hubbard, Roger W. "Effects of Exercise in the Heat on Predisposition to Heat Stroke." *Medicine and Science in Sports and Exercise*, Spring 1979.

Jackson, Robert W. *The Scope of Arthroscopy*. Warsaw, Ind.: Zimmer, 1982.

James, Stanley L., and Clifford E. Brubaker. "Running Mechanics." *Journal of the American Medical Association*, August 28, 1972.

Jokl, Ernst. *What Is Sportsmedicine?* Springfield, Ill.: Charles C Thomas, 1964.

Journal of the American Medical Association, editors of. "Increasing Numbers of Physical Changes Found in Nation's Runners." *Journal of the American Medical Association*, February 13, 1981.

Kulund, Daniel N., David Rockwell, and Clifford E. Brubaker. "The Long-Term Effects of Playing Tennis." *The Physician and Sportsmedicine*, April 1979.

Lundberg, George D. "The Medical Case for Ending Boxing." *New York Times*, January 16, 1983.

Lutter, Lowell D. "Foot-Related Knee Problems in the Long-Distance Runner." *Foot and Ankle*, September 1980.

Lyons, John W. "Cross-Country Ski Injuries." *The Physician and Sportsmedicine*, January 1980.

McGregor, Rob Roy, and Stephen E. Devereux. *EEVeTeC*. Boston: Houghton Mifflin, 1982.

Mack, Robert P., ed. *The Foot and Leg in Running Sports*. St. Louis: C.V. Mosby, 1982.

McLaughlin, Loretta. "Knee Injury: A Revolution in Treatment." *Boston Globe*, October 3, 1983.

Martin, Bruce J. "Effect of Sleep Deprivation on Tolerance of Prolonged Exercise." *European Journal of Applied Physiology*, Vol. 47, 1981.

Michener, James A. *Sports in America*. New York: Random House, 1976.

Mirkin, Gabe, and Marshall Hoffman. *The Sportsmedicine Book*. Boston: Little, Brown, 1978.

Nadel, Ethan R. "Control of Sweating Rate While Exercising in the Heat." *Medicine and Science in Sports and Exercise*, Spring 1979.

Nelson, Richard C. "A Glimpse of Sport Science and Medicine in the People's Republic of China." *Sports Medicine Bulletin* (American College of Sports Medicine), January 1980.

Nigg, Benno M., and Barry A. Kerry, eds. *Biomechanical Aspects of Sport Shoes and Playing Surfaces*. Calgary, Canada: University of Calgary, 1983.

Oriard, Michael. "Why Football Injuries Remain a Part of the Game." *New York Times*, November 20, 1983.

Pandolf, Kent B. "Effects of Physical Training and Cardiorespiratory Physical Fitness on Exercise-Heat Tolerance: Recent Observations." *Medicine and Science in Sports and Exercise*, Spring 1979.

Person, Burton L., et al. "An Epidemiologic Study of Squash Injuries." *American Journal of Sports Medicine*, Vol. 9, No. 2, 1981.

Priest, James D., Vic Braden, and Susan Goodwin Gerberich. "The Elbow and Tennis." (Two parts.) *The Physician and Sportsmedicine*, April and May 1980.

Richardson, Allen B., Frank W. Jobe, and H. Royer Collins. "The Shoulder in Competitive Swimming." *American Journal of Sports Medicine*, May–June 1980.

Rose, Richard C., III, et al. "Heat Injuries Among Recreational Runners." *Southern Medical Journal*, August 1980.

Rost, R. "The Athlete's Heart." *European Heart Journal*, Vol. 3, Supplement A, 1982.

Roy, Steven. "Muscle Pulls and Cramps." *Runner's World*, September 1983.

Ryan, Allan J. *The Physician and Sportsmedicine Guide to Running*. New York: McGraw-Hill, 1980.

——, and Fred L. Allman, Jr., eds. *Sports Medicine*. New York: Academic Press, 1974.

Sandelin, J., Kiviluoto, and S. Santavirta. "Injuries of Competitive Skiers in Finland: A Three-Year Survey." *Annales Chirurgiae et Gynaecologiae*, Vol. 69, 1980.

Sharkey, Brian J. *Physiology of Fitness*. Champaign, Ill.: Human Kinetics Publishers, 1979.

Siegel, Arthur J., Lawrence M. Silverman, and Robert E. Lopez. "Creatine Kinase Elevations in Marathon Runners: Relationship to Training and Competition." *Yale Journal of Biology and Medicine*, Vol. 53, 1980.

Stulberg, S. David, et al. "Breaststroker's Knee: Pathology, Etiology and Treatment." *American Journal of Sports Medicine*, May–June 1980.

Subotnick, Steven I. *Cures for Common Running Injuries*. Mountain View, Calif.: World Publications, 1979.

——, and Oded Bar-Or. "Thermal Illness in Fun Running." *American Heart Journal*, December 1980.

Tutko, Thomas, and William Bruns. *Winning Is Everything and Other American Myths*. New York: Macmillan, 1976.

Valliant, P.M. "Personality and Injury in Competitive Runners." *Perceptual and Motor Skills*, Vol. 53, 1981.

Weisenfeld, Murray F., with Barbara Burr. *The Runner's Repair Manual*. New York: St. Martin's Press, 1980.

Welsh, R. Peter, and Judy Clodman. "Clinical Survey of Achilles Tendinitis in Athletes." *Canadian Medical Association Journal*, January 26, 1980.

Wolpa, Mark E. *The Sports Medicine Guide: Treating and Preventing Common Athletic Injuries*. West Point, N.Y.: Leisure Press, 1982.

Yuroki, Y., et al. "Current Trends in Ski Injuries." *Orthopedics*, Vol. 30, 1979.

CHAPTER 13: The Gadgetry of Sport

Alsofrom, Judy. "Forecasting Future Athletic Achievements." *American Medical News*, November 29, 1976.

Amdur, Neil. "Racquets Problems for Pros." *New York Times*, May 2, 1983.

Boling, Rick. "Skis That Think." *Outside*, November 1983.

Brewster, Barbara. "Nature's Fibers and the New Synthetics." *Nordic Skiing*, November 1980.

Brody, H. "Physics of the Tennis Racquet." *American Journal of Physics*, June 1979.

Chase, Anthony. "A Slice of Golf." *Science 81*, July–August 1981.

Clarke, T.E., E.C. Frederick, and L.B. Cooper. "Effects of Shoe Cushioning Upon Ground Reaction Forces in Running." *International Journal of Sports Medicine*, Vol. 4, 1983.

Clarke, T.E., E.C. Frederick, and C.L. Hamill. "The Effects of Shoe Design Parameters on Rearfoot Control in Running." *Medicine and Science in Sports and Exercise*, Vol. 15, No. 5, 1983.

Clarke, T.E., E.C. Frederick, and H.F. Hlavac, "Effects of a Soft Orthotic Device on Rearfoot Movement in Running." *Podiatric Sports Medicine*, Summer 1983.

Cooper, Laura Kessler, and Anne L. Rothstein. "Videotape Replay and the Learning of Skills in Open and Closed Environments." *Research Quarterly for Exercise and Sport*, Vol. 52, No. 2, 1981.

Dalton, Anne Walsh. "The Right Stuff: The Runner's Annual Holiday Guide to Equipment and Other Gifts." *The Runner*, December 1983.

Discover, editors of. "Running by the Beeper." *Discover*, October 1981.

Falsetti, Herman L., et al. "Hematological Variations After Endurance Running with Hard and Soft-Soled Running Shoes." *The Physician and Sportsmedicine*, August 1983.

Fish, Mike. "Royals' Reputation as Killers on Carpet Is Partly Artificial." *Kansas City Times*, May 13, 1983.

Frederick, E.C. "Body Size and Biomechanical Consequences for Runners." In *Sports Medicine, Sports Science: Bridging the Gap*, edited by R.C. Cantu and W.J. Gillespie. Lexington, Mass.: Collamore Press, 1982.

Freifeld, Karen. "Body Management." *Personal Computing*, August 1983.

Goldsmith, Werner, and J. Michael Kabo. "Performance of Baseball Head-gear." *American Journal of Sports Medicine*, Vol. 10, No. 1, 1982.

Jackson, John. "Music in Motion." *SportsWise New York*, December 1983.

Jakush, Judy. "Can Dental Therapy Enhance Athletic Performance?" *Journal of the American Dental Association*, March 1982.

Johnson, Robert J., et al. "Trends in Skiing Injuries." *American Journal of Sports Medicine*, Vol. 8, No. 2, 1980.

Kaufman, Richard S. "Case Reports of TMJ Repositioning to Improve Scoliosis and the Performance by Athletes." *New York State Dental Journal*, April 1980.

Keene, J.S., et al. "Tartan Turf on Trial: A Comparison of Inter-collegiate Football Injuries Occurring on Natural Grass and Tartan Turf." *American Journal of Sports Medicine*, January–February 1980.

Klemesrud, Judy. "Gym Clothes: Exercises in Style." *New York Times*, March 2, 1983.

Mechanical Engineering, editors of. "Mechanical Design in Sports." *Mechanical Engineering*,, April 1982.

Moore, Mike. "Corrective Mouth Guards: Performance Aids or Expensive Placebos?" *The Physician and Sportsmedicine*, April 1981.

Nolan, Gerald N., and Barry T. Bates. "A Biomechanical Analysis of the Effects of Two Paddle Types on Performance in North American Canoe Racing." *Research Quarterly for Exercise and Sport*, Vol. 53, No. 1, 1982.

Runner's World, editors of. "Charting the Top Training Aids on the Market." *Runner's World*, August 1983.

————. "Runner's World Guide to Training Aids." *Runner's World*, August 1982.

Sanders, Michael T. "Comparison of Two Methods of Training on the Development of Muscular Strength." *Journal of Orthopedics and Sports Physical Therapy*, Spring 1980.

Schwartz, Robert, and Max M. Novich. "The Athlete's Mouthpiece." *American Journal of Sports Medicine*, September–October 1980.

Scimone, Francis S. "Effect of a Mouth Appliance on Athletic Performance." *Journal of the Massachusetts Dental Society*, Vol. 30, No. 3, 1981.

Stipe, Peter, ed. "Cushioning in Athletic Shoes." *Nike Research Newsletter*, Summer 1982.

————. "The Effect of Shoe Weight on the Aerobic Demands of Running." *Nike Research Newsletter*, Fall 1982.

————. "The Effects of Midsole Hardness, Heel Flare and Heel Height on Rearfoot Control." *Nike Research Newsletter*, Spring 1983.

————. "The Prediction of Vertical Impact Force During Running." *Nike Research Newsletter*, Spring 1982.

————. "Running Economy on Air-Soles." *Nike Research Newsletter*, Winter 1982.

————. "Scaling of Body Size and Cushioning in Running Shoes." *Nike Research Newsletter*, Spring 1982.

————. "Vertical Impact Force and Basketball." *Nike Research Newsletter*, Spring 1982.

Stoddard, Gordon. "Protective Equipment." In *Sports Medicine*, edited by Allan J. Ryan and Fred L. Allman, Jr. New York: Academic Press, 1974.

Tilden, William T., 2nd. *Match Play and the Spin of the Ball*. Port Washington, N.Y.: Kennikat Press, 1969. (First published 1925.)

Time, editors of. "A Boom in Low Tech and No Tech." *Time*, May 30, 1983.

Vecsey, George. "Pro Football Braces for Newest Fashion." *New York Times*, December 31, 1983.

Weltman, Arthur. "Exercising Safely in Winter." *The Physician and Sportsmedicine*, January 1981.

CHAPTER 14: Outer Limits

Allman, William F. "Steroids in Sports: Do They Work?" *Science 81*, November 1981.

Alsofrom, Judy. "Predicting Future Athletic Achievements." *American Medical News*, November 29, 1976.

Amdur, Neil. "Using Science in the Service of Sport." *New York Times*, November 15, 1983.

Baer, L. "Effect of a Time-Slowing Suggestion on Performance Accuracy on a Perceptual Motor Task." *Perceptual and Motor Skills*, Vol. 51, 1980.

Banister, E.W., and T.W. Calvert. "Planning for Future Performance: Implications for Long Term Training." *Canadian Journal of Applied Sport Sciences*, Vol. 5, No. 3, 1980.

Brooks, R.V. "Problems in Detection of Anabolic Steroids." *Medisport*, Vol. 2, No. 67, 1980.

Chass, Murray. "[Rich] Gossage Pact at $6.25 Million." *New York Times*, January 17, 1984.

Cooper, Laura Kessler, and Anne L. Rothstein. "Videotape Replay and the Learning of Skills in Open and Closed Environments." *Research Quarterly for Exercise and Sport*, Vol. 52, No. 2, 1981.

Epstein, Sue Hoover. "World Records: Any Limits?" *Science 84*, April 1984.

Frederick, E.C. "[Alberto] Salazar's Predictable 2:08." *Running*, March-April 1982.

International Journal of Bio-Medical Computing, editors of. "Computers to Aid Athletes' Performance." *International Journal of Bio-Medical Computing*, Vol. 12, 1981.

Moore, Kenny. "Projecting from Mozart." *Sports Illustrated*, September 13, 1976.

Nawrocka, W., and G.D. Olszewska. "Female Sport Today: Psychological Considerations." *International Journal of Sport Psychology*, Vol. 10, 1979.

Nideffer, Robert M., et al. "The Future of Applied Sport Psychology." *Journal of Sport Psychology*, Vol. 2, 1980.

Riegel, Peter S. "Athletic Records and Human Endurance." *American Scientist*, May–June 1981.

Segal, Doralie Denenberg. "Physical Performance: What Are the Limits?" *Running and Fitness*, December 1983.

Whieldon, David. "Biomechanics: Space Age Sports Medicine." *The Physician and Sportsmedicine*, May 1979.

Index

About the Author

JAMES F. Fixx wrote six other books, including the record-breaking best seller *The Complete Book of Running*. He was a consultant to the President's Council on Physical Fitness and Sports, a regular contributor to national magazines, a frequent television and radio guest, and the author of the annual *The Complete Runner's Day-by-Day Log and Calendar*.

Mr. Fixx died in August 1984, just after completing this book.